AND EVERY WORD IS TRUE

AND EVERY WORD IS TRUE

Gary McAvoy

LITERATI
EDITIONS.

2019

First Edition

Hardcover ISBN 978-0-9908376-0-2
Paperback ISBN: 978-0-9908376-1-9
ebook ISBN: 978-0-9908376-3-3

Library of Congress Control Number: 2018911995
Publisher's Cataloging-in-Publication Data
Names: McAvoy, Gary, author.
Title: And Every Word is True / Gary McAvoy.
Description: Includes bibliographical references and index. | Bremerton, WA: Literati Editions, 2019.
Identifiers: LCCN 2018911995 | ISBN 978-0-9908376-0-2 (Hardcover)
| 978-0-9908376-1-9 (pbk.) | 978-0-9908376-3-3 (ebook)
Subjects: LCSH Murder—Kansas—Case studies. | Murder—Kansas—Olathe. |
Crime—United States—History—20th century. | Kansas Bureau of Investigation—History. | Law enforcement—Kansas—History. | Capote, Truman, 1924-1984. |
BISAC TRUE CRIME / Murder / Mass Murder | TRUE CRIME / Historical
Classification: LCC HV6533.K3 M3 2019 | DDC 364.1/523/0978144—dc23

Published by:
Literati Editions
PO Box 5987
Bremerton, WA 98312-5987
Email: info@LiteratiEditions.com
Visit the author's website at www.garymcavoy.com

Cover design by John Burgess/2Seventy
Printed in the United States of America

NOTE TO THE READER

This book is the result of over six years of research relying on a generous collection of source material, including the personal investigative notebooks of Kansas Bureau of Investigation Special Agent and former director Harold R. Nye; official State of Kansas law enforcement reports, prison records, photographs, and other largely-inaccessible documents published here for the first time, as permitted by Kansas court ruling; reports found in the preserved files of the Finney County Sheriff's office, including photos, copies of KBI investigation reports, copies of memoranda written by local police and KBI investigators; the original research papers of Truman Capote and Nelle Harper Lee archived in the New York Public Library and the Library of Congress, and the product of that research, Capote's nonfiction novel *In Cold Blood*; Richard Hickock's Death Row letters; Perry Smith's personal journals and correspondence; publicly available records and news reports; books and articles published over the past 60 years specific to the subject matter; and extensive interviews with scores of individuals related to the events or hypotheses contained herein. Where appropriate—and without revealing the identity of certain sources who have requested anonymity—all references are cited in the narrative or in endnotes. Unless otherwise attributed, opinions expressed in this work are solely those of the author.

— Gary McAvoy

This book is dedicated to
the career and memory of

Harold R. Nye

"*In Cold Blood* is the story of these six people—the Clutters, who died together November 15, 1959, and Perry Smith and Richard Hickock, who were hanged April 14, 1965. And my book is the story of their lives and their deaths. It's a completely factual account and every word is true."

– Truman Capote

"Capote has, in short, achieved a work of art. He has told exceedingly well a tale of high terror in his own way. But, despite the brilliance of his self-publicizing efforts, he has made both a tactical and a moral error that will hurt him in the short run. By insisting that 'every word' of his book is true he has made himself vulnerable to those readers who are prepared to examine seriously such a sweeping claim."

– Phillip K. Tompkins[1]

Table of Contents

Table of Figures

Acknowledgments

Having just one name on a book's cover as the author is never quite accurate, since no writer works in a vacuum. Invariably each of us turns to others, to hear or read the words we write, or just patiently listen to our grousing about such a solitary process. I am guilty on both counts.

In a very literal sense, this book would never have been possible without the new friend I made in Ron Nye, when in 2012 he turned to me in a time of need to reluctantly sell his father's books and letters from Truman Capote, an innocent effort that landed us both in court for the next four years. His patience and faith in the process were rewarded, but at great cost to both of us. Ron kept me motivated even at our lowest points, and for that I will be forever grateful. I hope this book gives him and his family closure on the churlish actions of an ungrateful State.

Nor would these pages have seen the light of day were it not for our tenacious legal team, Yale Lewis of Hendricks & Lewis in Seattle, and Tai Vokins of Sloan Law Firm in Lawrence, Kansas, who fought our battle with Kansas in protection of our First Amendment rights. Their business partners (and respective spouses) Kate Hendricks and Krystal Vokins also deserve credit for their essential contributions of time and expertise. Yale, in particular, was a constant presence throughout, and for his support, encouragement, and genuine caring on a daily basis, I owe him a debt beyond words. And Tai's obliging skill at unearthing hidden material gives new meaning to the word *discovery*. To His Honor Judge Larry Hendricks, whose patience with and understanding of the complex issues in our case led him to rule in our favor, making him (in my estimation) the wisest jurist in the land.

Sally Keglovits, my unfailing sister in crime, went above and beyond her calls of duty with enthusiasm and without complaint.

Her trips to the New York Public Library for fact-checking, her sensible guidance on dealing with the criminal mind, her cautions on where to draw the line, and her pumpkin pretzel pie will never be forgotten.

My trusted friend and brilliant editor, Phil Shallat, deserves much of the credit for making me sound smarter than I am. Editorial tussles are legendary, but despite occasional stubbornness to have it my way, his way usually prevailed.

From day one and for several years on, Kevin Helliker at the *The Wall Street Journal* taught me a veteran reporter's way of playing chess with facts: challenging perilous moves I was about to make, suggesting new lines of engagement across the board, warning me when my king was in danger. His skill and inspiration gave me the courage to see this through.

To the gifted documentary filmmaker, Daniel Birman, thanks for years of wisdom and advice. You were always there when I needed a shove in the right direction, and your passion for this project means more than I can express here. Good luck to you and Megan Chao on the next phase of our journey. Sincere appreciation to Gary Brown for his unflagging enthusiasm and efforts, and to Sandi Mendelson for her wisdom and deep connections in the book world. And to Michael Ohoven, producer of the milestone film *Capote*, my gratitude for championing this project in other meaningful realms (and for what yet may come).

Very special thanks to my dear Подруга, Lily "Red" Mashkova, whose wisdom belies her years, and whose knowledge of all things *In Cold Blood* is humbling. And to my lifelong friend Kathleen Costello, the meticulous Miss Grammar, who rapped my knuckles time after time, instilling my work with precision where the nuns had failed so many decades before. Robin Kobaly and Doug Thompson, your tolerance of my constant interruptions of fellowship on the hobbit deck is deeply appreciated.

Special thanks to Mark Denchfield for his assistance, and to his parents, Keith and Carolyn Meier Denchfield, for their invaluable firsthand history as they lived it in Garden City,

Kansas, during the time the events described here took place. And posthumous credit goes to Carolyn's parents, Wendle and Josephine Meier, for being such good custodians of the many historical documents entrusted to my care and featured in these pages.

Directly or indirectly, I turned to many experts in my research for this book over the years, and to each of them I extend my deepest appreciation for their insights, advice, and assistance: to Alan Schwartz, literary executor of the Truman Capote Estate, for his generous permission to quote from *In Cold Blood* and the Capote Papers at the New York Public Library; the late Joanne Carson, in whose arms Truman died in 1984, and who graciously allowed me intimate perspectives on her friend; Gerald Clarke, Capote's biographer, who kindly clarified an important point in correspondence between Truman and Harold Nye, and whose book, *Capote: A Biography*, served as invaluable research.

For their gracious time in exploring my theories: Dr. W. Mitchell Jones, the psychiatrist who personally interviewed Richard Hickock and Perry Smith during their 1960 trial; neuropsychologist Dr. James Walker, for his fresh analysis of Richard Hickock's letters; and author and professor of forensic psychology Dr. Katherine Ramsland, who indulged my curiosity about psychopaths. Thanks to Alex Heard of *Outside* magazine for his encouragement and kind introduction to Donald Lamm, one of the sharpest publishing minds in the business—and to Don for sharing his wisdom on sensible structure; Stuart Hinds, Assistant Dean for Special Collections & Archives, University of Missouri at Kansas City; Ashley Boggan Dreff, PhD, for her clarifying historical views on United Methodist culture of the era; Sheila Krohe, Kansas researcher-extraordinaire; Ted Blankenship, former ace reporter for the *Hutchinson News*, whose faithful live reportage during the Clutter murder trial was immensely helpful; Dr. Keith Collins, former USDA chief economist; the Kansas Historical Society; the Olathe Historical Society; and Mary Rasenberger, Executive

Director of the Authors Guild, for the Guild's legal assistance with the Hickock letters. Thanks to Lou Aronica of The Story Plant, whose publishing advice tipped the scale on which path to take; Fran Libra Koenigsdorf, who has taught *In Cold Blood* to young Kansas scholars for some thirty years, and upon whose expertise I often called; and for their encouragement in this project, a few of the talented writers I am honored to call friends: Tawni "P.L." O'Dell, T. Jefferson Parker, and Adriana Trigiani.

To Gray County Sheriff Jim Kramer, and his brother, former Sheriff Bill Kramer, whose late father Marvin "Squirt" Kramer provided the most crucial witness report mere hours after the Clutters were murdered; as well as Jack Curtis and Ken Curtis, sons of Garden City photographer and writer, Jack Curtis, whose fine work both Capote and I depended on. To Finney County Sheriff Kevin Bascue, local historian of the Clutter murder case, who obligingly assisted our legal team; investigative reporter Pat Shannan, whose 1966 interview with Floyd Wells at Mississippi's Parchman prison provided me with revelations on the most enigmatic character in the book; Dr. Richard Adler, for his kind introductions and keen observations; Michael Nations, son of *Wichita Eagle* reporter Starling Mack Nations, and his father's strongest advocate; Dr. Phillip K. Tompkins, Professor Emeritus of the University of Colorado at Boulder who was among the first to critically review *In Cold Blood* in 1966, for his engaging correspondence; Dean Rohleder, the son of the real hero of the Clutter investigation, Garden City Assistant Chief of Police Richard Rohleder; and Jon Craig, who interviewed Rich Rohleder and kindly shared with me many of his observations (and whose father was Finney County Sheriff Grover Craig); John Burgess for his unfailing photographic mindfulness and all the rest; JW Sternickle and Melanie Hansen with the Taro Leaf Society of the 24th Infantry Division Association; Kimberly McGath, former Sarasota County Sheriff detective and cold case consultant, for her thoughts on the Walker family murders; Tara Scott at the Mississippi Department of Archives and History; Stacia Lay, Mark Washburn, and Brenda Nixdorf of Hendricks & Lewis for strengthening our triumphant legal efforts; Meredith Mann and Brandon Westerheim at the Manuscripts and Archives Division of the New York Public Library, for facilitating frequent access to the Truman Capote papers; Mary O'Sullivan of the Society of Former Special Agents of the FBI; and to one historically significant contributor who wishes to remain anonymous.

To the cadre of friends, colleagues, and muses who lent me their ears, eyes, or voices in the wake of various revisions, or who contributed to this project in ways I couldn't begin to calculate: Marshall Bell, Renee Bell, Dr. Kurt Billett, Connie Calabrese, Megan Chao, Gene Dueber, Mimi Dueber, Karen Flannery, Dennis Foreman, Tony Francis and the Guides, Brad Gray, John Grissim, Mary Anne Gunter, Michelle Harden, Alex Heard, Joanne Hopkins, JT Hunter, Dr. Kent Kiehl, Sarah Lewis, Travis Lively, Mitchell Maxwell, Gregory McDonald, Sandi Mendelson, Joyce Nye, Lecia Nye, Byron Rabin, Mali Sastri, Gordon Taylor, Jenny Tharp, Albert Treskin, Peter Vartabedian, Seth Weber, and Ron Weekes. Thanks to each and all of you.

Finally, to Ron's father, Harold R. Nye, I extend posthumous admiration for his dedication to duty during the Clutter murder case. The exquisitely detailed handwritten notes he penned with every step taken in his investigation were infinitely valuable, giving up clues to various mysteries that would not reveal their relevance until decades later—a true literary treasure hunter's dream.

As Ron has claimed on several occasions, it felt as if his father was nudging us in certain directions, defending our cause as we were defending ourselves against the organization he was most proud to serve—sadly, one that turned its back on him after his death. Harold Nye's legacy is a lesson in undivided loyalty, one that should serve both as an inspiration to the men and women who dedicate their lives to law enforcement, and perhaps a caution to the agencies who take their service for granted.

Foreword

By Ronald R. Nye

In 1886 my great-great-grandfather, Henry Nye, loaded his family's worldly possessions into a covered wagon, bid farewell to friends and family, and left their home in Chillicothe, Iowa, for the fertile plains of western Kansas, homesteading a farm near Oakley, about 50 miles north of Garden City. Their son, my great-grandfather Charley William Nye, was just 19 years old at the time, and like so many other persevering, self-reliant German immigrants who settled in the grassland prairies of the Midwest, he, and his sons after him, became farmers as well.

My father, Harold Nye, was also raised on the farm. But he never saw himself taking over the family business. Since childhood, his dreams were associated with police work. Generations of stern northern European upbringing had instilled in his DNA an unyielding sense of law and order, of right and wrong. As a career law enforcement officer, he took that ethic to work every day, and brought it back home every night. And that's how I was raised, to respect the rule of law, a characteristic that has served me well throughout my life.

As far back as I can remember, Dad kept a more or less continuous diary, writing in hundreds of spiral-bound steno pads. His entries, which he frequently recorded at night, included his thoughts about pretty much everything: to-do lists for household chores and repair jobs, vacations, job-related tasks and observations from when he was a detective, and continuing with the practice when he became director of the Kansas Bureau of Investigation (KBI) and beyond into retirement. Dad kept these journals in a locked closet. None of us were ever allowed to go in there, because he said not to. (It was the same with his

service revolver. Visitors to our home were often shocked seeing
Dad's holstered weapon slung over the back of a living room
chair. Asked if he weren't concerned that my sister or I might
handle it: "No," he told them matter-of-factly, "because I told
them not to.")

When KBI Director Logan Sanford retired in 1969 it
surprised no one that the attorney general, Kent Frizzell, chose
Harold Nye as his replacement. Politically, however, Dad's
rigorous adherence to the rule of law didn't earn him many
friends, and he stayed in the job for just a few years. He would
never have sacrificed his principles for political gain; his only
objective was faithfully serving the people of the state his great-
grandfather helped settle nearly a century before, and he did so
with honor and distinction from 1947 until his own retirement
in 1975.

After Dad's death in 2003, my mother—as so many widows
do when their husbands pass—had to deal with some 50 years of
Dad's "stuff." And my dad was a legendary keeper of stuff,
including well over a dozen large boxes filled with copies of
documents from cases he had worked on throughout his career,
as untold numbers of investigators do in case they are ever called
to testify on former cases. Mom had wanted to get rid of them
for years, but Dad insisted on keeping them in the event he ever
got to write his memoir of police work. So, she had a huge
dumpster delivered for disposing of odds and ends in the garage
and attic—and also called a shredding company, who
indifferently fed so many years of my dad's life into their efficient
machines—and that was that.

Except for one box.

Truman Capote had an aloof but cordial relationship with
my father, and during the time he was working on *In Cold Blood*,
Truman—and I use the name familiarly here because he told me
to, having visited our home when I was a boy—would often
write letters to Dad, amiable letters chatting him up on various
aspects of the case and the trial, trying to draw out details from
him about the investigation—details which rarely satisfied
Truman's expectations (though he did have better luck with

Alvin Dewey). He also sent Dad first editions of two of his
books, both of them signed with warm inscriptions. That last
box, one I salvaged from the trash my mother had set out,
contained those books and letters, along with two note-filled
steno pads my father maintained during the Clutter murder
investigation. I was grateful beyond words that they had survived
a tragic fate with the shredders, for I had little else by which to
remember my father.

Frankly, I would just as well have preferred to keep my dad's
memorabilia than sell it, but my family's mounting medical
expenses came first, and I believed there was likely some value in
that box. I called Christie's, the esteemed auction house in New
York, but this was outside their area of interest, so they referred
me to the Seattle dealer Vintage Memorabilia.

Over the next few days the owner of that company, Gary
McAvoy, and I had many long talks about my father and the
Clutter case, and I knew I'd found the right home for my dad's
legacy. Gary has an authentic reverence for history and takes
seriously his role as provisional custodian for the objects left in
his care. I have no doubt he's invested far more time and effort
preparing my items for auction than he was likely to get out of
the deal. But his keen interest in Capote's legacy and, frankly,
empathy for my personal situation, inspired him to produce a
first-class presentation that was viewed by thousands of people
online and covered by media all over the world in the summer of
2012.

But then, inexplicably and at no small effort or expense, the
State of Kansas filed a lawsuit against us in a no-holds-barred
grab for my dad's personal notebooks regarding the Clutter
murder case, punishing his reputation with lies and insinuations
in the process. Rather than submit to their abusive and
threatening behavior, I did what my dad taught by example all
my life: I fought for what was right. And with the grateful
support of Gary and his company—and a first-rate legal team—
we chose the high road. After years of litigation, the District
Court of Kansas ultimately affirmed our First Amendment

rights to publish Dad's papers and notebooks—retaining possession of everything in the process—so that we could continue this work of which I am certain my father would have approved.

Over his long career in law enforcement Dad had many more interesting cases than this one, and he was always bewildered by the attention the Clutter case received. It was, after all, thought to be just a small-time robbery gone terribly wrong....

Ronald Nye
Oklahoma City

Introduction

"You often meet your fate on the road you
take to avoid it."

—French proverb

Introduction

Over a half century ago, Special Agent Harold R. Nye of the Kansas Bureau of Investigation (KBI)—who would later become that agency's third director—was thrust into an investigation to help solve what would eventually become an iconic tale of true crime in America: the brutal slayings of a Kansas wheat farmer, Herbert Clutter, and his wife and two children in November 1959.

A little more than fifty years later—as a dealer of rare historical letters, photographs, manuscripts, and books—I was contacted by Harold Nye's son, Ronald, in March 2012, who revealed who his father was and what materials he had to offer for sale. As an ardent collector of distinctive autograph memorabilia since the 1980s, with a particular appetite for literary manuscripts and signed first editions, I felt privileged to be handling the sale of the rarest books and letters by Truman Capote—presentation copies personally given by the author to one of the principal investigators, during the time history was being made.

The books, first editions of both *In Cold Blood*[2] and Capote's earlier work *Selected Writings*,[3] were each warmly inscribed by Truman to Harold Nye and his wife Joyce. That alone would generate solid interest in the sale, but this particular copy of *In Cold Blood* was also signed by twelve other people, including KBI Director Logan Sanford and three principal investigators in the case, among them Special Agent Alvin Dewey (who fared remarkably well in the story), and the director, actors, and crew of the eponymous 1967 movie, which used the Clutter house and other area locations to produce on film a chillingly authentic portrayal of what appeared on the page. As of this writing, only three such books signed by all principal figures are known to exist.

But the two personal letters Truman had written to Agent Nye were the most tantalizing of the lot. Both were sent in 1962 from his villa in Spain, on the Costa Brava overlooking the

Mediterranean, where he spent three springs and summers writing much of his book. In one letter, neatly composed on thin pages the color of wheat, Capote laments having to suffer yet another delay in finishing his book, with the Kansas Supreme Court having issued a stay of execution for the killers. For the frustrated author, this meant he would not yet have an ending—one way or another—for his book, and he was to endure another three years before realizing that goal, with the hanging of Richard Hickock and Perry Smith in April 1965. For a collector, this is the most vivid form of autograph correspondence: handwritten documents richly infused with intimate historical association and solid provenance.

The second letter, also in Capote's cramped, childlike scrawl but this one on 3-holed, blue-lined composition paper, teasingly informs Nye how often he appears in the book, and that "...*my editor said: 'Aren't you making this Mr. Nye just a little too clever?'*"

Along with the two signed books, these letters were to form the centerpiece of the auction. The rest of the material, though interesting on its own, held little tangible value to serious collectors. But it did contribute historical relevance and an in-person, chronicled authority to the auction as a whole, so we chose to offer all materials to the winning bidder—and only one bidder, since Ron Nye felt the material should stay together for historical continuity.

Sensing the gravity of the task ahead, like an eager historian I began educating myself more deeply in Capote's legacy. As I paged through Harold Nye's investigative notebooks and copies of actual case reports he had written—not yet digging deep, just skimming the material—I was reminded of key passages in Capote's masterwork—but they were hazy, since my first and last reading of it was the year it was published, in 1966. So, I reread the book with new vigor. This time, every word seemed to have fresh perspective, since I was privy to actual handwritten notes describing Nye's interviews, his discovery of clues and gathering of evidence, his random thoughts, and a hastily penned transcript gleaned while extracting a confession from one of the killers—all of which made the experience as visceral as being on the scene in 1959.

I watched the indelible 1967 film *In Cold Blood*, as well as the 1996 TV production of the same name, followed by 2005's film *Capote* and 2006's *Infamous*. I absorbed Ralph Voss's skillful examination of Capote's book,[4] Gerald Clarke's rich biography,[5] George Plimpton's interviews with Capote's "friends, enemies, acquaintances and detractors,"[6] Charles Shields' portrait of Harper Lee,[7] and anything else I could find that brought objective viewpoints to the table—along with many not so objective.

As prepared as one could be, then, I began assembling the material for an online catalog exhibiting the auction. After much consideration, Ron and I decided to exclude the crime scene photos, most of which were simply too gruesome to release "into the wild." We realized well before the auction went live that we would have no control over how they might be used in the future. Not wishing that burden on our shoulders, we removed the photos from the auction, and instead voluntarily sent them to the KBI for archival disposition.

To our surprise and dismay, a few days later we were served with a cease and desist letter from the Kansas attorney general at the instigation of the KBI, claiming among other things that Harold Nye's personal journals were state property and were possessed of "highly confidential information." On the face of it this was a farcical claim at best, since they had never seen the notebooks, not to mention that it had been well over fifty years since the case was closed and those charged with the crime had been executed, as the Court itself would ultimately point out. Our position, obviously, couldn't have been more at odds with Kansas's reckoning, and believing we were on the right side of the law, we took on their challenge. After a grueling legal battle, lasting years, it's clear now that Kansas thought Ron and I would just roll over and be done with it. That was their first mistake.

Over the time we prepared our defense—all the while baffled as to why Kansas was so vigorously mounting an expensive, and unusually high-level campaign of suppression and intimidation—a new thesis emerged that seemed at odds with the State's declared rationale. And the deeper we looked, the clearer that proposition became. To our thinking—not to mention the views of independent lawyers, journalists, forensic criminologists, and others who in some way touched our case—it looked more and more as if Kansas had something to hide. At the very least there was something more to this story, and I intended to find out what it was.

And therein lies their second mistake and the irony of this cautionary tale: Had the State of Kansas simply avoided such heavy-handed tactics as pressing the lawsuit against us, and publicly tarnishing Harold Nye's good name, we might never have discovered the sensational "new" details of the Clutter case that time and opportunity revealed as our own investigation deepened. Had they not interfered in our legitimate business—to provide for the Nye family's medical needs by selling the books, letters, and notes that rightfully belonged to his father—the KBI would not now be suffering under the weight of any potentially embarrassing disclosures being made here.

Throughout his life Truman Capote maintained that his book was "immaculately factual," as he told George Plimpton in a January 1966 interview.[8] Shortly after *In Cold Blood* first appeared in print—in September 1965, when the story was serialized in four consecutive issues of *The New Yorker* magazine—critics, pundits, and others assessing the work were already taking Capote to task for inaccuracies found in his account, or as one reviewer put it, "reaching for pathos rather than realism."[9] Not least among these was Harold Nye, who not only lived it, but whose prominent role in the book ultimately ensured a firsthand evaluation of the known facts.

But for as much as Capote added to or reshaped the brilliant telling of his story, in analyzing Harold Nye's notebooks I found that much had been omitted from *In Cold Blood*, and in many cases there were surprisingly crucial details that, at the time, might have appeared in the eyes of many to be of little value. It was only when other documents came into my possession that we were able to connect the dots, alluding to something very different than was passed on to readers of *In Cold Blood*.

In a striking coincidence, within a matter of weeks another new client—a grandson of Garden City Undersheriff Wendle Meier, one of the central characters in the story—consigned to me the Death Row diaries, family photos and correspondence, poetry, and a whole passel of riveting memorabilia given to Wendle Meier and his wife, Josephine, by one of the killers, Perry Edward Smith, on his way to the gallows. To be clear, I have no interest dealing in the so-called "murderabilia" market. But this was becoming more of a literary mystery the likes of which few people in my position could resist.

By this point any writer would feel grateful to have such an abundance of material to work with. But later, as a result of the media coverage our case had sparked, synchronicity struck again. I came into possession of copies of handwritten letters by Smith's partner in crime, Richard Eugene Hickock, which had originally been sent to *Wichita Eagle* reporter Starling Mack Nations. Hickock had contracted with Nations to write his "life story" while he was on Death Row. To the chagrin of both Hickock and Nations, however, no publisher showed interest in the book, titled *High Road to Hell*. But it's clear from Hickock's remarkable memory and his command of precise details, which both Capote and case investigators marveled over, that he did have compelling things to say.

As of this writing neither the Smith diaries nor the Hickock letters have been published, and only a handful of people have seen Hickock's letters to Mack Nations. But at least one thing is clear from putting all this material together—it appears there was a good deal more to the foundations of Capote's story than was originally told. And if there were any doubt as to whether Ron

Nye and I would just give in to the bullying tactics of a comparatively well-funded state government—saving ourselves a lot of time and money fighting a senseless battle—the new evidence coming at us from all directions made it unambiguously clear that we were on to something. And we had to believe Kansas suspected it, too.

Presented here, then, are several new hypotheses—undoubtedly bound for controversy, while nonetheless supported by facts— including one in particular that would surely have given authorities in Kansas every reason to fight as hard as they did to keep this material from being published: that Herbert Clutter may have been the victim of a murder-for-hire.

Despite an abundance of leads pointing in this darker direction, it appears that the original KBI investigation either overlooked or concealed such a fundamental possibility, one that no responsible law enforcement agency would ever rule out, given the circumstances. Indeed, this was and remained for some time the strongest opinion of coordinating investigator Alvin Dewey, and he personally knew Herb Clutter very well.

Yet despite new information becoming known to authorities years later, even before the killers had been executed, the Kansas attorney general at the time appears to have adopted a stance of letting sleeping dogs lie, without further investigation. But why? As is often the case with powerful institutions, could a keen drive for self-preservation have overshadowed a full accountability of justice?

Now, nearly six decades later, and with the passing away of nearly every involved character since 1959, it's unlikely any final determination can be made, short of a "Deep Throat"[10] insider emerging from the shadows of time. But much of what you find here will present compelling new arguments, and I leave it to readers to draw their own conclusions.

Forensics

"The truth is rarely pure
and never simple."

— Oscar Wilde

Case File

On November 16, 1959, a young writer in Brooklyn named Truman Capote was reading *The New York Times* when the headline of a brief article on page 39 caught his eye: **"WEALTHY FARMER, 3 OF FAMILY SLAIN: H. W. Clutter, Wife and 2 Children Are Found Shot in Kansas Home."**[11]

Capote, who at the time was enjoying fame as a minor literary figure after publishing *Breakfast at Tiffany's* a year earlier, had been experimenting with a novelistic style of nonfiction for *The New Yorker* magazine, but had yet to find a subject of "sufficient proportions"[12] that appealed to him. The murder of a Kansas farm family—its "ordinariness," and its impact on a local community frightened and bewildered by the crimes—provided the fresh perspective he sought in his writing, magnified by a completely foreign setting, for Capote had never set foot in the Midwest and knew little about it.

Thus began the work that would largely define Capote's life and, to some extent, his reputation after death 25 years later. Serialized in four consecutive issues of *The New Yorker* magazine beginning September 25, 1965, *In Cold Blood* was a huge sensation, selling out all copies published. By January 1966, the critical reviews were so strong that the initial print run of some 240,000 hardcover copies flew off the shelves. Since then, the book has never been out of print, having sold millions of copies. Even today it is required reading in countless high schools throughout the world and is used as case study material for college-level courses in fields such as law, criminology, and sociology. *In Cold Blood* is commonly ranked among the Top 100 best American books of all time in countless surveys (categorized as either fiction or nonfiction). As author Ralph Voss has noted, "*In Cold Blood*'s ongoing relevance stems from its unmatched role as a touchstone for enduring issues of truth, exploitation, victimization, and the power of narrative."[13]

American journalism at the time was in its nascent stage of becoming "mass media," nothing at all like today's ubiquitous news coverage. By 1960 only 40% of homes had a television, and those offered at most twelve channels whose broadcasts ended at midnight (to various renditions of *The Star-Spangled Banner,* while an American flag fluttered on the screen). By and large, radio and newspapers were the primary ways Americans learned what was happening in the world.

Mass murders were virtually unheard of. The only notorious modern crime preceding the Clutter atrocity was a two-state murder spree carried out in December 1957 and January 1958 by 19-year old Charlie Starkweather and his 14-year old girlfriend Caril Ann Fugate. The two teenagers drove through Nebraska and Wyoming, claiming eleven lives in their murderous rampage. For the first time in the early television era a serial killer was at large, and residents of surrounding states were terrified. Adding to the dread was the random nature of the victims, with no common denominator. Anyone could be next.

That same pervasive fear dominated much of the news following the brutal Clutter family killings, even in *The New York Times,* which is how Truman Capote learned of it. It is no exaggeration to say that the murder of the Clutters—an archetypal, God-fearing family in the Heartland—deeply affected millions of Americans who, before that dark moment in 1959, had no reason to lock their doors at night.

In view of the KBI's full-throated embrace and deference to *In Cold Blood* as conforming to the bureau's own official account, a critical examination of the errors and omissions in the KBI's investigation of the Clutter murders is, by necessity, a critique of Capote's work. Consequently, it seems important for the reader of this work to have, close at hand, a summary of the Clutter murders and the ensuing KBI investigation that is consistent with Capote's story (except as noted).

As you read this summary, two things should be kept in mind. First, it does not come close to, nor attempt to replicate, the indelible images, haunting prose, and genre-defining heft of *In Cold Blood*, which should be read in its entirety, in Capote's own words. Secondly, aspects of Capote's account differ significantly with the new evidence and hypotheses to which you will be introduced later in this book. Indeed, we have seen these new disclosures take people's breath away simply at the mere possibility of them, especially since most readers of *In Cold Blood* have accepted its conclusions as fact. Accordingly, you are advised to read the following as a primer, suspending for now a reflexive acceptance of the enduring mythology that has formed around the KBI-sanctioned account.

The Events and Circumstances Underlying
Truman Capote's
"In Cold Blood"

In the late 1950s, Herbert W. Clutter was a highly respected
farmer and pillar of his community in Garden City, a small town
in western Kansas. His three-thousand-acre River Valley Farm
produced wheat, alfalfa, barley, and grass for pasture, which fed
his 800 head of cattle. By any measure he was among the largest
and most successful ranchers in Kansas at a time when many
others were losing their farms.

Clutter's wife, Bonnie, was a nervous woman who suffered
from depression and slept in her own bedroom, where she also
spent much of her time. The Clutters had four children, two of
whom lived at home: 16-year old daughter Nancy, a bright and
popular high school student; and their 15-year old son Kenyon, a
quiet introvert who, like his sister, Nancy, was active in the 4-H
club. The Clutters' two remaining children, both older
daughters, had left home; one was married, the other was about
to be.

On November 14, 1959, two young ex-cons, Richard
Hickock and Perry Smith, drove four hundred miles west from
Kansas City with a plan to rob Mr. Clutter's office safe, based on
a tip given to Hickock by his former cellmate at Kansas State
Penitentiary (KSP) named Floyd Wells. Wells had worked for
Clutter eleven years earlier and told Hickock, among other
stories about the family and his time employed there, that
Clutter kept a safe in his office containing $10,000, often more
at harvest time.

Hickock, intrigued at the prospect of such a big score, had
convinced Smith, also a former cellmate at KSP but since
paroled, to help him do the job. The two men arrived at Clutter's
farm around midnight, entered the house through an unlocked
door, and using flashlights as their only illumination, began
looking for the safe.

After a failed search, Hickock, his anger mounting, woke Mr. Clutter, demanding he show them the safe, but Clutter is mystified, claiming truthfully that he has no safe. Smith, skeptical of this "perfect" score ever since Hickock pitched it to him a month earlier, quickly realized they were duped. Waking and rounding up the rest of the family, Smith and Hickock murder the family one by one, starting by gruesomely slashing Mr. Clutter's throat, then delivering close-range shotgun blasts to the head of each victim. After just over an hour in the house, Smith and Hickock flee the scene and soon make their way to Mexico.

Word of the crimes had spread quickly. With a population shy of 12,000 citizens to protect and serve, Garden City's local authorities were ill-equipped to handle the demands of an investigation gaining national interest. Finney County Sheriff Earl Robinson turned to Alvin Dewey, Jr., an agent of the Kansas Bureau of Investigation who lived in Garden City, to coordinate the case. KBI Director Logan Sanford assigned another 17 investigators to the case, among them three of the bureau's most skilled men: Special Agents Harold Nye, Clarence Duntz, and Roy Church. Together, these three agents carried out most of the field work while Dewey coordinated the investigation from the Sheriff's office in Garden City.

Herb Clutter was no ordinary farmer. He had also been president of the Garden City Co-op, founder of the Kansas Association of Wheat Growers, and former president of the National Association of Wheat Growers. In 1954, President Dwight Eisenhower appointed Clutter to the nation's first Federal Farm Credit Board.

It was, in fact, Clutter's prominence in the agricultural industry, both nationally and locally, that raised early suspicions that his murder might have had something to do with his political involvements. From the beginning of the investigation, Agent Dewey believed the crime was not a robbery, but a grudge killing that had gotten out of hand. Other findings at the crime scene did suggest robbery might have been the motive—Mr. Clutter's empty wallet left on the bed; Nancy's purse lying open on the kitchen floor; Kenyon's missing portable radio and binoculars. But a gold wedding band and diamond ring, probably the most valuable items to be found, were still on Mrs. Clutter's left hand. Why hadn't those been taken?

Investigators weren't alone in suspecting motives other than robbery. Many townspeople who were interviewed reported stories of personal vendettas against Mr. Clutter; of widely known arguments and hostile feelings in the wake of business transactions, some even involving specific threats to the farmer's life.

Richard Rohleder, assistant chief of police for Garden City and the principal crime scene investigator, had perceptively discovered the only clues authorities had to go on: two boot prints found in the dried blood on the dusty cardboard box laid beneath Mr. Clutter's body—one having a diamond pattern, the other bearing the distinctive Cat's Paw brand—indicating there were at least two perpetrators.

Two days after the murders, Floyd Wells, Hickock's old cellmate still serving time at Kansas State Penitentiary, heard about the Clutter murders on the radio, and word soon reached the warden that Wells believed he knew who committed the crimes. The KBI, now in possession of the names of two suspects, expanded its investigation into the backgrounds of Richard Eugene Hickock, 28, and Perry Edward Smith, 31.

KBI Special Agent Harold Nye, who had taken on the bulk of investigative field work, tracked down the growing number of leads authorities had accumulated on the suspects: interviewing Smith's sister in San Francisco and his father in Alaska; Hickock's parents in Olathe, Kansas; the owner of the body repair shop where Dick worked; hotels where they had spent the night; and the many pawn shops where they fenced stolen merchandise bought on check-kiting sprees. Nye visited most of these people and places himself, carefully noting details gleaned from each interview in the spiral-bound reporter's notebooks he always carried. Overall the investigation required hundreds of interviews, produced some 700 leads, and involved countless witness reports. Nye's own notebooks on the Clutter case comprised some 400 pages, front and back, packed with investigative minutiae.

On December 9, 1959, Nye and his team, armed with a search warrant, descended on the Hickock farm and took into evidence the hunting knife and Savage 12-gauge pump-action shotgun believed to have been used in the Clutter murders.[14]

On December 30, 1959—after traveling six weeks throughout the U.S. and Mexico—Hickock and Smith were arrested in Las Vegas by two observant police patrolmen who recognized the stolen vehicle from an all-points bulletin. The next day Agent Nye flew to Las Vegas to recover what evidence he could find, while Agent Dewey and other KBI investigators drove from Kansas to Nevada to assist Nye in interrogating the prisoners.

Both men eventually confessed to participating in the crimes. Hickock adamantly claimed that Smith had killed all four Clutters by his own hand. Smith said each killed two: he shot both father and son in the basement, while his partner shot the mother and daughter in their beds upstairs. After conferring with Hickock the next day, however, Smith changed his statement to accept blame for all four murders, purportedly to save Hickock's family from further grief.

The Garden City Sheriff's office was situated on the fourth floor of the Finney County courthouse. Since proximity and convenience benefited both the town and its sheriff, one perk of Sheriff Earl Robinson's job was a small furnished residence, which the sheriff chose to offer to the undersheriff and his wife, Wendle and Josephine Meier. The residence was adjacent to the jail, a secure block of cells equipped to handle some 30 prisoners. One of the cells—separated from the others by a solid steel door and dubbed the "ladies' cell"—was situated just off Mrs. Meier's kitchen.

The trial was set for March 22, 1960. Until then, the KBI wanted Smith and Hickock separated and unable to speak to each other, so Perry Smith was confined to the ladies' cell. From there, he could talk with the undersheriff's wife, Mrs. Meier, as she prepared meals for her husband and any prisoners in residence.

Over the two months before the trial began, Perry developed a fondness for his jailers, especially "Josie" Meier—as she did for him, despite her husband's caution to keep her distance, to remember what those boys had done. Regardless of Perry's terrible actions, Josie found in him a sort of lost boy, one who'd had a rough go in life. She often made his favorite meal, Spanish rice, and—as Perry later wrote in his journals—they became convivial, or at least as friendly as two people could be in that situation.

The weeklong trial began, the Honorable Roland H. Tate presiding. The evidence presented against Hickock and Smith was overwhelming. Neither defendant testified on his own behalf.

The State's star witness, the last to take the stand, was Floyd Wells, Hickock's former cellmate at KSP. Up to that moment the identity of this "mystery man"—the tipster who broke the case by fingering Hickock and Smith as prime suspects—had been kept secret, mainly for his own protection as an informer, lest some harm come to him in prison.

Wells's testimony was well-rehearsed. He laid out the bones of the story he told the KBI when first interviewed,[15] about the time he worked for Mr. Clutter in 1948; about how generous the man was and how good the family was to him. He then talked about his time in prison with Dick Hickock, whom he claimed showed keen interest when Wells revealed that Clutter was a wealthy man who kept as much as $10,000 in cash in a safe behind his desk.

When prosecuting attorney Duane West[16] asked him about the safe, Wells responded, "It has been so long since I worked out there. I thought there was a safe. I knew there was a cabinet of some kind."[17] When asked if Hickock told him how he was going to rob Mr. Clutter, Wells said Hickock was not going to leave any witnesses, going into further detail about Hickock's plan. Wells's graphic description told the jury all it needed to know.

Defense attorneys had sought and obtained psychiatric evaluations of both Hickock and Smith. The evaluations revealed serious incidents in the earlier lives of each man, and the presence of psychoses that may have sufficiently influenced their actions to warrant the jury's considering a penalty other than death.

But the twelve men on the jury were never allowed to consider psychosis as a contributing factor to the defendants' mental capacity. Kansas law permitted only "Yes" or "No" responses to specific questions. Dr. W. Mitchell Jones, the psychiatrist from Larned State Hospital who had volunteered to examine the men, offered to elaborate on the defendants' mental state, but the judge allowed only a determination as to whether each defendant knew the difference between right and wrong. Dr. Jones had spent only one hour with each man; regardless, he could offer no response other than "Yes."

It took the jury just forty minutes to render a verdict: Guilty on all counts, sentenced to death by hanging.

Over the next five years both Hickock and Smith filed a series of appeals that eventually reached the U.S. Supreme Court. None of the appeals offered sufficiently reasonable grounds to overturn the original convictions and sentence. Their options exhausted, the final execution date was set for April 14, 1965.

"The Corner" at the Lansing state prison was a grim, shadowy building, a windowless brick-walled warehouse where stacks of lumber and other out-of-the-way surplus was kept. It was an all but neglected setting with just one important though rarely-used function, carried out upon a tall wooden structure erected in one corner of the building. At the base of the structure, the first of thirteen steps rose to a ceiling-high scaffold, over which a thick spar of timber was suspended from opposite corners by two sturdy posts. Casual observers might have found little noteworthy about the structure, hidden in the shadows as it was, but for two pale nooses hanging from its crossbeam. On the scaffold stood a thin, leathery executioner wearing a capacious knee-length coat, a sweat-stained cowboy hat perched on his head.

Around midnight a somber group of men gathered at the base of the gallows, waiting expectantly: a few prison officials; a handful of reporters; KBI agents Harold Nye, Roy Church, Clarence Duntz, and Alvin Dewey; the Finney County sheriff; and the psychiatrist, Dr. W. Mitchell Jones. Also present was one individual whom both condemned men had invited as their personal witness, someone each had befriended in his own way over the years leading up to that moment—Truman Capote.[18]

A sudden cloudburst pounded the roof of the wooden building as a vehicle approached the entrance, its headlights piercing the heavy rain. Richard Hickock, handcuffed and trussed in a leather harness embracing his torso, emerged from the vehicle surrounded by several guards.

The warden recited the death warrant and Hickock mounted the scaffold. The executioner placed a hood over his head while the chaplain intoned a prayer. Then, as another heavy shower of rain pummeled the wooden roof, the hangman sprang the trap door. All eyes below followed Hickock's body as it plunged down through the opening. He was dead in twenty minutes.

A hearse removed Hickock's body as a second car pulled up behind it. Shackled and harnessed as his partner was, Perry Smith exited the car, his jaws working a spent stick of chewing gum. His expressionless eyes peered first around the dark warehouse, then up at the waiting noose and the gaunt man who would place it around his neck, and finally down to the assembled group.

The warden repeated the reading of the warrant, and before the executioner placed the hood over his head, Smith spat out the gum into the chaplain's outstretched hand. The noose was fastened around his neck and he took his last breath.

Cohorts

"Tis the only comfort of the miserable to
have partners in their woes."

— Miguel de Cervantes

Defendant

Beyond having a direct lineage to one of the founding families of Kansas, Ronald Nye's name is forever linked to history through his father, Harold Nye, the lead field investigator for the Kansas Bureau of Investigation during one of America's most famous early criminal cases.

Ron was nine years old when the Clutter family was murdered on November 14, 1959. And although he was just a boy, the date of the crime is not something he is likely to forget, for the 14th of November happens to be his birthday. What's more, he was born in Garden City, Kansas, the same town and hospital that Nancy and Kenyon Clutter were born in, just a few years before Ron:

> It must have been sometime in 1959 when I first became aware of the Clutter murders. I was nine years old then and I remember the moment so well. My mother drove a 1950-something Dodge coupe to take my sister and I to school every day. My sister and I did not get along... not at all. To keep her more than an arm's length away I would sit in the back seat of that old brown car and wait for my sister to get dropped off first, she was a few years older than I was and her school was closer.
>
> My dad was gone a lot in those days. He never really said much about what he was working on, but one day when he came home he had put something in the back seat of Mom's car—a very large piece of cardboard with stuff stuck all over it. It had a large black stain from some kind of liquid that had dried on it, like it had been poured on it. There were bits of something in black,

some of them small, like little bugs, and some larger, like chips of wood.

If you asked my dad a straight question about something, he gave you a straight answer. You might not understand it, but still, he gave it to you "with the bark on it." So, the next time he was at home for supper I asked him what was all over that cardboard in the back seat. He said some of it was part of a man's brain and skull...and the black liquid was his blood. That was enough information, and where that conversation ended.

When I was in my early teens, I heard some friends talking about the movie *In Cold Blood*. They said that Mr. Clutter had been killed while laying on a mattress box in the basement of his home. It rang a bell with me all those years later. The timing was right, and the description was right. The piece of cardboard in the back of my mom's car must have been what my friends were talking about. I waited for another opportunity to ask Dad about the cardboard that had been in the back seat of Mom's car. He simply stated that, yes, it was the one Mr. Clutter had been killed on, destined for the KBI lab in Topeka for tests. Dad had to return to the Clutter farm before being able to check it in to the property room at headquarters, however, so he dropped it off at home for safekeeping.

I also remember another evening when my dad brought a slide projector from the office with a box of transparencies he needed to analyze. We had finished dinner and Dad waited for the dishes to get washed. He told my mother and sister that he was going to look at some autopsy slides on the kitchen wall and asked them to leave

the kitchen. They left, and as I got up Dad
asked if I wanted to stay and view them with
him.

Those slides are as vivid in my mind
today as they were that evening. Not
because I knew they were the Clutter family,
but because this was the first time that Dad
let me watch an autopsy of naked females.
Believe me there was nothing erotic about
what I was watching. The pictures revealed
the step-by-step process of layers of flesh
being peeled back to locate objects that had
stuck in the flesh and bone. I still remember
the close-up pictures of the heads with large
pieces missing or just barely hanging on.[19]

In the seven years from the Clutter murders in 1959 to his
sixteenth birthday in 1965, Ron had not seen much of his father.
Promoted to assistant director of the KBI just months after
winding up the Clutter investigation, Harold Nye's caseload—
indeed, the KBI's entire crime fighting caseload throughout the
state—was outpacing the meager capabilities of the bureau's
dozen or so field agents.

Fighting crime was what Harold Nye was built for. But the
cost to his family life was a bitter trade. His wife, Joyce, never
knew when she might see her husband again for dinner; she
fretted over the grim and ever-present possibility that he might
fall in the line of duty. Joyce Nye struggled with persistent
anxiety as long as Harold had the job. Young Ron, who slept at
the foot of her bed each night when Harold was away, bore the
brunt of safeguarding his mother from her imagined dangers.
Since childhood, Joyce had been warned that if she wandered too
far from home the gypsies would steal her, thus beginning a life
filled with groundless fears.

As a son whose dad, for years, had never come to any of his
sporting events at school, Ron had his own melancholy. Lacking
other interests at home or school, and with a family life that held

more strictures than it did stability, Ron felt stifled.

Rebellious adolescents looking to find their place in life often dream of escaping the confines of family, of metaphorically "running away to join the circus." At age fifteen Ron harbored similar dreams of independence, but when he chose to act on them, the circus he ran off to join was a literal one—he jumped at the chance to become a "carney" for Royal American Shows, the largest traveling circus troupe in the world.

Over the next few decades Ron lived a life not unlike most middle-class Americans. He had three children from two marriages, four grandchildren, and three great-grandchildren. His career as a rehabilitation counselor fulfilled him, and his hobby of fixing up old cars kept his mind content. The discipline instilled in him by his father (nascent in youth, when little else mattered except girls and sports) ultimately applied itself admirably in college, where Ron graduated magna cum laude. Following graduate school, he was credentialed as a National Certified Counselor and later certified by the American Board of Medical Psychotherapists and Psychodiagnosticians.

Like his father, Ron chose a life of service, but he never sought the kind of spotlight that rivaled his father's. His more discreet calling came, unbidden, on the morning of April 19, 1995. Working as a licensed professional counselor for HealthSouth Rehab Hospital in Oklahoma City, he was discussing patients with a colleague when, at exactly 9:02 a.m., a Ryder rental truck parked three blocks away, in front of the Alfred P. Murrah Federal Building, exploded with such violence that—as would be accounted for later—324 buildings in a sixteen-block radius were damaged or destroyed.

Starting almost immediately following that pivotal event in American history, and for the next several years, Ron and his team counseled and treated nearly every survivor of the bombing, including first responders. He was later nominated by the Oklahoma Counseling Association for the Humanitarian of the Year Award for his work with the survivors and was named Counselor of the Year by HealthSouth Oklahoma City.

As the epicenter of tornadoes in the U.S., people living in Oklahoma are ever vigilant for abrupt weather changes, especially in May, when rotating columns of air touching the earth appear with little warning, often causing massive destruction in their wake.

But in 2005 the entire state was spared from the threat of even one twister. Spring, brief as it usually is there before the hot, humid days of summer press in, had favored Oklahoma City with a picture-perfect day on the 10th of May, and the sun had just settled above the horizon when Ronald Nye pulled up to his mother's house in Warr Acres, a tidy suburb northwest of the city.

Obviously, his mother was doing a thorough job of cleaning house. An imposing green twenty-yard dumpster, already brimming with household detritus after just a few days on site, hugged the side of the driveway where his mother and sister had parked their cars. Risking a ticket from the ambitious patrols scouting the neighborhood, Ron nosed his Dodge Caravan in behind the dumpster, its tail jutting out into the street, and shut the engine off.

It had been a long day counseling patients at the hospital, and as the early evening's lingering warmth swirled around him, he closed his eyes and leaned back for a moment. The mellow percussive slap harmonics of Michael Hedges' acoustic guitar, winding down on the CD player, braced him for the certain chaos waiting inside the home his father died in two years earlier.

Harold Nye passed away in 2003. For his wife, Joyce, the house they had shared for 28 years had grown too big and become too empty with the kids grown and gone. Alone and increasingly apprehensive, her anxiety spells were more frequent, unpredictable, and often tormenting. She looked forward to living closer to her son in Edmond, north of the city, where he could look in on her after work.

His moment of bliss over, Ron switched off the ignition and got out of the van. Behind his mother's car a row of trash cans had been put out for collection, jutting haphazardly into the street. Figuring his van might be enough ticket for one day, he pulled the bins in closer to the curb.

Peering inside the bins, Ron spied stacks of paper—old photos, fingerprint cards, an assortment of documents—and two spiral-bound reporter's notebooks, the kind his father had used for years. Notebooks he was never permitted to see as a young boy; notebooks he had completely forgotten about since leaving home to join the circus.

Reaching down, he snatched a thick, worn, chestnut-brown folder with an elastic tie cord enclosing it, shaking off scraps of garbage partly obscuring it.

He set the folder on the hood of his van, exposing two familiar hardcover books his mother had also discarded—and suddenly a memory surfaced: a vision of Truman Capote sitting in his family's living room in 1960, talking about his famous Hollywood friends, names like Humphrey Bogart and Marilyn Monroe.

From beneath the jetsam of household rubbish, Ron pulled out the two books—signed first editions of *In Cold Blood* and Capote's *Selected Writings*—both inscribed and given to his father by Truman many years before, when Ron was eleven years old. Beneath those books was yet another brown clasped folder identical to the first, but this one was stuffed with yellowed newspaper clippings about the Clutter murders.

For years, Harold Nye had saved copies of reports from every investigation he'd ever worked on, an entirely permissible practice under Kansas statute and—more relevant to law enforcement professionals—a sensible policy in the event they might later be called to testify in court.

After a long and rigorous career, reams of musty old paperwork filled some 15 sturdy banker's boxes Harold had diligently kept stored up in the attic for decades, and which had agitated his wife Joyce to no end, anxiously convinced the KBI would one day come a-knocking. Despite her husband's assurances that he was in compliance with the law, she remained unsettled by their presence in her home. Joyce Nye did not trust the KBI.

Ron's reverie was broken by the distant sound of clanging garbage cans, followed by the high-pitched whine of a hydraulic packer blade, compacting the hopper in a garbage truck approaching the house. Seizing the books and the second folder out of the trash, Ron stowed everything in his van and went inside to join his mother and sister in clearing out the house, packing up what was left of her worldly possessions:

> Before I got a chance to say anything to Mom about the folders and books I fished out, she just came out with it. "You're going to be mad at me, I just know it," she said. "But I got those boxes of your dad's down from the attic and had them professionally shredded. I called a company and they brought a shredding truck out to the house last week and destroyed all of them while I watched!" She announced this with a certain measure of pride, as if it had been on some years-long checklist she could finally mark off and be done with.
>
> I just never regarded my father's files in the attic like she did. Mom said many times that she wished they were gone. I told her it was fine that she had them shredded, but that I'd found the two books and Dad's papers on the Clutter case in the trash. She said she hadn't discovered them until after the truck left, because they were on the shelf in Dad's office.
>
> Because I knew this was a sensitive issue for her, I asked if she had any problem with me taking them out of the trash. She said *"No, as long as you don't bring them back into my house!"*
>
> I didn't bring them back into my mom's house. Instead, I took them home.[20]

Six years later, in 2009, Ron learned from his son Will that his ex-wife Lecia was fully disabled, suffering from lupus and early onset Alzheimer's, and living in federal housing, a scaled-down "apartment" the size of a walk-in closet. Despite being divorced from her for thirty years, Ron had never stopped caring for her:

> I'd always told Lecia that when I sleep and dream about a girl, that girl is always her. She is literally the girl of my dreams, always has been. But thirty years ago I was young and foolish, so self-absorbed that I couldn't see myself tied down with a sick wife for the rest of my days—so I left her and filed for divorce. To this day I agonize over that decision more than any other in my life. But at the time Lecia also thought it was the right thing to do, for she could be neither wife nor mother due to her illness. So, we parted amicably.[21]

Decades later, Ron still carried the burden of abandoning his ex-wife. He decided to visit her, looking for any way he might help. When he discovered her living in such shabby, degrading conditions, he couldn't bear it. He implored her to move in with him so he could take care of her properly, proposing that they spend their remaining days together.

Despite everything, Lecia knew Ron still loved her. She was also aware that her quality of life was diminishing, and that Ron's offer was the most sensible option she had out of not very many good ones. She accepted Ron's offer. He moved her into his home that day.

After three years living together, and with the approach of their fourth winter, Ron knew that the insulation in his drafty home was inadequate for Lecia's comfort. The insulation of his home was inadequate to stave off the constant drafts:

When the wind blows through this old house

you can hear all the windows rattle. No amount of caulk would seal them up; they needed replacement, but I didn't have that kind of money.

Then I remembered those books Truman gave my father, the ones I dug out of the trash. There were also two letters I found tucked inside the pages of one of the books, part of an exchange of correspondence Dad had with Truman while he was in Spain working on *In Cold Blood*, and I figured they might have some value.

My dad also had a lot of official papers, copies of reports he filed during his investigation of the Clutter murders, and two reporter's notebooks he kept all his notes in. All of these papers, by the way, dealt only with the Clutter investigation. There was nothing remaining in what I pulled out of the trash—the only surviving materials that didn't get shredded—that discussed anything but the Clutter case.

So Lecia and I gathered everything I'd salvaged from my mother's trash bin several years before—the books, the letters, documents, photos, notebooks, clippings— all of it. While I worked up an inventory list, she started making calls to auction houses to see if there was any interest they might have in the material.

After a few calls we finally reached someone at Christie's in New York who was personally intrigued by what I'd told her— about my father having worked on the famous murder case that sparked *In Cold Blood*—but she admitted the material wasn't really the kind of thing Christie's handled.

She did, however, suggest I call Gary McAvoy, a dealer of historical memorabilia in Seattle.[22]

And that's when our long journey began.

Motive

Ron and I forged an easy rapport over the next few weeks. We made arrangements to have his father's notebooks and other documents sent to me in Seattle, and even discussed the possibility of writing a book about Harold Nye's role in the famous murder case. Although interest in Truman Capote's work had remained high for well over five decades, not one of the principals had ever written anything more than a few articles about the case.

As I came to discover, Harold Nye did have a story to tell, one he'd wanted to write after he retired from the KBI. There were things about the Clutter case that had nagged him for years, pieces of a puzzle that didn't quite fit together, especially for a man trained to recognize which tabs interlocked with their corresponding blanks, making the puzzle whole. Sadly, his goal to write a book laying out only what he knew never materialized.

But for now, any thoughts of helping Harold achieve that dream posthumously had to wait.

With the approach of another frigid Oklahoma winter, Ron more than ever wanted to install double-paned windows throughout the house to protect Lecia from drafts. Understanding it might take a while to find a buyer for his father's historical cache, and with Lecia's medical expenses mounting, we determined that an auction would be the quickest way to get top value in the shortest time.

Over the next few weeks, I prepared an online catalog of the items being auctioned and posted it on my company's website. A few friends and colleagues helped test it and by all accounts it presented well.

Ron and I spent much time considering how to display the

original crime scene photographs, the very photos taken by Officer Rich Rohleder in 1959 which were used to convict Hickock and Smith. Each bore the signature of *"Harold R. Nye"* penned on the back, for it was Nye himself who had developed them in the KBI photo lab.

Few people have seen all photos from the Clutter murders. Those of the victims, in particular, hold a lurid attraction for many. In my research, I found a cultish fascination existed in locating those specific images. Exposing this underbelly of the internet did little to mitigate my reluctance in displaying them at all. As a compromise, I reduced each photo to the size of a postage stamp, expunging any detectable detail but sufficient as a practical disclosure to potential buyers that they did exist and were part of the auction.

That these photographs were being offered at all troubled me, not just on a personal level but for the reputation of my business. Again, I sought the opinion of friends and colleagues. A majority believed the crime scene images were essential to the auction process, that they intensified the historical significance while attesting to the brutal consequences of the crime. After all, went the rationale, it wasn't as if we never saw grisly images like that on TV or in movies. Precedent had long been settled on that score. In November 2017, in fact, SundanceTV aired filmmaker Joe Berlinger's four-part documentary series, *Cold Blooded: The Clutter Family Murders,*[23] featuring many of the same more controversial images.

A minority, however, felt that exhibiting the photos might be indelicate and surely impolitic in some circles, despite the minuscule size of the images. My instincts squared with the minority view. But I am, at the end of the day, in the business of representing my clients' best interests, and this particular client not only needed but deserved the best return we could achieve at auction. We kept the images discreet.

Ready to launch the event, then, tempting fate on Friday, July 13, 2012, we issued an arresting press release announcing a sealed bid auction ending on August 31:

...The sealed bid auction, comprising the
extensive personal investigative archives of
Special Agent Harold Nye, the youngest of
four Kansas Bureau of Investigation
detectives assigned to the case—features
never-before-seen letters sent from Truman
Capote to Agent Nye discussing intimate
details of the case years before the book
was published. In one letter Capote
laments, *"...I assume the Kansas Supreme
Court will have set a new execution date for
Perry and Dick. And now I suppose they will
go into the federal courts, and the whole
thing will drag on into eternity! No, I'm not
bloodthirsty either, but I do wish the damn
thing would end. So that I can finish the
book before I'm too old and feeble to hold a
pen."*

Also highlighted in the auction are
hundreds of pages of investigative
notebooks and documents, transcripts of
interviews with and confessions of the
murderers, original crime scene
photographs long shielded from the public
(and which have been obscured in the
online catalog out of respect to the surviving
family), fingerprint sheets, mug shots, and
rare first editions of Capote's books,
including *In Cold Blood* signed by the
principal KBI detectives as well as the cast
and crew of the 1967 film of the same name
starring Robert Blake and Scott Wilson as
the killers....

A full, detailed inventory accompanied the online catalog,
listing the contents of each of several document packets, along
with scanned images of various items that might elicit dramatic
appeal for bidders. Having decided to keep the entire lot together
for sale to just one buyer, we expected a minimum bid in the low

5-figures, an amount that, to use an apt metaphor, would separate the wheat from the chaff in terms of potential bidders. But it's safe to say, interest in the auction exceeded our expectations.

Within days, the release sparked excitement in newspapers and websites around the world. Thousands of visitors watched the online presentation. Email messages and phone calls poured in daily inquiring about the items, people asking if they could just buy one thing or another, media outlets asking for further details, teachers requesting class materials for their students.... Clearly interest was building; more interest, in fact, than we were prepared for.

But before the auction hammer could fall, a hammer of a different sort came down on us.

Search & Seizure

"He who controls the past controls the future. He who controls the present controls the past."

— George Orwell

Shamus

Within days of news breaking about the auction, Ron received an unexpected phone call at home, and at a rather peculiar time: after 8:00 p.m. on Saturday night, July 28, 2012. The caller identified himself as Kirk Thompson, director of the Kansas Bureau of Investigation—the man holding the same office Ron's father held until 1971.

The KBI has some 300 employees. That the director personally made the call got our attention. It also made us curious. Why would the chief executive of the KBI, who reports directly to the state's attorney general—two steps down from the governor—make such a call himself?

Thompson got right to the point. News of our auction had reached him, and he wanted to meet with Ron to discuss the materials being offered. Ron, ever amiable, invited Thompson to meet at his home in Oklahoma City to discuss the matter. Thompson agreed, saying he would drive down the next morning—an eight-hour round trip by car from KBI headquarters in Topeka, *on a Sunday*. Clearly there was some urgency guiding his mission.

It then occurred to Ron that, as field representative for the State of Oklahoma's rehabilitation counseling programs, he had already arranged meetings with affiliate agencies in Topeka later that week, so he offered instead to meet Thompson there, if the director wanted to save eight hours of his own time on the road. The two agreed to meet at Ron's hotel in Topeka on Monday, August 2, 2012.

Ron recalls their meeting that day in the lobby of the Hampton Inn:

> Our appointment was set for 5:00 p.m. but with my state business done I'd arrived early, waiting in the lobby, when a tall bald man approached me. Thompson introduced

himself and we took a table in the lounge, sitting across from each other. He looked pretty fried, confessing he'd been in a budget meeting all day.

Like he did in our phone call, Thompson got right to the point, telling me he was troubled by the pending sale of some of my father's materials. As background, I walked him through how all this started: rescuing Truman's books and letters to my dad from the trash, along with his notebooks, photos, and other papers; how I was now the sole caretaker for my ex-wife, whose medical expenses were the reason I put Dad's materials up for sale; and how Lecia and I organized and boxed them up for shipment to Seattle.

I even described how, as a little kid, Dad would take me with him to KBI headquarters on weekends; this would be some time in the late 1950s. Dad had authorized access to everything, and as he looked through boxes of closed case files in the underground archives he would set some boxes aside, taking them to offices upstairs where secretaries could later copy items he needed to work on a book. He'd always wanted to write a book about his investigations, and for years asked me to help him. But being a teenager then, I didn't really have interest in any of that.

Several times during the conversation Thompson probed for ways he might preempt our sale and commandeer all the items he had highlighted on the inventory list, which a month earlier had been posted on the website's auction page. But I had to remind Thompson, several times, that I had already turned over my dad's entire archive to Vintage Memorabilia in preparation for sale, and that I no longer had any control over the material.

I had learned the art of "purposeful conversation" from one of the best. My dad was a gifted interrogator, and he would often try to break me, getting me to acknowledge whatever adolescent mischief I'd gotten into. My father was a master of the third degree, with a piercing gaze so intimidating that even the most resistant subjects eventually collapsed. I was the only one he could never get to fold, which frustrated him to no end.

And while that skill has come to be useful in my job as a counselor, sitting there with Thompson I sensed I might be in an adversarial position, so my instincts were on full alert. I was not going to let this guy put me in a one-down position.[24]

Our conversation went on for over an hour, and all that time Thompson was bent over in his chair, his neck leaning forward as he rubbed both hands across his shaven head which, like his face, was getting redder and redder as I spoke. Having worked in a hospital for over 20 years, observing the physiological condition of people I'm interacting with had become second nature to me. And it was obvious this was one stressed and exhausted man. I kept thinking it was a good thing I knew CPR.

At the end of our time together, Thompson pointedly told me that, while Capote's books and letters didn't matter to him, he was committed to taking possession of my dad's investigation records, which he claimed were state property—and that included Dad's personal notebooks.

Of course, I had a different notion. My

> father had devoted his entire life in service
> to Kansas. There was no way I'd let them
> lay claim to his personal papers.
>   On my way back to Oklahoma, I called
> Gary to fill him in and give him a heads up.
> Thompson would be calling him next.[25]

I did not have to wait long. Director Thompson called the very next day, and a couple more times after that, leaving messages with my service. I had been busy traveling that week but returned his calls when I got back home to Seattle.

Introducing himself, Thompson told me—as he told Ron—that he was calling on behalf of "the families of the victims and the defendants." By "the defendants" he obviously meant Smith and Hickock—the killers—which I thought was an odd collaboration of influence by any measure. As I later found out, Perry Smith's family, what was left of it, had estranged itself from anything to do with him—which only left the Hickocks, though any concerns they might have had about the disclosure of Harold Nye's notebooks on the investigation were a complete mystery to us.

It's relevant to note here that I had not yet thoroughly read any of Agent Nye's materials. A student of history, I did skim through the two notebooks, taking in the moment of proximity to one of literature's most enduring true crime stories. But aside from the long-standing admiration I had for *In Cold Blood* as a gripping narrative, I had little interest in crime as a genre, whether true or fictional. I did glance through the unsettling photographs of the murdered Clutter family, though with dispassionate interest. All of which is to say that I had no clue yet what information these materials possessed. Anything irrelevant to the auction itself had simply been inventoried by type, and that was that.

Since Ron had explained the background of his circumstances to Thompson, I took him through my own role in the transaction which, as for all historical items I take in, involves careful vetting to best insure that ownership is free and clear, while establishing as strong a provenance as possible to prospective clients. In my discussions with Ron, I was assured he had rights to the materials, and there was no doubt about their authenticity.

I had also researched Kansas law regarding the disposition of materials of this nature. Since these records were prepared long before any specific statutes governing their disposition were in place—and being *file copies*, not originals—I was reasonably convinced that we were on solid ground; that this material did belong to Harold Nye, and that it lawfully passed to Ron from his mother after Harold's death.

I also confirmed that, as Thompson would have found in the online presentation for the auction, we had terms in place forbidding the eventual buyer from any rights to publication of any kind, essentially to safeguard public exposure and misuse of the crime scene photos.

Since those images seemed to be the KBI's main concern—and, as mentioned earlier, we had reservations about offering them in the first place—I explained we would be happy to oblige him by delivering all materials on his list, especially the photos. Frankly we were just as glad to have that responsibility out of our hands. The only exceptions we made, and would not turn over under any circumstances, were Nye's two steno notebooks. These were Harold Nye's diaries and represented material value to Ron, especially with the generous inscription of a prominent party to the events—Nelle Harper Lee—who on one clean page penned a personal sentiment to Harold Nye six months *before* the publication of *To Kill a Mockingbird*, the book that lifted her from obscurity to winner of the Pulitzer Prize for Fiction in 1961.

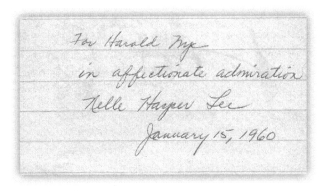

Figure 1. Nelle Harper Lee signed inscription to Nye
Harold R. Nye Archives

By the end of our conversation, Thompson appeared to be agreeable, and pleasantly so, indicating that he would relay this offer back to "the families" and that return of all other materials, excluding the notebooks, would likely resolve the situation. He specifically added that he "didn't think it would go any further."

That isn't how things turned out. Three days after our fairly cordial conversation, Thompson called again. This time his voice had a different timbre to it, clearly more subdued, less confident, even somewhat chastened, I felt, given his more cooperative and optimistic tone just a few days earlier. If I were to speculate, I'd say he had been directed, in no uncertain terms, to procure *all* materials at any cost.

Thompson now made clear that the attorney general had demanded that all materials be "returned" to them—an odd claim, given that Nye's personal notebooks were originated by him and had never been seen by anyone else.

First, though, the KBI wanted to send someone out to Seattle to inspect our cache of documents "just to see what we have." I was told "an agent who knew the files intimately" would arrive at my office three days hence, at 9:00 a.m. on Monday.

This was not an appealing prospect, to say the least. It was an intrusive and undiplomatic tactic, and for Kansas to act so brazenly, especially when our discussions had been moving along amicably, made me less inclined to accommodate any of their demands.

This peculiar change in their approach was our first indication that someone wanted these materials pretty desperately. Instead of opening my door to one of his agents, I offered to send Thompson a DVD containing a digital copy of all material, to which he agreed, though I gather with some reluctance.

I'd seen enough political thrillers to know that when the stakes are high enough, the person who possesses incriminating evidence is likely to find himself the victim of some "misfortune." To even the bargain, that person often takes out an "insurance policy."

While I didn't feel my life was in danger, I did think it might be prudent to get a copy of these materials into the trusted hands of someone in the media—just in case it was all snatched out of ours without due process.

I didn't have to wait long for another stroke of synchronicity. Two days after my conversation with Kirk Thompson, I received a call from Kevin Helliker at *The Wall Street Journal*. A University of Kansas graduate who grew up just a mile from the Hickock farm, Helliker has had a lifelong interest in the Clutter murders. When word of our auction reached him, he asked me if he could see some of the Nye materials.

Helliker had won a Pulitzer Prize for his past work, so I was delighted to share our cache of documents with such a respected journalist. But since Helliker's beat was largely health and sports, I didn't hold much hope for his writing an article about our auction or the legal peril surrounding it. But at least whatever Kansas wanted so badly would be in the hands of an independent third party, a senior reporter for a prominent newspaper the State of Kansas would be hard pressed to coerce.

Based on the KBI's interest in our little auction—and put on guard by the director's unsettling assertions to Ron about a preemptive strike, as well as his puzzling change of attitude—it was clear we might need some legal advice. I figured our best strategy was to find someone with expertise in taking on public agencies, and—given our proximity to Truman Capote and his work—someone skilled as well in intellectual property law.

Though Seattle is teeming with lawyers, for our particular needs one firm stood out: Hendricks & Lewis. The firm's partners, O. Yale Lewis, Jr. and his wife Katherine Hendricks, had won major cases against cities, states, and the federal government, as well as litigating complex estate issues for the Jimi Hendrix family, the rock band Nirvana, and Kurt Cobain's wife, Courtney Love—all successful wins in defense of intellectual property.

Having been a Navy submarine officer, Yale knew, literally and figuratively, how to work in tight spaces—and we were definitely in one of those. He also hails from Alabama, not far from where Truman Capote and Harper Lee grew up, another touch of synergy to the unusual case encircling us.

Yale, a Southern gentleman to the core, listened carefully as I ran down the latent menace descending on Ron and me in those early days. I laid out Harold Nye's notebooks, the Clutter crime scene photos, and scores of other documents on his conference room table, and while his team stood in awe of the documents spread out before them (all past readers of *In Cold Blood*), I marveled at the impact historical materials have on those who rarely come in contact with such potent objects.

Legal minds have little tolerance for ambiguity. And the first question everyone raised was: *What is in here that Kansas does not want exposed?*

One developing theory for why the KBI was so keen on acquiring our documents was the possibility that, odd as it may seem, they may not have had much at all in their own official file dealing with the Clutter case. We had solid grounds on which to base this assumption, including court testimony by KBI personnel who were unable to offer informed responses to simple, relevant questions by our attorneys and even the judge, about what the official case records contained.

Indeed, Logan Sanford, director of the KBI until 1969, once lamented, "Law-enforcement and crime records in Kansas through the years have been seriously inadequate .... In many cases an outgoing police chief or sheriff just destroyed his records or took them with him. We've found many cases in the state where a crime has been committed but where there is no written record."[26]

Our suspicions in that regard proved to be correct. The KBI later admitted that, in fact, there were surprisingly few documents in their own Clutter investigation file. In a series of internal KBI email messages discussing our case,[27] a revealing exchange took place [initials are used in place of the writers' names]:

> **MM:** There wasn't much in the file folder when [it was] [micro]filmed... All we had at the time were a couple of reports (I remember one by Dewey) and some of Perry Smith's poetry.

> **JW:** TEK or LW destroyed the bureau's file. [Thomas E. Kelly (TEK), and Larry Welsh (LW) are both former directors of the KBI.]

> **BB:** It wasn't TK who destroyed the bureau's files... I didn't think we had any of the case other than the evidence in the display case. Seems AG Curt Schneider took them from agency to lock up and "protect" downtown.

> **JW:** One of the two, TEK or LW, destroyed, nobody knew why. Can only guess.

One wonders why anyone in the bureau or the attorney general's office would go to such lengths to ensure that the Clutter case file—undoubtedly the most high-profile murder investigation in Kansas history—be *"locked up and 'protected' downtown,"* or even *"destroyed."*

Another suspicion that persisted throughout was that an ever-baffling escalation of activity had been mandated by some authority higher up the chain of command in Kansas state politics, some entity beyond the KBI. This was later confirmed by a credible source who informed us that the directive to pressure us—in any way that prevented these materials seeing the light of day—came from *above* the office of Attorney General Derek Schmidt.

Meaning, ultimately, that we had been targeted either by the governor, or by someone representing Kansas in the United States Congress.

The nagging question persisted: Why?

Interrogation

On September 11, 2012, my lawyer and I walked into the decorous offices of the Washington State attorney general in Seattle, summoned there by the attorney general of Kansas, who had demanded a formal accounting of every document consigned to me by Ron Nye, one of my business clients. Such reciprocal courtesies are apparently accorded attorneys general in other jurisdictions, but I was none too happy to be there.

After signing in at reception, we were buzzed through the fortified glass doors shielding the main offices. An escort appeared, leading us down long wide hallways, the solemn faces of previous attorneys general peering down from their frames on the walls lining the route to our destination.

On arrival we entered a large, well-appointed conference room, where *thirteen* state officials sat around an enormous U-shaped table furnished with pencils and pads, laptop computers, cell phones, and water glasses. On the wall facing the table, two formidable video conferencing monitors and cameras stared down silently on the group.

Leading this official cluster was an assistant attorney general for the State of Washington, along with his senior counsel and several more state lawyers, at least three forensic investigators, a court reporter, audio/video specialists, and what may have been a few interns or possibly just curious personnel from other offices.

Apparently, the videoconferencing equipment wasn't an option, so an assistant placed a phone call to the Kansas attorney general's office. Once connected, through a strategically positioned speakerphone names and titles were offered up as introductions went around the table in Seattle. Then a disembodied voice from Kansas called out their own cast of attendees 1500 miles away: an assistant attorney general, the director of the KBI, various attorneys and special agents—seven people in all (or so they said) were present and accounted for in Topeka.

My lawyer and I were seated at one end of the table, somewhat taken aback by the startling number of people (now at least twenty) assembled for what we had presumed would be a simple review of documents.

Only then did it hit me: This was a big deal for a lot of people. The leather messenger bag slung over my shoulder contained something every person in this room wanted to see, which likely meant the same eagerness pervaded the opposite room in Kansas.

All eyes turned in my direction as I withdrew a hefty six-inch stack of historical documents from my bag: copies of reports yellowed with age from various agencies; mug shots and fingerprint cards of the killers; personal and official correspondence; various photos; and finally, Agent Harold Nye's personal notebooks comprising in detail his cryptic investigation notes, the reason we were here.

Everything was sealed in clear Mylar sleeved packets, numbered 1 through 22, which I had previously organized as best I could, given the diverse nature of the collection which, as Ron mentioned in the Foreword, had survived the dreaded shredders of Oklahoma. The whole historical heap was reverently passed down to the assistant AG at the center of the conference table. Then the tedious litany began.

Unsealing the first packet, the assistant AG inspected the first of hundreds of document pages yet to go. But just as he was about to start reading to the group, one of the vigilant investigators across from me interrupted his boss and, in a firm voice aimed at the phone, posed a simple question: *"Kansas, are you recording this?"* After a 3-beat pause, a thin, metallic voice from the speaker uttered a faintly tense, *"Yes."*

All around me to a person, eyes rolled, and a few pencils flew in the air. Some groaned, a few sighed. This was proving to be more entertaining than I'd expected.

Recovering his composure, the now-irritated assistant AG stoically announced, "Kansas, Washington is a two-party consent state. Standby, we have to go around the room here..."[28]

Which he then did with every person present, asking if each of us consented to having our conversation recorded in Kansas, by who knows who and for what purposes. For a moment I flirted with objecting just to be poke the bear but assumed they would probably record it anyway.

Over the next four hours—as Kansas presumably followed along, matching the stack of copied documents I had provided them to the set under review here in Seattle—the assistant AG removed sheet by single sheet of paper from the topmost packet, flatly describing each in surprisingly fussy detail:

> *One page stationery, a logo at the top reading "State of Kansas, Office of the Kansas Bureau of Investigation, Topeka;" typewritten on one side of what appears to be an onionskin carbon copy; beige in color, a single staple mark in the upper left corner, with the imprinted word COPY centered vertically one inch from*

the left margin; dated 25 January 1960,
this is a report by Harold R. Nye, Re:
HICKOCK, Richard Eugene & SMITH,
Perry Edward – Suspects, the Herbert
Clutter Family Murder; signed at the
bottom in black ink by Harold R. Nye,
Special Agent.

After describing each page, the assistant AG passed it to the person on his left, who in turn reviewed it, silently concurred with a nod that the description was accurate, made some notes on his pad, and passed it on to the next person on his left. Around the room it traveled, each person distinctly aware they were holding something of historical magnitude. And at the tail end of that gauntlet, *two* people took photocopies of each document for the record.

And on it went, for another four hours. No wonder the room was mobbed. This kind of show-and-tell had to beat the drudgery of dealing with the state's common everyday criminals.

From time to time a discarnate voice from Kansas would pipe in, asking for particular details on one or another of the pages being described. I took careful notes as to the objects of their interest, for later review.

Prosecution

On September 27, 2012, sixteen days after that torturous inquisition at the Washington State Attorney General's offices, the Kansas attorney general obtained a temporary restraining order:

"IT IS, THEREFORE, BY THE COURT CONSIDERED, ORDERED, ADJUDGED

AND DECREED that...the Defendants...be and they hereby are...restrained from any sale or distribution, replication or publication of any portion of the KBI crime file related to the Clutter Murders and the investigation thereof...including but not limited to any digital images or copies thereof..."

Within days, both Ron and I personally, as well as my company—along with Ron's sister, who had nothing at all to do with the matter, and his infirm mother who was confined to an assisted-living home in Oklahoma—had been served with a summons, shutting down the auction until the Court could review the merits in a formal hearing.

The temporary restraining order eventually became a preliminary injunction, and so began the four-year odyssey that has consumed thousands of hours at no small expense, and which suspended our efforts for two years, until November 2014.

Claiming that its interest was solely in the preservation of Nye's physical records themselves, the State requested and obtained a "gag order" from the Court as part of its temporary injunction, then fought tooth and nail using various bizarre tactics—including a refusal to comply with discovery orders demanded by the Court itself—to maintain the gag order.

Among the more spurious claims pressed by the State was: "Any possession of Clutter Investigative Records by Harold Nye other than work related would accordingly have been the result of his wrongdoing or a default in the performance of his duties as a special agent of the KBI," an oddly bogus claim, as will be shown.

It quickly became clear, however, that simply seeking legal advice for the escalating events now facing us would be insufficient. Ron and I were anguished at the prospect of being dragged into court over half-a-century-old documents that were acquired legally by his father, and which, at the time they were written, were deemed routine and of little importance. But given the emerging David and Goliath magnitude of what lay ahead, we had two choices: capitulate to the State's demands and avoid a long and costly court battle; or stand our ground and take our chances.

Since we had already taken the high road, we stayed our course.

Neither of us had the resources for what would likely be a costly and tedious crusade, but we knew we were on the right side of the law. The auction was one thing, but the book we'd planned to work on together, highlighting Harold Nye's investigative work on the Clutter case, would be based largely on his personal notes. Losing access to these would not only cloud our vision but infringe on our rights protected by the First Amendment.

Sharing that vision, persuaded that we could win, Hendricks & Lewis agreed to take our case. Ron and I were elated, confident we had the right team. But with me based in Washington and our adversaries in Topeka, we would also need a member of the Kansas State Bar to handle local matters there, if it came to that. And if it did, I wanted a pit bull.

As luck would have it, we got "a real bulldog," the lusty attribution former Kansas Attorney General Stephen Six gave to his then-staff attorney, Tai J. Vokins.

Tai, a young lawyer from Lawrence, Kansas, was for several years an assistant attorney general for the State before going into private practice. He and his wife Krystal specialized in litigation helping ordinary people who are treated unfairly in a system that hopes they will lose their grip and fall. Even in those early weeks, I had little doubt Kansas would be hell-bent on us losing our grip, but game for a challenge in a state bureaucracy he knew well, Tai found the prospect appealing. The bulldog joined our team.

Thus began our coordinated resistance to a vigorous campaign of suppression and intimidation by the State, whose political machine had signaled an ambition to win at any cost. *Kansas v. Nye, McAvoy et al* landed on the Shawnee County District Court's docket in October 2012, the Honorable Judge

Larry D. Hendricks presiding.

Owing in part to some residual hostility toward Truman
Capote's book (and very likely toward the author himself), any
news related to the Clutter murders can be counted on to rile the
good citizens of Kansas.

Keenly aware of this, Kansas newspapers rarely fail to sniff
out fresh stories on the old topic, whipping up frenzy anew.
Then come the reader comments. As the saying goes, everyone
has a right to his own opinion but not his own facts. To that end,
I offer clarity.

In the wake of each new article, Ron and I were disparaged
for all manner of heinous acts. Headlines such as "Judge Blocks
Use of 'In Cold Blood' Files" ... "Clutter Case Documents
Should Go to the State" ... "Company is Auctioning Off
Documents from Murder Case" ... appeared on front pages
throughout Kansas and elsewhere. And beneath each article
readers weighed in, with even measures of support and
indignation, most of the latter largely uninformed as to the actual
merits of the lawsuit. So, to set straight the record and quench
any residual mania, here are the facts:

> ✎ The well-publicized centerpieces of the
> auction were Truman Capote's signed
> books and handwritten letters. The rest of
> the materials, including the Nye notebooks,
> were included for historical association.

> ✎ The KBI investigation documents in
> Agent Nye's possession were *copies* of
> official reports that he had written or
> received, consistent with his official duties.
> At the time, nothing in Kansas statutes
> prevented agents from keeping copies of
> their reports, which many officers rely on
> should they later be called to testify in court
> regarding cases they've worked on.

✎ As mentioned, the crime scene photographs were delivered to the KBI voluntarily, presumably resolving the KBI director's main concerns he expressed at our first meeting.

✎ Contrary to the attorney general's wild assertions accusing Harold Nye of theft of official case files, Nye never stole a thing, as later affirmed by the Court.

Harold Nye's personal papers and reports held nothing confidential, and as also later held by the Court, no privacy issues were at stake, despite the State's repeated assertions to the contrary.

As for the charge of making money off crimes, and especially the Clutter murders, that was a moot point, since my company, like many trusted dealers, routinely handles the sale of important memorabilia on behalf of collectors worldwide. And had it not been for Kansas intervening, this book would have been an altogether different kind of project.

That said, writing about crimes—and the Clutter murders in particular—has been a well-traveled path for decades. One former director of the KBI even published a true crime memoir featuring a chapter on the Clutter murders (using *In Cold Blood* as his only source material, as its author acknowledged to a reporter).[29]

Americans have a seemingly insatiable appetite for the sensational, legalistic, and forensic details in the true crime genre, and until human nature attains some form of enlightenment diminishing that interest, such an appetite is not likely to vanish.

Since its publication in 1966, *In Cold Blood* routinely appears in Top 100 bestseller lists every year, and a May 2017 article that appeared in *Publishers Weekly* even ranked it #1 in a Top 10 List of true crime books. *The Guardian* has ranked it #84 on its list of the 100 Best Novels in English. And of all books available on Amazon.com, *In Cold Blood* regularly ranks in the

Top 10 of all relevant categories—True Crime, American History, Social Sciences, Biographies & Memoirs, and Criminology—as well as moving in and out of its Top 100 lists in Literature & Fiction (since lists are updated hourly).

Beyond sales of the book itself, fans of *In Cold Blood* flock to theaters for more. In 2005 the blockbuster film *Capote* grossed $30 million in its box office run alone (against a $7 million production budget), earning the late Philip Seymour Hoffman an Academy Award for his role playing the title character.

In addition to *Capote*, to date there have been four other films or documentary series', numerous theatrical productions, graphic novels, countless magazine and newspaper articles, and, as of this writing, at least two documentary features are in the works by prominent studios.

For better or worse, the Clutter murders and *In Cold Blood*'s legacy have energized a cottage industry of its own, one that shows no signs of letting up. And this book surely won't be the last on the subject.

Discovery

"Once you eliminate the impossible, whatever remains, no matter how improbable, must be the truth."

— Sir Arthur Conan Doyle

Detection

While an engrossing and superbly told story, parts of *In Cold Blood* have long been laid bare as exaggerated, contrived, wrong, or plainly fabricated. Of course, the author can be forgiven his immodest swaggering about the book's being "immaculately factual" since he did produce a sensational form of narrative nonfiction journalism comprising the best elements of fiction: setting, plot, and character.

To Capote's credit, his artful use of the phrase "non-fiction *novel*" in describing his new genre goes a long way toward reconciling these problems with the facts. Yet, truer facts remain.

Had Capote not pressed his repeated assertion about the book's accuracy, much of the negative criticism might have stayed at a lower volume. Indeed, the title of this book is taken from an actual quote Truman gave to *Newsweek* reporter Karen Gunderson, who interviewed Capote at his home on Long Island for the 1966 documentary *With Love from Truman*.[30]

In the interview, the author emphatically states about his book that, *"It's a completely factual account and every word is true."* Claiming such a lofty standard, however, demands being held to account for it. And held accountable he was.

In Cold Blood had taken the literary world by storm in 1966, making Truman Capote the most famous writer in America. As noted critic Irving Malin observed, "...some consider *In Cold Blood* a 'lightweight' effort; others praise it as a 'grave and reverend book.'"[31] Malin's superb anthology includes ten notable reviewers who contrasted the book's "public ambiguities and American life in general," in good company with other prominent writers appraising the Capote oeuvre in relation to his new masterwork.

In Cold Blood had been on bookstore shelves only a month when Phillip K. Tompkins, writing for *Esquire* magazine, rebutted Capote's daring claim of accuracy in a scholarly critique titled "In Cold Fact."[32] Tompkins, after reading Capote's book, had set off on a nine-day trip to Kansas to determine the veracity of the author's declaration that, "One doesn't spend almost six years on a book, the point of which is factual accuracy, and then give way to minor distortions."[33]

But the unveiling of minor distortions, along with several major errors in fact, form the hallmarks of Tompkins's incisive work.

There is one assertion Dr. Tompkins makes, however, that does bear reconsideration, as confirmed by documents now available to which he did not have access at the time: the intimate correspondence between Perry Smith and the Meiers.

As Tompkins relates: "During our telephone conversation, Mrs. [Josephine] Meier repeatedly told me that she never heard Perry cry; that on the day in question she was in her bedroom, not the kitchen; that she did not turn on the radio to drown out the sound of crying; that she did not hold Perry's hand; that she did not hear Perry say, 'I'm embraced by shame.' And finally— that she had never told such things to Capote. Mrs. Meier told me repeatedly and firmly, in her gentle way, that these things were not true."[34]

The notion of the undersheriff's wife being friendly, even overtly caring for one of the Clutter murderers would have been viewed, at best, as indecorous for the time and place. So Josie Meier may have told the young journalist, many years later, what she had to in order to deflect any perceived improprieties by friends and, politically, for her husband's career as former Finney County sheriff and, at the time, an officer of the Garden City Police Department.

Despite the undersheriff's early cautions to his wife, however, it appears that both Meiers came to better know and care for Perry Smith in the years leading up to his execution—in correspondence, holiday cards, and at least two personal visits to him on Death Row at Kansas State Penitentiary (a 750-mile round trip they undertook by car).

Prior to his execution, Perry handed a leather satchel to Josie Meier containing his personal journals, some family photos, a few handwritten pages of poetry, and what meager possessions he had remaining, saying, "Here. Take all this stuff. I won't need it."[35]

Figure 2. Perry Smith's journals and memorabilia
Courtesy of and photo © 2018 Lily "Red" Mashkova

Truman Capote has been quoted as saying that as much as 80% of his research for the book was never used.[36] Even so, it's very likely that neither he nor Harper Lee were aware of the facts that appear here.

It has been well established that Alvin Dewey, the KBI agent coordinating the investigation, provided Capote with ample confidential details of the crimes, including those with highly sensitive elements, the kind that gave the book such human intimacies as passages from Nancy Clutter's private diary, containing her last entry written an hour before a shotgun blast ended her life. Apart from this ongoing and widely acknowledged ethical breach lasting years, given what follows, one is left to wonder if Dewey hadn't actually been the guiding hand behind the story that ultimately appeared in print; the story the KBI itself has eagerly promoted for decades.

When I began helping our legal team build our defense in 2012, I dug into the task wholly exasperated at the time and effort it would take away from my business and my life. Reading and digesting all that "closed-case" documentation might have been a true crime devotee's idea of a good time, but it wasn't mine. The lawyers, however, urged a thorough index of everything, and doing that required a submersion into material that, over time, both challenged and intrigued the lay historian in me.

Peeling back the layers, each scenario laid out here made little sense on its own. But, as with many mysteries having too many threads, when woven together properly a different tapestry began to emerge. And it wasn't just me seeing new patterns. Others of note to whom I turned for periodic sanity checks— criminologists, legal experts, journalists, law enforcement officials, psychologists, crime writers—all professed astonishment when presented with new and materially relevant facts to a story that had been pretty well known. Or so they thought.

Custody

Figure 3. Harold Nye's notebooks on the Clutter case
Photo © 2012 Gary McAvoy; Harold R. Nye Archives

As we were now on our way down the long and combative path to litigation—and the Nye archives would remain in our possession until the Court ruled otherwise—I laid out the stacks of documents on my desk, contemplating the strategy we might take. I had given this material only token attention thus far since there was no compelling need to read every page word for word just for a simple auction. After all, at the time these appeared to be only supplemental artifacts, bit players in a supporting role to the headlining letters and first edition books inscribed by

Truman Capote to Harold Nye.

But then there were the gruesome crime scene photographs, harsh and sobering reminders of the great cost involved, tempering my anticipation. The photos called to mind a question that has lingered in the minds of many readers of *In Cold Blood*, myself included: given the pitiful spoils for which the Clutters' lives were exchanged—reportedly less than fifty dollars—why were the murders so extravagantly brutal? The official explanation did nothing to make that question less relevant.

For my part, I couldn't imagine there might be new details among the auction items in my possession that would materially change Capote's story or the KBI's hand in the investigation.

I began with Harold Nye's two steno pads, a worthy challenge alone since Nye's handwriting was meant only for his own reference and later interpretation. Apart from what could more easily be read, a profusion of cryptic scribbles, references, and abbreviations will forever be unknown to anyone but Nye himself, and he's no longer alive.

I dedicated the next few weeks to reading every page, jotting down notes when a particular detail caught my attention. The deeper I got into Nye's chronicle of events, the more profoundly I was struck by the history spread before me—a contemporaneous, first-person account by a sharp young investigator at the top of his game, laying out the bones of what would ultimately become, from the viewpoint of another, an American literary classic in master storytelling.

Nye's notes from his interrogation of Hickock in Las Vegas, for example, reflect a calculated precision, illustrating the art of capable, old-style sleuthing techniques. For several hours (and pages) Nye and his partner, Roy Church, allowed Hickock to spin his factitious cover story, replete with false alibis—until they pounced on him, stating the real reason for his detention:

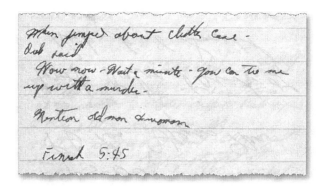

Figure 4. Nye "jumps" Hickock on the Clutter murders
Harold R. Nye Archives

"When jumped about Clutter case - Dick said
Now now - wait a minute - you [can't] tie me
up with a murder -
Mention old man & woman
Finish 5:45"

One early discovery in Nye's notebooks revealed a pivotal discrepancy in timing during the investigation, a key fact first gleaned by the *Wall Street Journal's* Kevin Helliker, with whom I'd shared the Nye materials early on. As recounted in his February 2013 article,[37] *"Capote Classic 'In Cold Blood' Tainted by Long-Lost Files,"* Helliker was first to note a previously unacknowledged gap between the time Floyd Wells revealed to the KBI who the murder suspects were, and when the KBI actually acted on that information.

Readers of Capote's book, and even viewers of the 1967 film, may recall the dramatic scene in which Harold Nye visits the Hickock farm alone and, talking with Dick's parents, spies the presumed murder weapon.

According to *In Cold Blood* and to the official version of events given by the KBI, this scene took place the day Wells spoke up about the crime. Inconvenient as they might be, however, the facts tell a different story. The KBI did not act on the same day they received Floyd Wells's information, but five days later. Alvin Dewey simply did not believe Wells's story, dismissing it as nothing more than contrived prison talk, so he gave the lead no pressing importance.

On the face of it, this recent revelation might not have merited the news it generated—clinching a front-page appearance in *The Wall Street Journal*'s weekend section and its repurposed syndication on hundreds of websites worldwide—were it not for two notable points.

First, Harold Nye never visited the Hickock farm by himself, an implausible scenario some in law enforcement consider might have been reckless if he had. But it did provide Capote with a riveting scene for the book (and an even more gripping treatment in the film). The official report shows that after obtaining a lawful search warrant, Nye and three other officers descended on the Hickock farm several days later, discovered the shotgun, then took the suspected murder weapon into evidence and tested it for ballistics.

Second, the KBI has for decades held up Capote's book as the bedrock version of events for its own investigation, even relying on *In Cold Blood,* flaws and all, as its primary source material for the bureau's official history published in 1980.[38] A cursory review of their own Clutter case summaries might easily have alerted someone over the years that the bureau was open to exposure when the official facts controverted what had already been widely asserted in one of the most famous books in modern literature—the book purportedly documenting the KBI's "landmark case." But to this day, claims persist that *In Cold Blood* portrays a faithful account of the investigation.

Despite the profusion of Clutter case documents in the Nye materials, there seemed at first glance to be little of value beyond what Capote had written. But then, as mentioned, another collection of documents came into my possession: Richard Hickock's Death Row letters to reporter Mack Nations. And as those revelations unfolded—with startling events corroborated by Harold Nye's notes and the KBI's own reports—it felt like a

Kansas twister was carving a path through everything I knew about the *In Cold Blood* saga.

Many of Hickock's extraordinary disclosures will be revealed in the pages to come, but as unlikely as it may seem, one event in particular stands out regarding a peculiar meeting described in one of Harold Nye's reports—a meeting that took place about an hour after the murders, fitting Hickock's stated timeline [emphasis added for discussion]:

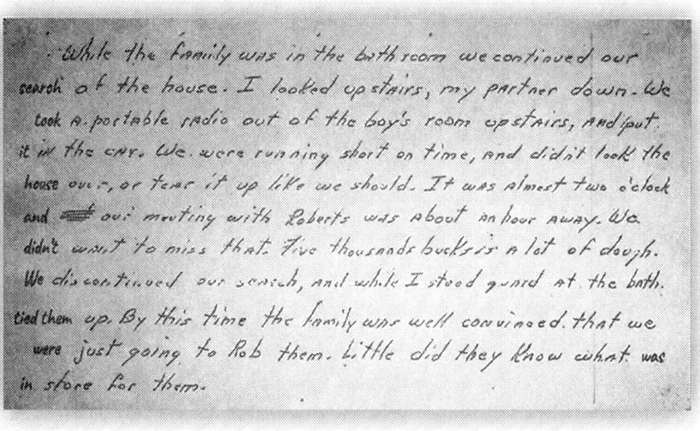
While the family was in the bathroom we continued our search of the house. I looked upstairs, my partner down. We took a portable radio out of the boy's room upstairs, and put it in the car. We were running short on time, and didn't look the house over, or tear it up like we should. It was almost two o'clock and our meeting with Roberts was about an hour away. We didn't want to miss that. Five thousands bucks is a lot of dough. We discontinued our search, and while I stood guard at the bath. tied them up. By this time the family was well convinced that we were just going to Rob them. Little did they know what was in store for them.

Figure 5. Hickock shows premeditation, hints at being paid

Author's archives [missing off-margin words; supplemented as presumed]

> While the family was in the bathroom we continued our search of the house. I looked upstairs, my partner down. We took a portable radio out of the boy's room upstairs, and put it in the car. We were running short on time, and didn't look the house over, or tear it up like we should. ***It was almost two o'clock and our meeting with Roberts was about an hour away. We didn't want to miss that. Five thousand bucks is a lot of dough....*** By this time the family was well convinced that we were just going to rob them. Little did they know what was in store for them.

The relevant part of this passage is Hickock's intriguing allusion to meeting up with someone named "Roberts" after killing the Clutter family. His additional unexpected disclosure about *"five thousand bucks"* will be discussed in the next chapter. But for now, what are we to make of this meeting, and the reference to someone named "Roberts"?

The timing here is pivotal, for as it happens, about one hour after the murders—but many hours *before* the bodies were discovered—a local marshal had observed a gathering of three suspicious men in the nearby town of Cimarron, which could very well have been the meeting with "Roberts" referenced by Hickock.

Dodge City, Kansas, "Queen of the Cowtowns," was the American Old West personified. This part of the country has a fabled history, calling to mind legendary figures like Wyatt Earp, Bat Masterson, Doc Holliday—and of course its most famous fictional lawman, Marshal Matt Dillon, who, along with his hobbling sidekick Chester and "Miss Kitty," were characters on the long-running TV-western series *Gunsmoke*. Real or not, all helped conjure a lasting image of Kansas as the heart of the Wild West, an image that still resonates fondly with anyone who grew up in the late 1950s and '60s.

Midway between Dodge City and Holcomb lies another historic town called Cimarron. Once a major transportation hub on the famed Santa Fe Trail, the Cimarron Crossing provided passage for wagon trains and stage coaches bound for major points of commerce in the mid-1800s, risking threats of Indian raids, rustlers, and outlaws along the way.

Within an hour after the Clutter family was murdered—making it between 2:00 a.m. to 3:00 a.m. that Sunday morning—Cimarron's Night Marshal Fred Voelker was just about to go off duty when he stopped in at the Western Cafe.

Figure 6. Western Cafe, Cimarron, Kansas, circa 1950s
Author's archives

Before doughnut shops became ubiquitous hangouts for cops working the graveyard shift, all-night diners served that noble purpose. Even in the early hours around 2:30 a.m., the Western Cafe in Cimarron was doing a brisk weekend business with locals and others passing through town.

Hours before the bodies of the Clutter family would be discovered, Night Marshal Voelker entered the cafe and took a booth seat as waitress Eunice Bell set down the first of two cups of coffee.

Another patron, Marvin "Squirt" Kramer, owner of the local beer tavern, had just closed his bar for the night and was sitting at the counter when three men walked in, also taking seats at the counter.

The following report was prepared by County Attorney Duane West with Undersheriff Wendle Meier, both of whom interviewed Voelker two weeks after the Clutter murders. *[Note: Kramer is misspelled in the report as "Krimer;" spelling is shown as reported; emphasis added for discussion]:*

> On December 15 Undersheriff Wendell Meier and the writer [West] made a trip to Cimarron, Kansas, to check information received on December 2, from Fred Voelker, Night Marshall at Cimarron,

Kansas. This information was in regard to three men who stopped at the Western Cafe in Cimarron sometime **between 2 and 3:00 o'clock a.m.**, Sunday morning, November 15. Marshall Voelker was interviewed and stated that he was in the cafe sitting in a booth on the east side. That 3 subjects, **one short, dark-haired, heavy set** and **two tall light-haired individuals** entered the cafe and sat on the 3 stools at the north end of the counter, which is on the west side of the cafe. Mr. Squirt Krimer, a tavern operator in Cimarron, was sitting at the counter and the 3 subjects asked Krimer if they knew where they could get gasoline. Krimer in turn asked Voelker if he could get into the station to get gas. Voelker left the cafe and went across the street to the Standard station. He stated that **the three individuals hurried out of the cafe, got into their car and drove east on the highway**. He stated that the waitress at the cafe indicated to him through the window that **the 3 had failed to get their hamburgers which they had ordered to go**. A short time later these individuals came back into Cimarron from the east, making a U-turn in front of the cafe, where they stopped while one of the individuals ran into the cafe for the hamburgers. Voelker jumped the driver about making a U-turn, but the driver stated that he was not from Cimarron and so did not know that there was a law against making a U-turn in the middle of the street. Voelker indicated that the subjects were driving a **1949 or 50 Chevrolet 2-door sedan Fleetline, a dark gray color**. He stated he believed the **license tag was a 1959 Kansas** Wyandotte County 67 or 57, remainder of numerals unknown. A small two-wheel trailer was being pulled by the subject's automobile.

… We talked with Squirt Krimer and his story was substantially the same as that related to us by Mr. Voelker…. **One of the other individuals had a scar on the left side of his face**.

Both Krimer and Voelker indicated that the dark, heavy set individual had a bad right leg, which they thought to be artificial. They indicated that they had observed this individual limping and saw some type of harness under his clothing which made them think the man had a artificial leg. Voelker indicated that all three of these men were rough looking and had a dirty, unkept appearance.

At Dodge City, Kansas, we interviewed Mr. Ben Hughes, an employee at the Phillips 66 Station which is on the south side of the highway as you go into Dodge City from the west. Mr. Hughes reported that he was on duty Sunday morning November 15 when 3 individuals drove into the station in 1949 or 50 dark gray Chevrolet 2-door Fleetline sedan. He indicated the car was pulling a United Rental Trailer from Kansas City, Missouri, and that **the car was bearing Missouri license plates**.

Author's Note:
In 1969 Marvin "Squirt" Kramer, the tavern owner, eventually went on to become sheriff

of Gray County, in which Cimarron is the county seat. As of this writing, Marvin's son Jim is Gray County Sheriff, as was his brother Bill before him.

In an interview, Sheriff Jim Kramer confirmed to me that his father, "Squirt" Kramer, had indeed spoken with the three men mere hours after the murders [which, of course, no one had known about yet].

"Dad had a good eye for details, and he just knew people," Sheriff Kramer told me in an interview.[39] "He would talk to anyone as long as they wanted to talk. I do remember Dad saying he felt like it was them."

That this crucial observation—an official eyewitness placing Perry Smith and Richard Hickock at the Western Cafe—has eluded entry in the official record (not to mention further investigation) simply adds strength to the hypotheses laid out in pages to come.

In a separate but factually equivalent report taken by Harold Nye, who interviewed Voelker the day after the Clutter murders, more specific details were gathered for each individual:

Voelker describes the three subjects as follows:

No. 1: White male, 21 to 25, 175 to 180 pounds, heavy build, rough-looking, artificial right leg, wearing a dark green jacket...reddish brown high topped shoes.
No. 2: Possibly Spanish, 21 to 25, 5 ft. 7 – 5 ft. 9, sandy blonde bushy hair, white shirt with design in it, black shoes, no coat.
No. 3: White male, 21 to 25, 5 ft 9.

Slender build, ducktail haircut, black shoes, white shirt with two inch black check in it, no coat....

The three subjects had moved one of the three's personal belongings from Kansas City to Garden City, Kansas, and were en route back to Kansas City, Missouri....

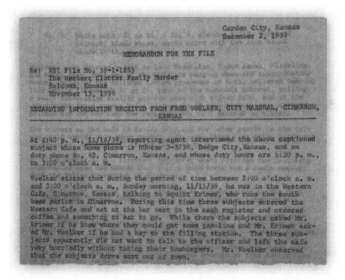

Figure 7. Nye report on Western Cafe sighting in Cimarron
Harold R. Nye Archives

The first point of interest here is the reported time frame. It took the killers just eight hours to get to Holcomb from Hickock's home in Olathe, yet the return trip took *eleven* hours. It was a 45-minute drive from Holcomb to where they buried the spent shotgun shells and other materials used in the crimes, just north of Garden City, and another 45-minute drive down to Cimarron. That leaves at least ninety minutes otherwise unexplained, which easily accounts for the meeting in Cimarron before Smith and Hickock made it back to Olathe at noon on Monday.

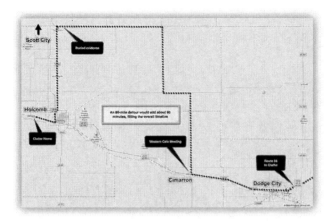

Figure 8. Plausible route taken after the murders
Map data © 2016 OpenMap Contributors. Detail by author.

Then we have descriptions of two of the three men in the Western Cafe, who bear striking similarities to Smith and Hickock. As Subject "No. 1," Smith could easily have passed for white (his father was Caucasian), and he looked young for thirty-one, his age at the time. His "limping" "bad right leg" reference is the clincher since Perry's left leg had been mangled in a motorcycle accident. Allowing for eyewitness fallibility, it would be easy to mistake *which* leg of a person seen limping was "artificial." And since Smith did wear high-topped black boots, they would likely have had blood smeared on them just an hour after the murders, which could account for the observed "reddish brown" color. Hickock himself commented on how much blood Perry had on him at the murder scene and how much he left on the floor of the car.

Subject "No. 3" distinctly corresponds to Hickock in age, height, build, his ducktail hair style, and most notably the scar beneath his left eye from an injury suffered in a bad car accident years before.

Which leaves the identity of the third man, Subject "No. 2," a mystery. Could this have been "Roberts"?

During the ensuing murder investigation, state Highway

Patrol officers were charged with canvassing area hotels and filed reports on what they found. An exhaustive review of these documents revealed surprising entries in the registers of two separate Garden City motels: the Wheatlands Motel and the Warren Hotel. Both had registered guests with the name "D. Roberts." Both guests checked out the day before the murders.

Figure 9. Wheatlands Motel Guest Register
Author's archives

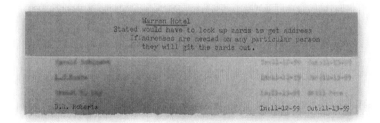

Figure 10. Warren Hotel Guest Register
Author's archives

Further research into the identity of "Roberts" yielded only dead ends. Who "Roberts" was remains unknown.

The suspicious behavior of the three men—rushing out of the cafe to avoid the marshal, leaving behind the food they ordered—is especially noteworthy. And though it may just be coincidence, in his letters Hickock wrote that, after killing the family, "... I was hungry. Boy was I hungry."

During his interrogation with Harold Nye after being captured in Las Vegas, Hickock did mention that he and Smith stopped at an all-night cafe, adding "but I don't remember the name." For someone whose mastery of such granular details so impressed investigators, as well as Capote and Lee, it seems odd that Hickock's memory would fail him for such a key moment in the chain of events.

The appearance of a 1949 Chevy Fleetline sedan plays prominently throughout this story. Hickock owned a black 2-door model, and ten years in the hot Kansas sun would have oxidized it to a dark gray, as was common then for black cars lacking modern paints with protective polymers. The three unidentified "Subjects" seen in the Western Cafe drove a vehicle that was identical in make, model, color, and condition.

As for the license plates, Kansas passenger car tags in 1959 were *yellow*, whereas Missouri plates that year were *black*, so they could hardly be confused, dampening the potential for flawed witness reporting. Given the time, proximity, and nearly identical description of the occupants and their vehicle at the Phillips 66 station in Dodge City, the possibility of that sighting being a different vehicle with different people, towing an identical trailer, is improbable. But how to explain the difference in license plates, unless Roberts had an otherwise identical car? Hickock had no qualms stealing license plates in the past, so they could easily have had another set on hand since they were on the run.

If one were to pose a plausible theory in light of this report—predicated on the credibility of Hickock's exhaustive letters to Mack Nations—after killing the Clutters, Hickock had prearranged a meeting with someone named Roberts to collect an agreed upon payment, presumably for the task of eliminating Herbert Clutter.

All of which opens up a Pandora's Box of yet more questions: Who hired him, and why? How did Wells fit into the scheme? Did Smith know anything about the plan? How do we account for any money Hickock claims to have received, since they appear to have had minimal funds for their trip to Mexico? Did the killers get paid at all? Why did they murder the entire family? What was the trailer used for?

And perhaps strangest of all: Why did neither Hickock nor

Smith mention any of this in their confessions, or in their defense at trial? If Mr. Clutter was the sole intended target, could murdering the entire family have upset the scheme of the contracting conspirator? One who may have threatened the lives of Hickock's and Smith's families should they ever breathe a word of truth? Are answers even possible after so many decades, with nearly all principal figures now long-dead?

From mid-November to the end of January is a miserable time to be a pheasant in Kansas.

Native to Mongolia, ring-necked pheasants were introduced in Kansas in 1906, and today as many as 150,000 hunters in just two months can bag up to three-quarters of a million birds in a bounteous season. Western Kansas in particular boasts some of the best brood rearing habitats in the country, so pheasant hunters are a common sight in the winter. The Kansas Game Commission carefully regulates each season in order to maintain healthy bird populations, so the length of permitted upland hunting and bag limits can vary. In 1959 just twenty days were allowed for hunting, starting on November 7.

On November 11, three days before Hickock and Smith invaded the Clutter home, two hunters were driving by the old Holcomb Bridge, just a half-mile from River Valley Farm, when they caught sight of a pheasant flying across the road. Stopping their car to chase the bird, they noticed an old faded Chevy Fleetline with a black license plate parked north of the bridge. The hunters reported seeing "three rough-looking individuals" all sitting in the front seat of the vehicle, so they waited, allowing them to go after the pheasant first. Several minutes passed, and as there was no movement from the occupants of the Fleetline, the hunters left their car to flush the pheasant themselves. Ninety minutes later they returned to their vehicle, and the three individuals were still sitting in the Chevy.

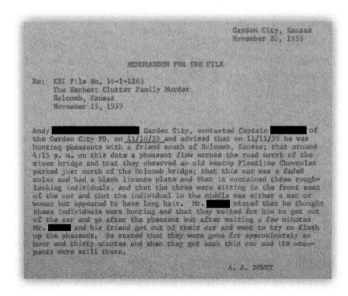

Figure 11. Pheasant hunters sighted days before murders
Author's archives

Garden City, Kansas
November 20, 1959

MEMORANDUM FOR THE FILE

…

Andy ▮▮▮▮▮▮▮▮ Garden City, contacted Captain ▮▮▮▮ of the Garden City PD, on 11/18/59 and advised that on 11/11/59 he was hunting pheasants with a friend south of Holcomb, Kansas; that around 4:15 p.m. on this date a pheasant flew across the road north of the river bridge and that they observed an old beatup Fleetline Chevrolet parked just north of the Holcomb bridge; that this car was a faded color and had a black license plate and that it contained three rough-looking individuals, and that the three were sitting in the front seat of the car and that the individual in the middle was either a man or woman but appeared to have long hair. Mr. █████ stated that he thought these individuals were hunting and that they waited for him to get out of the car and go after the pheasant but after waiting a few minutes Mr. █████ and his friend got out of their car and went to try to flush up the pheasant. He stated that they were gone for approximately an hour and thirty minutes and when they got back this car and its occupants were still there.

A. A. DEWEY

There are surprising similarities to the reported sighting of these men and the "three rough-looking individuals" at the Western Cafe. If, as in Nye's report, they were supposedly moving one of their number from Kansas City, Missouri, to Garden City, Kansas, taking time out to hunt pheasant would seem a strange diversion, one especially dubious when not taking advantage of a prime opportunity as a pheasant flew right in front of their car.

In his 2010 memoir, *In the Shadow of My Brother's Cold Blood,*[40] Hickock's brother David writes poignantly about the family's annual tradition of hunting pheasant in western Kansas, noting "... the last pheasant hunting adventure took place exactly one week before November 15, 1959."[41] *In Cold Blood* also describes this hunting trip—to Grinnell, Kansas, a small town ninety miles north of Garden City, where the shotgun David purchased as a gift for his brother Dick was first used.[42]

The second and last time it was used was one week later, inside the Clutter home.

Lineup

"Very few of us are what we seem."

— Agatha Christie

Truman Capote & Nelle Harper Lee

On his arrival in Kansas, it was little wonder that Truman Capote—whose homosexuality was tolerated if not embraced in his New York social circle—was received with tense apprehension by Kansans already on edge with, as many thought, a killer among their own kind. Having never traveled to the heartland but fully conscious of its social strictures, Capote was surely aware that he could be entering hostile territory, one not especially welcoming to his flamboyant effeminacy.

One might assume that is precisely why he asked his childhood friend Nelle Harper Lee to join him in researching the impact of the Clutter murders on the people who lived in and around Garden City.

But the fact is, the first invitation to accompany him to Kansas was extended to his best friend, Andrew Lyndon,[43] a fellow Southerner and former intimate companion of the playwright Tennessee Williams. Lyndon was an aspiring writer who happened to be, as Williams described him to a friend, "extraordinarily beautiful" and "a charming little creature—breast of milk-fed chicken!"[44]

If Andrew Lyndon had not had a prior commitment preventing him from accepting Capote's invitation, one could just imagine the prospect of two such men making meddlesome inquiries among the already suspicious local folk, a pursuit that might well have resulted in a different book entirely—if they had gotten anyone to talk to them at all.

Ultimately, having Lee at his side was the best choice Truman could have made. Nelle's authentic Southern charm would do more to open doors than the specter of a colorful, splashy highbrow from New York City. And the exquisite details found in her research notes reflect such potent intellectual contributions to his book, it's hard to believe Capote could have done it without her at all. Indeed, as others have recently brought to light, he very likely didn't.

Harper Lee's contributions to the making of *In Cold Blood* have been given fair reappraisal in recent years, and as long surmised by many, Lee did far more work than Capote gave her credit for, undoubtedly explaining the shadow cast over their lifelong friendship following publication of his book.[45]

Such a claim can't be fully appreciated until one actually sees her work firsthand, most of which can be found in the New York Public Library's Capote archive. Lee's more nuanced eye for discrete mannerisms, for the emotional idiosyncrasies of people she met, distinguish her observations from Truman's in very different yet complementary ways. She conducted countless extensive interviews on her own, noting subtleties that shaped the characters who appeared on the pages of *In Cold Blood*, sketches that could not have materialized without her insightful reportage. Notes that, in the end, amounted to some 150 single-spaced pages she turned over to Capote.[46]

As Lee's biographer Charles J. Shields noted, "Nelle's gift for creating character sketches turned out to complement Truman's ability to get people to open up...." Their collaboration was reciprocal, prodding each other's recall to "get it right" together.[47]

That is not to say that Capote's research wasn't exhaustive on its own. Despite ongoing arguments about truth and fiction in the final published book, his obsession to detail is apparent, including such things as the recipe for the cherry pie Nancy baked on the day of her death; a meticulous inventory of the Clutter house including Bonnie's precious miniature knick-knacks; and how one navigates the prison to reach Death Row ("reached by climbing an iron spiral staircase").

Whatever compelled him, Capote not only failed to mention Lee's indispensable collaboration in the book's acknowledgments, he referred to her reductively as his "assistant researchist" and "protégé." Their friendship would never be the same after Lee discovered she shared the book's dedication with Capote's lover, Jack Dunphy.

It was, in fact, Lee herself who wrote and published the first in-depth account of the Clutter murder investigation in March

of 1960—almost six years before *In Cold Blood* was published—
in an article that appeared in *The Grapevine*, a magazine
produced by the Society of Former Special Agents of the FBI.[48]
One could speculate that Lee's pre-emptive exposure of the
material, at least in part, accounted for Capote's diminution of
her efforts in helping to shape his book. Having established
herself as one of the twentieth-century's leading literary figures
mere weeks after turning over her exhaustively organized notes to
Truman (*To Kill a Mockingbird* was published in July 1960), Lee
might have expected more in the bargain.

Shields's biography on Lee contains an insightful exchange
between Harold Nye and Capote that made the latter's stand on
the matter quite clear. Toward the end of his work on the book
Capote had visited with Nye at his home in Topeka. As they
were discussing Truman's work, Nye remarked "Well, Nelle will
certainly play a part in all this."

"No," Capote said emphatically, "she was just there."

Harold Nye, who had developed a respectful fondness for
Lee, was disturbed by Capote's discourteous treatment. "As well
as they knew each other," he said, looking back, "there is no
reason not to give some credit to her."[49]

Nelle's own tolerance of Truman up through their shared
time in Kansas was the product of her southern congeniality. But
with the pressing burdens of her own fame, and Capote's
narcissism wearing thin as his life spiraled downward, Lee
widened the distance between them.

That two such titans of literature had come to this isn't that
uncommon. Think Ernest Hemingway and William Faulkner;
Jane Austen and Mark Twain; Gore Vidal and Norman Mailer;
or Gore Vidal and Truman Capote, for that matter. All held
their respective nemeses in the highest contempt, saving some of
their best vitriol for their counterpart. (Commenting on
Capote's death, Gore Vidal once remarked, "Good career
move.")

Still, a deep friendship of nearly forty years vanished in the
evanescent bubble of fame each endured following publication of

their one big book. After *In Cold Blood* and *To Kill A Mockingbird*, neither Capote nor Lee published anything comparable for the rest of their lives.

Herbert W. Clutter

[Nye] had been assigned what he called "the damned delicate business" of interviewing the Clutter kinfolk: "It's painful for you and it's painful for them. When it comes to murder, you can't respect grief. Or privacy. Or personal feelings." [50]

In his book, Truman Capote took great pains to depict Herbert Clutter as a man standing on high moral ground. Indeed, Clutter enjoyed a reputation as a strict Methodist who demanded untarnished purity from those around him, a solemn but good-natured man revered by nearly everyone in his community. By all accounts, Clutter was self-assured and confident, a man who, in the vernacular of the Midwest, was enjoying life in tall clover.

Born in 1911, Clutter graduated from Kansas State University in 1933 with degrees in agronomy and economics, and the next year, at just twenty-three years old, he served as agricultural agent for Finney County, counseling and educating farmers on the most advanced farming and marketing methods of the day.

By any measure, Clutter was a successful farmer at a time when the industry was undergoing dramatic change. Despite the post-Depression havoc, agriculture in the United States was enjoying somewhat of a peak in the mid-1930s, with nearly seven million family farms providing some thirty million jobs.

In the twenty years that followed, however, the number of American farms declined to just over five million, with a comparable number of jobs, five million, lost largely to consolidation. Other causative factors included improved technologies for planting, cultivating, and harvesting crops—tasks made easier and more efficient by machines instead of manpower—and some to outright failure, with the vagaries of weather, and crops dependent on it, exacting a final, punishing toll on hard-working farmers whose hopes had just run out.

Post-war agriculture in the plains, however, was booming. In 1947, Kansas produced the largest wheat yield in the state's history, a "miracle crop" of nearly 287 million bushels. Larger operations like Clutter's 3000-acre River Valley Farm were integrating the new technologies he championed to help meet the rapidly growing family-table demands of millions of returning war veterans—a phenomenon setting in motion the Baby Boom and its ravenous appetite. Clutter's operation alone that year boasted its best wheat yield ever, 50,000 bushels.

Like most farmers dependent on the shifting fortunes of agriculture, Herb Clutter cultivated a widely diversified cropping plan with a constant three-year outlook. In addition to wheat he grew alfalfa, barley, milo, and maize, as well as grass, both to sell as certified seed and for pasturing his 800 head of cattle.

He was also forward-thinking in securing that most crucial element crops cannot live without: water. Clutter's shrewd business acumen was aptly described in a wide-ranging *New York Times* feature on the state of farming in 1954:

> There is plenty of water under his land but normally it would be fairly costly to pump up. But a while ago Mr. Clutter leased drilling rights to a natural gas company. In exchange he was entitled to a one-eighth share of the profits. But he uses some of the gas himself to run a big pump. He is charged for this gas of course, but the cost runs slightly under his royalty receipts. So he is getting both gas and water for nothing.[51]

It was this kind of savvy that established Herb Clutter's reputation in agrarian circles, not just throughout Kansas and the Midwest but well beyond, to the halls of Congress and even the White House.

That kind of influence tends to pay off, as it did in 1953, when President Eisenhower appointed Clutter to the Federal Farm Credit Board. By this time, he had already served as president of the National Association of Wheat Growers and as founder and president of the Kansas Association of Wheat Growers and several local co-ops.

He was also a director of the Farm Credit Administration, and served on both the USDA Grain Advisory Committee and the International Wheat Advisory Committee, two influential groups under the direction of the controversial Secretary of Agriculture Ezra Taft Benson, who held that post from 1953 to 1961.

It was widely known that Benson and Clutter loathed each other's policy positions, however; feelings which conceivably extended to each other personally, despite the common but separate bonds of their deeply-held religious beliefs: a closely aligned heritage in missionary work. Clutter was a prominent and lifelong Methodist, while Benson was a highly-ranked member of the Mormon Church, with a privileged seat on the Quorum of the Twelve Apostles (and who later became its 13th president).

But Ezra Taft Benson was also a virulent anti-communist crusader, strongly opposed to government agricultural subsidies, which he held to be a noxious form of socialism. By contrast, Herb Clutter's own vocation was to ensure price parity for American wheat farmers, a fight he appears to have lost, and which may have accounted for his declining reappointment to the Farm Credit Board when his term expired.

Religion and politics aside, few people achieve such pinnacles in life without making enemies along the way, and Herb Clutter was no exception.

In the final weeks of his life, Herb Clutter became

uncharacteristically anxious, even surly, and as his worried daughter Nancy confided to her home economics teacher, Polly Stringer, Clutter had even taken to smoking cigarettes, a vice so personally repugnant that he had fired employees for having the habit.[52]

There may have been good reason for his inconsistent mood, however, for it appears Mr. Clutter was having an affair with the wife of Kenneth Lyon, his banker, business partner, and executor of the Clutter estate.

The KBI certainly had evidence pointing to the likelihood, as found in official "memoranda" taken by Alvin Dewey— reports which, for whatever reasons, were never acknowledged in final investigation summaries.

At least two eyewitnesses observed Mr. Clutter at a co-op party at the Allis Hotel in Wichita, dancing and "smooching" with Kenneth Lyon's wife, Mildred, and neither of their spouses were in attendance. After dancing the pair were seen heading upstairs together in the hotel elevator.[53]

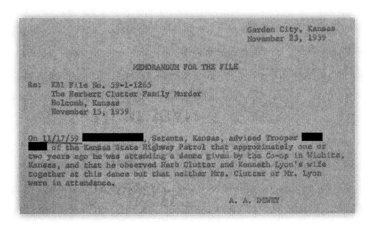

Figure 12. Clutter & Mrs Lyon observed without spouses
Harold R. Nye Archives

Garden City, Kansas
November 23, 1959

MEMORANDUM FOR THE FILE

...

On 11/17/59 ███████████, Satanta, Kansas,
advised Trooper ██████████ of the Kansas
State Highway Patrol that approximately
one or two years ago he was attending a
dance given by the Co-op in Wichita,
Kansas, and that he observed Herb Clutter
and Kenneth Lyon's wife together at this
dance but that neither Mrs. Clutter or Mr.
Lyon were in attendance.

A. A. Dewey

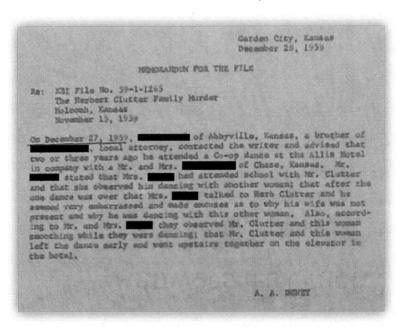

Figure 13. Clutter "dancing...smooching" with Lyon's wife
Author's archives

Garden City, Kansas
December 28, 1959

MEMORANDUM FOR THE FILE

...

> On December 27, 1959, ███████ of
> Abbyville, Kansas, a brother of ███████,
> local attorney, contacted the writer and
> advised that two or three years ago he
> attended a Co-op dance at the Allis Hotel in
> company with a Mr. and Mrs. ███████ of
> Chase, Kansas. Mr. ███████ stated that
> Mrs. ███████ had attended school with
> Mr. Clutter and that she observed him
> dancing with another woman; that after the
> dance was over that Mrs. ███████ talked
> with Herb Clutter and he seemed very
> embarrassed and made excuses as to why
> his wife was not present and why he was
> dancing with this other woman. Also,
> according to Mr. and Mrs. ███████ they
> observed Mr. Clutter and this woman
> smooching while they were dancing; that
> Mr. Clutter and this woman left the dance
> early and went upstairs together on the
> elevator in the hotel.
>
> A. A. Dewey

A dalliance of this gravity seems to have been a poorly kept secret around town. Lee's interview notes with Nancy's teacher, Mrs. Stringer, are frankly revealing on the subject: "He had his fun on the side, and Bonnie probably knew it."[54]

Reasons for infidelity are as common as locusts in a plague. Herb Clutter had his. His wife was enervated by mental illness, often forced into self-imposed seclusion in the family home. Physically and emotionally absent, cursed with chronic bouts of anxiety, Mrs. Clutter was hardly inclined toward coital pursuits in the later years of their marriage.

In an interview with Agent Dewey two weeks after the murders, Kenneth Lyon, who knew the Clutters intimately, was of the opinion that "Herb and Bonnie had not lived together as man and wife for the past ten years."[55] Lyon's observation was, in fact, confirmed in unambiguous detail by the Clutter's own family physician, Dr. V. A. Leopold, whose professional opinions are documented in an interview with KBI Agent Wendell Cowan:[56]

> Dr. Leopold stated that he had been the Clutter family doctor for many years, and had delivered all the Clutter children. Mrs. Clutter had a bad time in childbirth with Nancy and became mentally ill following that birth. She improved a little then gave birth to Kenyon. Dr. Leopold stated that he told both Mr. and Mrs. Clutter that Mrs. Clutter should not have another pregnancy due to her physical and mental condition. Mrs. Clutter was complaining of severe backaches and headaches, but Dr. Leopold stated he could find nothing radically wrong…. that he recommended that she consult a psychiatrist as it was believed her trouble was mostly emotional.
>
> Dr. Leopold stated that it was his firm belief that there was sexual incompatibility between Mr. and Mrs. Clutter for many years following the birth of Kenyon…. He stated Mrs. Clutter entered menopause about a year ago. The Dr. further stated that he doubts that there was much sexual activity insofar as Mrs. Clutter was concerned because of her mental condition and she probably does not feel very sexy….[57]

Moreover, Capote's and Lee's own research notes, supported by numerous KBI interviews, show that apart from his otherwise commendable reputation as a pillar of the community, many with whom Clutter had done business made specific threats against him as retribution for various grievances. Alvin Dewey acknowledged that over 700 leads had poured in over the weeks following the murders, suggesting all manner of reasons someone might have wanted to see Herb Clutter dead. Some interviewed even thought his murder may have had something to do with the Kansas Association of Wheat Growers.[58] Such swift and abundant reactions bring to mind that time-honored axiom, *Where there's smoke, there's fire.*

Lester McCoy, owner of Burtis Motors, Garden City's Ford dealership at the time, was blunt in his assessment, telling Capote in an interview that Clutter's strong power drive made him a challenging man to deal with, someone who didn't do much for others that wouldn't reward himself first. McCoy also revealed that Clutter, like most farmers in western Kansas, suffered under significant debt.[59]

Despite the realities of debt, Herb Clutter was unquestionably a wealthy man, with an estimated net worth, according to his own records, of nearly $2,000,000 (adjusted for inflation). As former USDA chief economist and agricultural policy expert Dr. Keith Collins told me, "Clutter appears to have been unusually successful at a time when many people were leaving farming. That success may have bred enemies through the methods he used to build his business or jealousy at his economic success."[60]

Given this new perspective, Mr. Clutter's decision to take out a double indemnity life insurance policy on the last day of his life is more than curious, especially since his New York Life agent, Bob Johnson, told the KBI that Mr. Clutter had been putting off getting the policy for two years. Why hadn't he attended to such an important matter in all the years preceding? Why *this* moment in time? Had he been threatened, perhaps endangering everything he'd spent a lifetime building?

Author's Note:
I must confess that Mr. Clutter's affair was

not a particularly pleasant discovery to have
made, nor is it gratifying putting it in print
here for the first time, having no wish to
injure his laudable reputation in the Kansas
farming community; nor should any
revelations appearing here detract from his
lifetime of good works.

Regardless, this observation alone, one
kept discreetly under wraps by Clutter's
friends who may have known or suspected
—and which was provably concealed by
those in law enforcement—sheds new light
not only on Capote's story, but the
investigation itself.

For historical purposes, then, such
statements are simply provided as they
appear in official documents.

Bonnie Mae Clutter

In official reports as well as documentation in the Capote
archives, an abundance of professional and anecdotal
observations makes clear that Herb Clutter's wife Bonnie
suffered for years from postpartum depression and physical
malaise. It's also apparent that she was unable to attend to her
home or family in any normal fashion, and responsibility for
domestic chores often fell to her children and the housekeeper,
Mrs. Helm.

Mrs. Clutter's physical and mental states are among the
more controversial topics Capote had written about; conditions
which, it's important to note, have been repeatedly denied by
family and friends of the Clutters. Of the acquaintances who
knew Bonnie personally and have publicly challenged Capote's

treatment of her, it's fair to assume most knew her in social settings when everyone puts on their best face. In Mrs. Clutter's case, her husband was a man of high standing, and, in what should be no great revelation, housewives of that era knew the importance of a dignified appearance, one that masked any personal troubles that might embarrass their husbands.

Setting aside *In Cold Blood*'s perceived sins on the topic, however, official reports, physician's statements, and many Garden Citians' observations support Capote's assertions, and do so quite specifically.

Mrs. Clutter's psychiatrist, Dr. Austin J. Adams of the Wesley Clinic in Wichita, confirmed that he had been treating her twice monthly for "nervous muscular spasms" over a period of six to eight years up to her death. Family friend Kenneth Lyon reported to Agent Dewey that "...due to Bonnie Clutter's condition she had to take a great deal of medicine, some of which were undoubtedly narcotics and barbiturates and that sometimes she would appear under the influence of this medicine."[61] This was the 1950s, after all, when as many as 1-in-20 Americans, predominantly women, were prescribed Miltown, a trendy tranquilizer for treating the widespread "afflictions of anxiety" apparently seizing the country (as paid tribute by the Rolling Stones in their hit song, "Mother's Little Helper").[62]

Even *The New York Times* mentioned Mrs. Clutter's condition in a 1954 article featuring her husband, noting that "...the teen-age daughters...are doing the housekeeping while the mother is away convalescing from a stay in the hospital...,"[63]—a three-month stay during which Mrs. Clutter had taken an apartment in Wichita while being treated by Dr. Adams.

In the years following World War II, as returning veterans married and reentered the workplace, housewives were relegated to homemaking, raising children, and coping with the mundane stresses of postwar America. Betty Friedan, the feminist author, famously termed this "the problem that has no name,"[64] referring to what sociologist Allan V. Horwitz described as "the ubiquitous malaise, tension, and anxiousness that results from the gap between the expectations of a fulfilling life and the realities of a stifling existence."[65] According to many, this "gap" may be where Bonnie Clutter found herself.

Harper Lee's research notes from interviews with Mrs. Polly Stringer, Nancy Clutter's high school teacher, are filled with such intimate revelations. By Lee's account, Mrs. Stringer cared deeply for Nancy, her star pupil, even taking on a stand-in role for the mother who, as Bonnie reportedly told her friend Wilma Kidwell,[66] was "a kind of ghost" to her own family.

According to Lee, Nancy was well aware that something was terribly wrong with her mother. Lacking the bond daughters typically have with their mothers, Nancy was happier when Bonnie was away, since she usually stayed in bed crying when she was home. Two other notes speak to Mrs. Clutter's condition:[67]

> ✎ Nancy bewildered by mother's insistence that there be twin beds in her room: "You're married, aren't you?" [To which Bonnie replied], "I'd go crazy if I had to sleep with your father." Apparently for several years Nancy had assumed most of the responsibility for running the Clutter household. She cooked and kept her (and Kenyon's?) clothes, and ran the house in general with aid of a maid who came in several times a week.

> ✎ [Stringer:] "Mrs. Clutter was a real mystery-like person. The sort of person you would think of as being kept in an attic."

Despite the bounty of contradictory evidence in his own research, Capote's sympathetic portrait of the Clutter family "fit" the wholesome American midwestern image he sought to portray, a depiction of sanctity cut down in the prime of its normalcy.

But those who knew the Clutters well appear to have told

their interviewers a much different story, and the intimate details recorded in Capote's own hand, along with those of Lee, reflect potent opposition to what ultimately appeared in print.

Kenneth Lyon

A longtime colleague and business partner of Herbert Clutter, Kenneth Lyon's final duty to his friend was to administer his estate after his death. While *In Cold Blood* makes no mention of him (nor was there any particular reason to, at the time), it was Lyon who opened the Clutter home for Capote and Lee to explore freely—favored access requested by Capote's lawyer, Clifford Hope, which, despite the KBI's having declared the farm off-limits, supplied firsthand details of the home so meticulously characterized in the book.

Lyon, a fellow farmer in western Kansas, owned 480 acres of his own irrigated land in northwest Finney County near Garden City. In the late 1940s and early '50s he was also manager of and a partner in Clutter's River Valley Farm, which at the time comprised over three thousand acres. In the months preceding the murders, presumably for reasons of debt, Lyon had urged Clutter to sell off some of his holdings. Gerald Van Vleet, River Valley's manager at the time of the murders, confirmed that Clutter had in fact sold 1080 acres earlier that spring.

Herb Clutter, as chairman of the board of the Garden City Co-Op in 1953, had named Ken Lyon as manager of that company, displacing the current manager to whom Clutter was opposed. Lyon, chairman of the Garden City School Board for several years, also served with Herb Clutter on the Federal Farm Credit Board. Both were prominent men of power and influence in their local, state, and national farming communities.

Having such stature goes a long way toward building one's career, and in 1959 Ken Lyon moved up from vice president to president of the Federal Intermediate Credit Bank in Wichita, one of twelve government-sponsored banks owned by its member-farmers, charged with providing loans to farms, ranches, and other agricultural industry organizations.

Left with few accounts of Lyon's life apart from the frequent accolades he earned in the press, and two interviews with Alvin Dewey, it's impossible to know now whether he was aware of a possible dalliance between his wife and Herb Clutter. In one of those interviews, however, Lyon told Dewey he had "never known Mr. Clutter to...have an association with another woman nor had he ever heard rumors to this effect."[68] Given the tight-knit community (and small town gossips few communities lack) it's hard to imagine Mr. Lyon would not have caught wind of it. (And practically speaking, if he had, would this have been the right time to disclose such knowledge?)

Kansas Bureau of Investigation

Like other Midwestern states during the Great Depression, Kansas in the 1930s was beset by roving gangs of bank robbers, cattle rustlers, and countless other thieves and outlaws bent on improving their fortunes. The names are legendary—Bonnie Parker and Clyde Barrow, Charles "Pretty Boy" Floyd, the Fleagle Gang, "Ma" Barker and Alvin Karpis—all manner of criminal infamy passed through Kansas while carrying out their crime sprees across the Midwest.

This burgeoning "public enemy era" gave rise to considerable expansion of the Federal Bureau of Investigation under J. Edgar Hoover and his "G-Men," as well as the formation of many statewide equivalents such as the Kansas Bureau of Investigation, an agency created in 1939 under the leadership of law enforcement veteran Lou Richter, its first director. Richter and his "K-Men," as the press soon dubbed them, would come to find their talents in great demand.

Established under the jurisdiction of the state attorney general's office—and thus subject to the AG's control and direction—the KBI was conceived as a state police organization formed to assist local law enforcement at all levels, and, mainly at the request of those agencies, to do so without interfering or superseding the authority of local officers.

By Kansas law, county sheriffs were the most powerful law enforcement officials statewide, and while the legislation creating the KBI did not invest it with authority over county sheriffs, it did give the agency broader jurisdictional and investigative capabilities to exercise its duties in any area of law enforcement anywhere in the state, even across state borders.

In the KBI's first year, Lou Richter handpicked a team limited by statute at the time to just ten agents. And with a total annual budget of only $46,000, their work was cut out for them. From day one, requests for assistance poured in from all over Kansas, a state burdened by a colorful variety of miscreants. Bootleggers, cattle rustlers, bank robbers, drug and gambling cartels, corrupt politicians, forgers, organized crime families...Kansas, the American heartland, served as the crossroads for villainy in the Midwest. In short order the KBI was pressed into action beyond its limits.

In the largest group hiring of personnel since its inception, the KBI hired several more special agents in 1955, among them four men who would become central figures in the Clutter murder investigation: Alvin Dewey, Howard Docker, Clarence Duntz, and Harold Nye.

At the time, with the bureau handling roughly a thousand cases in 1955 alone and growing steadily, agents were expected to put in long hours, while being conversant in the skills of others to fill in where needed—in such disciplines as fingerprint analysis, photo lab processing, evidence forensics, firearm ballistics, and, as might be expected, the endless filing of detailed investigative reports, often based on personal notes taken by agents themselves at the scene of the crime or when needed elsewhere.

From what remains of the Clutter murder investigation files today, it is abundantly obvious Harold Nye was one of the bureau's most prolific notetakers, and proficient in all disciplines required by the call of duty.

For decades, the Kansas Bureau of Investigation has actively promoted *In Cold Blood* as its official doctrine on the Clutter case. One recent KBI director, furious that Harold Nye's investigative work "dominated the narrative" in a 1997 A&E television documentary (upstaging Al Dewey's coordinating role), even issued a stern letter forbidding agency involvement with any Clutter-related project unless a KBI "technical advisor" was present to ensure that it would be "faithfully accurate in the portrayal of the case and the KBI."[69]

Moreover, both the KBI's official 50-year history published in 1990,[70] and one former director's own book,[71] clearly used *In Cold Blood* as their only source material on the Clutter case (both burdened with factual inaccuracies), ensuring that history is favorably defined from the perspective of the very agency who handed Capote the package it wanted delivered, neatly omitting parts of the story that did not fit the more heroic narrative.

Granted, a bold assertion. But the influence of Kansas authorities protecting their "landmark case" isn't limited to the KBI. As shown earlier, a secretary for one former director stated that Attorney General Curt Schneider, after his 1974 election, had the KBI's entire Clutter case file removed from agency custody and transferred to the attorney general's office "to lock up and 'protect' downtown."[72]

In December 2012—just two months after Kansas initiated its lawsuit against us—Florida law enforcement officials brought the Clutter case back into the headlines when Sarasota County investigators requested the exhumation of Perry Smith's and Richard Hickock's bodies, buried forty-seven years earlier, in hopes of connecting the killers' DNA to that state's unsolved Walker family murders of December 1959.

In a perfectly-timed act clearly intended to stall our own legal due process, the KBI inexplicably "reopened" the long-solved Clutter case, ostensibly to accommodate Florida's exhumation request, but which conveniently prevented us from pursuing discovery for nearly a year. The judge later fined and censured the Kansas attorney general *personally* for his defiance, noting "an investigation into the Clutter murders cannot be reopened when the killers have been captured, tried, convicted and executed."[73]

While it's reasonable to assume that current leadership at the KBI did not have a hand in the events of the early 1960s (nor were they very likely aware of the facts unfolding here, at least before demanding a full accounting of them in court), the agency's aggressiveness in suppressing our release of Harold Nye's materials cannot be adequately explained, especially when couched in deference to the privacy issues of surviving families and protection of "confidential" investigative documentation of a case long closed.

Harold Nye

Figure 14. Kansas Lawmen
Courtesy of Wendle & Josephine Meier Family

From an early age, Harold Ray Nye had set his sights on a life in
law enforcement. In December 1943 he enlisted in the U.S.
Army Air Corps. At the end of World War II, Harold married
his childhood sweetheart, Joyce Fechner, and soon after began
his life in police work as a night marshal in his hometown of
Oakley, Kansas. A year later he joined the Garden City Police
Department, serving from 1948 to 1951, during which time his
son Ronald Ray was born.

Nye embarked on his career in much the same way all
rookies begin, as a beat patrolman at a salary of $220 per month.
He was ambitious to learn everything he could about police
work, and soon took up classes under the aegis of the Federal
Bureau of Investigation, assimilating a broad range of
criminology studies including witness and suspect interrogation,
collection and preservation of physical evidence, fingerprint
analysis and classification, polygraph techniques, and other
"modern" mid-twentieth century investigative systems. Nye also
became proficient in crime scene and investigative photography
as well as advanced photo processing, later establishing Garden
City PD's first forensic photo lab. Only seven months on the job,
Nye was promoted to detective. He was 23 years old at the time.

One hundred seventy miles due east of Garden City lies
Hutchinson, then the fourth largest city in Kansas with a
population of around 35,000, three times that of Garden City.
Hutchinson was thriving, with a growing community's need for
more law enforcement.

In 1951, Harold Nye moved his young family to the heart of
the heartland to join the larger and more advanced Hutchinson
Police Department, again starting as a rookie patrolman—but
this time, to his delight, on a black-and-white Harley-Davidson
74 motorcycle—and now possessing an arsenal of formidable
skills acquired from many of the best FBI agents at the time.
(Nye kept close relations with the FBI for the rest of his life,
working directly with Director J. Edgar Hoover on several
occasions.)

Nye served as captain of detectives and assistant chief of police at Hutchinson until he was recruited for the KBI by Director Lou Richter, who appointed Nye a Special Agent on July 1, 1955. At 29 years old, Harold Nye was the youngest agent on the team, but every bit the archetypal lawman. A by-the-book professional with a photographic memory, Nye was already a highly-praised investigator, able to piece together disparate elements of a case to establish means, motive, and opportunity, the three bedrock essentials to winning criminal prosecutions.

In the years following Richter's retirement, succeeding director Logan Sanford found Nye to be one of his most capable and trusted agents, and put him in charge of the Investigations Division. Within months of closing the Clutter case, Nye was promoted to assistant director in January 1961 and was ultimately appointed director of the KBI by Attorney General Kent Frizzell when Logan Sanford retired in September 1969.

In a book commemorating the KBI's official 50th anniversary, Logan Sanford, while praising all the agents who worked under him, singled out Nye saying that he "...had men 'work 70-hour weeks as a routine thing, once they started on something they live with it and work it. Harold Nye went five days and nights without ever lying down while on the Clutter case.' That, to Director Sanford, was the reason the KBI had been successful."[74]

Even in his earliest years at the bureau, he was widely respected as an ordered, practical, and loyal public servant. He was also a meticulous investigator, verging on the obsessive in his quest for facts and answers, renowned for relentlessly chasing down leads and ferreting out clues to solve cases. Questions pleading for answers swirled through his mind day and night until each found its resolution, if it ever did. Rarely did he let up until "**CLOSED**" was stamped on the jacket of a case file. Even then, nagging details that didn't set right might gnaw at him for long periods, even years, as in the case of the Clutter murders.

Law enforcement agencies in the 1950s did not have the benefit of computer technology, not to mention cell phones and other modern devices that make fighting crime considerably different today. It wouldn't be until 1967 that the Federal Bureau of Investigation would launch the National Crime Information Center,[75] a centralized database of wanted persons, stolen weapons, vehicles, art works, and other valuable items. Large-scale computerization of law enforcement agencies did not emerge until the 1970s. In thousands of cities and small towns across America, detectives relied exclusively on telephones and police radios, teletype machines and typewriters, film cameras and fingerprints, and mostly, shoe leather and steno pads.

Early on in his thirty-year career, Harold Nye developed a methodical practice of journaling. Brief, incisive notes capturing whatever he felt he might need to reference at some future time were diligently recorded in his ever-present notebooks, always the slim, blue-lined steno pads that newspaper reporters used, spiral-bound at the top. These fit easily into Nye's coat pocket, ready to be plucked out to record the profusion of details he observed in his daily life and in every investigation he worked on.

As one of Nye's notebooks reveals, for example, it was a Sunday evening at 7:00 p.m. on November 15, 1959, when he received a call from Director Logan Sanford at the KBI's Topeka headquarters, dispatching him straightaway to Holcomb, a small village on the western edge of Garden City, Kansas, sixty miles east of the Colorado border. It was an uncommon murder scene, and Sanford wanted Nye's personal involvement in the investigation. It took Nye six hours to drive across the state from Topeka, arriving in Holcomb at 1:00 a.m. And what began on that high Kansas plain would occupy Harold Nye's thoughts for the rest of his life.

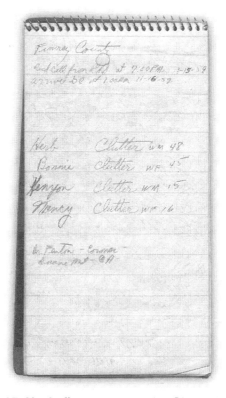

Figure 15. Nye's first notes on the Clutter murders
Harold R. Nye Archives

From the onset of the investigation, Nye's assiduous reliance on facts and figures, on his respect for structure and policy and process, is amply revealed in the cache of documents he left behind.

Apart from his personal notebooks, the Clutter case-related documents Nye retained include file copies of arrest records; summary reports he prepared, signed, and submitted; interview reports; crime scene photographs he himself processed in the KBI photo lab; fingerprint cards of Hickock and Smith; photos of Nye in Mexico with the secret police he met with on his evidence recovery mission; general correspondence related to the case and Nye's role in it; and the sundry ephemera that finds its way into the chronicle of a lawman's life.

His investigative work on the Clutter case, which ultimately earned him a promotion to Assistant KBI Director, is intimately detailed in those two steno notebooks and numerous reports, little of which has been made public before now.[76]

While Alvin Dewey coordinated the investigation from a borrowed desk at the Sheriff's office in Garden City, Harold Nye handled the brunt of investigative field work, often alone or with his KBI partner Agent Roy Church. Nye's notes reveal interviews with scores of townspeople and the families of both the victims and killers; details of his flight to Mexico to track down and retrieve items stolen by Smith and Hickock from the Clutter home; and his interrogation of Dick Hickock in Las Vegas, where Nye and Church skillfully extracted a confession.

Much of this appears in Capote's book, admirably reflecting Nye's own notes and reports (though Truman's access to this information can only be attributed to Alvin Dewey). Among those documents, however, are several surprising details probably unknown to Capote, among them:[77]

> ✎ On November 11, three days before the murders, a hunter reported an unusual sighting: while stalking pheasants around the old Holcomb bridge, just a half-mile from the Clutter house, he observed three people sitting in the front seat of a vehicle matching the make and model of Hickock's car, an older Chevy Fleetline. Returning ninety minutes later to his own car parked nearby, the hunter noticed that both the car and its occupants were still sitting there.

> ✎ The night marshal in Cimarron, a town just twenty-five miles from the scene of the crime in Holcomb, reported three suspicious men entering the Western Cafe at around 3:00 a.m., an hour after the murders. Though it wasn't realized at the time, descriptions of two of the men bore uncanny

resemblances to Smith and Hickock.

✎ Though Mr. and Mrs. Clutter did not sleep together and, as noted, had likely not had intimate relations for years (a consequence of Bonnie's mental and physical infirmities), the coroner's report shows that spermatozoa had been found on the back of Mrs. Clutter's light peach-colored nightgown—the one she was wearing when she was murdered (among the linens her fastidious housekeeper, Mrs. Helm, laundered twice weekly).

These three pieces of compelling information alone, as reported by Harold Nye, appear not to have been more thoroughly investigated, and may have contributed to Nye's later frustrations that left him with an unresolved conscience.

Owing to the unusual demands of his job, Harold's wife Joyce rarely knew what time her husband would be coming home, or if he would come home at all on any given night. The family was most likely to see him on weekends when he would typically drive up in his state car, unannounced, hauling in a week's worth of laundry with him. Whether day or night, Joyce would dutifully start the washing machine in case Harold got called out on some kind of emergency, which was more likely to happen than not. If the family had already eaten when Harold arrived, she would always have dinner waiting for him. After eating and watching a little television, Nye fell asleep quickly.

But even getting a good night's sleep couldn't explain the peculiar behavior his colleagues detected on the job. Nye's ability to fall asleep was legendary. He could be discovered in the arms of Morpheus anywhere and at any time. Co-workers often found him dozing peacefully, head down on his desk, while activity buzzed all around him. Though not diagnosed until some years later, it was the puzzling disorder known as narcolepsy that accounted for Harold's spontaneous napping, earning him the endearing nickname given by fellow officers: "Nappy" Nye.

His family, however, had long been aware of Harold's tendency to drop off with little warning, and much of the time it was a relief, for it spared his children the endless lectures and discipline expected of them while he was awake.

Unless, of course, they were in the car while Harold was driving, as his son Ron vividly recalls:

> Whenever the family traveled with Dad, we all took turns watching him. My sister and I sat in the back seat, and our job was to watch for his head to bob. Sitting in front, from the corner of her eyes Mom was alert to his lids starting to droop—even just a long blink might trigger her, and then she was on him like a tick on a hound dog: *"Harold!"* she'd hoot. And Dad would always protest *"I was just resting my eyes,"* which gave Mom her opening. *"I've been watching you for the last mile,"* she'd say, *"and your eyes have been closed practically the whole way!"* None of us ever felt we could rest while he was driving, which made every trip feel like it might be our last.
>
> I wanted to spend as much time with Dad as I could. So, a lot of that time had to be in the car—going to KBI headquarters in Topeka, visiting police departments and courthouses in other Kansas towns, running household errands for Mom. But there were rules, always rules, especially in the car.
>
> Upping the fear factor, most rides were always against the clock. So Dad would back out of the driveway at exactly 8:45 a.m., and say the goal was to hit the Oakley

city limits in under five hours or whatever. The highway was two lanes that wound this way and that, up hill and down dale. My mom and sister would often get motion sickness, but it never bothered me. Dad would tear up the road, the car leaning side to side on shocks that should have been replaced years ago, intent on making the self-imposed deadline just to see if he could. Any one of his three police-band radios would erupt in coded chatter throughout the ride, while two whip antennas crowning his state car lashed in the wind, just adding to the whole clown car adventure.

Harold Nye's attraction to law enforcement aligned with a natural inclination to serve his community. Of the many stories Ron shared with me about his family, the following stands out:

As early as six or seven years old, I remember Dad having a large wooden photo album that he made to keep pictures from his career in police work. The album had photos of Dad wearing his various police uniforms and the state cars he had driven. He loved his uniforms. My favorite was him in his uniform riding the police motorcycle. I remember looking into his face as he told of times past and could see that he was calling up good memories.

Dad would tell me a little about each picture in the book. With minimum encouragement, he would relate the most interesting stories, always filled with the kinds of details that painted a clear picture in my young mind.

One of my favorite photos was of Dad in a Boy Scout uniform with about a dozen young boys standing around him, all in jeans but each with a scout shirt and tie. The first thing I noticed was that none of the boys were white; all the faces were either black or Indian or Hispanic. Dad told me that when he learned there was no Boy Scout troop in the area where these boys lived, he decided to take it upon himself to start one. He petitioned the regional Boy Scout director and was approved to start a troop. He taught himself several languages—Spanish, German, even American Sign Language—because many of these boys spoke no English.

Over the years Dad would drag that album out from time to time, just to paste in more pictures and look over his earlier work, savoring his personal history. As he turned the pages, he always stopped at that photo of the Boy Scout troop he'd started, his eyes tearing up as he ran his finger across the picture.

As his son Ron learned all too well growing up under this particular lawman's roof, the one thing Harold Nye could not abide was a lie. When he first read *In Cold Blood*, what he found angered him so much that he threw the book across the room, calling it "a fiction." (Contrary to persistent media reports that Nye never read the entire book, it appears he did; his personal notes reveal numerous page references through to the last chapter.)

It was no secret that Harold Nye did not care much for Truman Capote. In an interview published in 1997, Harold Nye pointedly told writer George Plimpton that "I did not get a very good impression from that little son of a bitch...and that impression never changed."[78] But when warranted, Nye could be open and cordial despite his personal feelings toward the author.

As for being homophobic, Nye was hardly alone on that score, in Kansas or anywhere else in mid-20th-century America. During the 1950s, communists weren't the only targets of McCarthyism's "Red Scare." Homosexuals were considered "subversives" as well. Thousands of gay men and women were either dismissed without due process or quit from government jobs under pressure of blackmail and exposure. The zeal of this "Lavender Scare" actually became official government policy in 1953, when President Dwight Eisenhower signed Executive Order 10450 allowing any federal employee or contractor to be fired just for being homosexual (alcoholics and neurotics need not apply, either).

This gave rise to widespread and even "acceptable" persecution by law enforcement officials across the country, but especially in Bible Belt states, of which Kansas, though on the fringes geographically, adopted the rigors of membership enthusiastically.

No apologies need be made here for anyone's view of others. But two rather amusing accounts will surely help set the stage for why Harold cast Truman in the light he did, and Truman did nothing to diminish the power of that wattage. On the contrary, he clearly enjoyed cranking it up.

The first episode has some confusion and controversy attached to it, which will be cleared up here for the record. George Plimpton, in his wondrous book *Truman Capote: In Which Various Friends, Enemies, Acquaintances, and Detractors Recall His Turbulent Career*, ostensibly quotes Harold Nye in an interview (some 35 years *after* the events):

Al Dewey invited me to come up and meet
this gentleman who would come to town to
write a book. So the four of us, KBI agents,
went up to his room that evening after we
had dinner. And here he [Truman] is in kind
of a new pink negligee, silk with lace, and
he's strutting across the floor with his hands
on his hips telling us all about how he's
going to write this book....[79]

However, Ron Nye—who, like his father, has a remarkable
memory—specifically recalls Harold telling him a slightly
different version of the story about that particular night:

One day Dad and I were talking about
Truman and the Clutter case, which was
unusual for my father, since he rarely ever
spoke about his work. He said that Truman
and his friend Nelle were staying in a motel
close by the Clutter farm. Dad was at the
Clutter farm with two other agents, Clarence
Duntz and Roy Church, when he received a
radio call from Dewey that Truman would
like to speak with them.
    When they had finished their work for the
day, all three went to the motel, thinking
perhaps that Capote might have something
to share about the investigation. When
Truman opened the room door to greet
them, though, he was wearing a pink
negligee. He laughed and laughed at the
look on the agent's faces when he opened
the door. Then Truman started asking a lot
of questions about the investigation, but of
course no one said anything about the case.
Realizing there was nothing to be gained,
they thanked Capote for his time and drove
on home.[80]

By the time George Plimpton interviewed Harold Nye, with the crimes then decades past, it's probable Nye mistakenly recalled Dewey being in the scene, when in fact Dewey was simply passing on Capote's request that they meet him at the motel.

This view is reinforced by Dewey's wife, Marie, who was quoted as saying (not without a touch of derision):

> "That was ridiculous," she told *The Topeka Capital-Journal*. "Alvin never called on Capote in his hotel room…. I don't know what's gotten into Harold Nye. To me it was just hilarious."[81]

It's entirely possible that Plimpton was either unable to reach Nye for confirmation, or that he simply decided to use his original interview notes without subsequent validation. In any case, it is evident that Plimpton simply got it wrong.

The second episode was a more audacious stunt, in which Truman took Harold and his wife Joyce out for a memorable night on the town in 1965.

The town in question was Kansas City, Missouri, and it may surprise many to learn that as early as the 1920s, Kansas City was home to a remarkably large number of gay bars, nightclubs, and saucy cabarets discreetly nestled between the east and west coasts, all largely controlled by the Mafia. In spite of the Midwest's reputation for entrenched religious fervor, Kansas City's "homophile" community of the 1960s is today considered the central catalyst for the evolution of America's gay liberation movement.

Capote knew of these establishments better than most (straight) locals at the time, since—like many gay men and women who lived where such discreet locales prevailed—he understood the code for finding and gaining access to such largely invisible rendezvous. It had been later reported that he also knew George Cauden, the show director for the legendary

Jewel Box Lounge, "a willowy 29-year-old...who went by the stage name Mr. Tommy Temple."[82]

In what was surely a prime example of understated branding, the Jewel Box billed itself far and wide as "Kansas City's Most Unusual Show," spotlighting a lineup of drag queens who sang popular tunes and performed comedy sketches for both straight and gay audiences. Even top celebrities of the era, names such as Rock Hudson, Eartha Kitt, Liberace, and Pearl Bailey, were spotted there when passing through town.

On previous occasions when visiting Kansas City, Nye often brought his wife, Joyce, with him, staying at the historic Muehlebach Hotel, and he did so for this trip as well. It's not clear whether their respective visits to Kansas City were planned or coincidental, but one evening Capote insisted the Nyes join him for "drinks on the town."

The three met in the lobby of the Muehlebach and from there took a taxi to Midtown. Finding his desired destination, Truman introduced his guests to a lesbian bar, where he slipped the doorman a hundred-dollar bill to get in. Nye recalled there were about a hundred people in the bar, mostly female couples, eating and dancing and "doing their thing."[83] Joyce Nye, unaccustomed to such liberal gatherings, was horrified, but she dared not say anything to their host, not yet anyway.

From there Truman took them to a male gay bar (likely the Colony Club [84]) where they took a table and ordered drinks. Within minutes three "young bucks" approached Capote and engaged him in conversation while "playing with his ears." By this time Joyce, getting more nervous by the minute, quietly urged Harold to make excuses so they could get out of there.

But Truman insisted they make one more stop—at the Jewel Box cabaret, where thirty female impersonators performed, much to the amazement of Harold, who, three decades later, told George Plimpton in an interview, "I mean they looked as good as any beautiful babes in New York. But at the end of these little skits they revealed that they were males...." [85]

Apparently, that was just one too many boundaries crossed

for Joyce Nye. Without saying a word, she stood up from the table, snatched her purse, stormed out of the Jewel Box and hailed a cab. When the taxi pulled up, Joyce opened the door and got in. Truman, who had pursued her out of the club, jumped in beside her to soothe her ruffled feathers. In numerous retellings of the story to her son Ron over the years, Joyce always insisted Truman had taken on "a normal, masculine voice," apologizing to her profusely for "jerking peoples' chains" just to get a reaction, and pleading that she not go back to the hotel angry at him:

> My mom so disliked Truman that it really doesn't fit that she was there at all. She had to have been bushwhacked. There must have have been some compelling purpose for the trip in the first place for her to break her own rule and get roped into a night on the town. She would not have gone unless she felt there was an absolutely necessary reason, going so far as to compare the experience as offering herself up for human sacrifice.[86]

When they all returned to the Muehlebach, Harold and Truman got into a thunderous quarrel in the hotel lobby over that evening's ambush, which only served to create more rancor in a relationship that was never measured in terms of much affection anyway. It was not long after this clash that Harold and his wife were disinvited from what was to be Manhattan's hottest ticket in town the following year: Truman's famed Black and White Masquerade Ball.

Whatever Capote's reasons for behaving the way he did that night—or why the Nyes put up with three progressively more distressing venues that clearly came as a shock to a "small town girl," as Truman described Joyce—it remains a curious testament to his well-known penchant for recrimination that the author chose Alvin Dewey as the protagonist for his story.

A closer, more objective view of the facts clearly establishes Harold Nye as the one who did the lion's share of investigative work in the case, not only as vividly depicted in *In Cold Blood*, but as revealed in the majority of official KBI reports.

In any case, Capote would find that Alvin Dewey made a much more compliant ally as the book's "hero."

Alvin Dewey

KBI agent Alvin A. Dewey, Jr. lived in Garden City, just a few miles from the scene of the Clutter crime. A former FBI agent and past sheriff of Finney County, Alvin and his wife Marie knew the Clutter family well.

On November 15, 1959, Dewey was assisting local police with a bombing investigation in Wichita, some 200 miles away, when he got a call at his hotel from Marie, who was at church that Sunday morning, informing him that the entire Clutter family had been shot and killed.

As resident agent, Dewey took on the role of case coordinator. He knew the local law enforcement agencies and, indeed, most of the townspeople who knew the Clutters, so it made practical sense for him to serve as the point of convergence. He was also as close a friend to Herb Clutter as either man could have at the time, both involved with the same Methodist church and various community activities. Had he not been investigating the nightclub bombing in Wichita, Dewey would have been teaching that morning's Sunday school class himself.

In 1959 Garden City had a modest population of just under 12,000. Home to the seat of Finney County, the Sheriff's headquarters served as the most sensible base of operations for coordinating the Clutter investigation.

Although his office comprised just three crowded rooms on the third floor of the courthouse building, Sheriff Earl Robinson assigned Dewey a temporary desk for him to liaise the efforts of city police, sheriff, and county personnel, and other KBI investigators, while fielding phone calls from the public and the media and filing reports back to KBI headquarters in Topeka.

But was Dewey really the "hero" of the investigation, as depicted by Capote in his book? Not so much, as it turns out. Now that we're able to see past the shroud of mythology that has cloaked *In Cold Blood* for decades—and which has been perpetuated in nearly every book, article, and film about the story since its publication—it's clear that others had measurably greater influence on the outcome. And yet the Dewey myth continues. As former Finney County deputy sheriff Keith Denchfield recalls, "Harold Nye, Clarence Duntz, and Roy Church did the real investigative work. Dewey was mainly there for public relations. Roy once told me he had given all the notes he made each day to Dewey, who then just handed them over to Truman...."[87]

It was Harold Nye, along with two fellow agents, Roy Church and Clarence Duntz, who quietly and efficiently handled the bulk of investigative field work, acknowledged not only by other principals involved, but as confirmed in official reports. In fact, for his service in the Clutter case Nye was promoted to assistant director of the KBI just a few months later, while Dewey remained a field agent.

As Harper Lee's biographer Charles Shields quoted Harold Nye shortly before his death in 2003, "Dewey was only supposed to 'take care of the press, the news media, take our reports in, send them to the office, and be the office boy.'"[88]

Dewey himself later downplayed his modest role quite plainly in the *Garden City Telegram,* responding to the disgruntled feelings many held about the disproportionate credit he was given in the book.[89]

Frankly, there was much to commend the former FBI agent to the role for the author's purposes, for despite Agent Dewey's later denials of any impropriety, Capote would have no better access to the ripest and most sensitive investigative details that made his book such a compelling narrative. A case could be made, then, that *In Cold Blood* was as much a product of the

KBI's guiding hand as it was Capote's flowing pen.

"For the KBI," former assistant director Larry Thomas told a reporter, "we call it our landmark case that put us on the map... It's the rung on the ladder we all strive for." [90]

As coordinator of the Clutter murder investigation, KBI Agent Alvin Dewey knew very well that his friend, Herb Clutter, had been seen dancing and "smooching" with Mildred Lyon. Dewey had taken an official report from a Kansas State Highway Patrol trooper who reported a witness's account of the event.[91] Dewey personally wrote at least two "Memorandum for the File" reports detailing several individual eyewitness accounts to that effect.

Moreover, Dewey was convinced from the start that Herb Clutter was murdered with premeditation. County prosecutor Duane West, who tried the murder case in 1960, recalled that when Dewey learned Floyd Wells had fingered Smith and Hickock as the killers, he dismissed it: "Dewey said it wasn't them. [He] was convinced it was somebody local who had a grudge against Herb Clutter."[92] Yet this possibility was never seriously considered as a motive.

Beyond not even being considered, reports supporting the possibility appear to have been deliberately concealed. Alvin Dewey never disclosed critical evidence alluding to his initial suspicions, which begs the question: Why not? Despite his considering the possibility in his investigation, Harold Nye appears not to have known about the Clutter affair, at least according to his detailed notes and official reports, but there is a very good reason for that: the interview memoranda recorded by Agent Dewey alone were found in the Finney County records, in the office where he coordinated the investigation, but never appeared in any official KBI report, not even the final investigation summary found in Nye's file archive (among numerous report revisions). One can only surmise, since there were multiple credible reports, that Dewey was protecting his friend, Herb Clutter, from any posthumous exposure to scandal. While that may be questionable on the basis of personal loyalty, it is hardly official protocol during a murder investigation.

Moreover, why did this otherwise respected former FBI agent continue to feed Truman Capote confidential documents and case details that would form the underpinnings of a story that in so many ways differed from facts Dewey knew at the time?

Richard Rohleder

Figure 16. Richard Rohleder in 1943
Photo © 1943 Richard Rohleder; courtesy of Dean R. Rohleder

Choosing Dewey as the protagonist put at risk the story's historical fidelity. Most principal figures—notably Duane West, the county prosecutor who built the case against the killers—

have uniformly singled out one individual, Garden City's assistant chief of police Rich Rohleder, as having the greatest impact on the case from day one.

Born in 1911, Richard G. Rohleder grew up on a farm in Hays, Ellis County, that part of western Kansas settled by European immigrants in the late nineteenth century. His Russian-born mother and father—whose own parents starved to death in Siberian gulags—fled the Russian revolution for a better life in Kansas, drawn by the prospect of homesteading its vast fertile lands. They were among the wave of Volga-German farmers who settled in the Great Plain states, seeding the hard red winter wheat, the grain that would sustain Kansas farmers through drought and pestilence; the basic grain used to make bread and all-purpose flour.

When Rich was seven years old, both his parents died of Spanish flu during the great pandemic of 1918. Along with his two brothers, he was taken in by a foster family, where the boys worked the farmstead while attending school. Though he never made it beyond the sixth grade, Rohleder found lessons of self-reliance and ingenuity working the land, experiences that, lacking more formal education, would come to shape his skillful but underrated career in law enforcement.

In 1943, with no previous training in police work at all, Rohleder joined the Hays Police Department, and after proving his mettle there as deputy sheriff, moved on to the larger Garden City force in 1951. Over the next two decades he advanced from patrolman to detective to assistant chief of police, all the while devising new methods for analyzing and solving crimes, years before the KBI or other such agencies had similar capabilities.

"My dad had a natural, God-given talent for finding things out," Rohleder's son Dean told me in an interview. "His ability to investigate and solve crimes was amazing. Besides photography, he was a skilled mechanic and gunsmith, managing all firearm maintenance for the police departments he served with."[93] Rohleder also taught himself the esoteric art of fingerprint matching, refining his own crime scene kit with print dusters made of ostrich feathers (which, as he discovered, are superior to other material for their innate static charge that attracts dust).

In a *Lawrence Journal-World* article memorializing Rohleder's legacy in law enforcement, Patrick Smith, a contemporary reporter who has written extensively on the Clutter case, observed: "Even though Capote gave him little credit, Rohleder's thoroughness and forward thinking left a legacy at the Kansas Bureau of Investigation. The KBI now 'brackets' crime scene photos—meaning the photographer will take one photo at the proper exposure, then one longer and one shorter...,"[94] in order to suss out details that might otherwise be missed.

Finney County prosecutor Duane West and others also credit Rohleder with being the only investigator who initially considered robbery a motive for the murders, and he was alone in his (accurate) speculation that the killers could be hundreds of miles away the day after the murders.[95]

Though relegated to just one meager paragraph in *In Cold Blood*, it was Rohleder alone who discovered the single most important contribution to solving the Clutter murders. Using his Graflex 4x5 Speed Graphic (recognizable as the typical "press camera" used by news photographers in the early- to mid-twentieth century), Rohleder meticulously documented the crime scene, producing seventeen black-and-white pictures that told the jury all it needed to bring a swift conviction at trial: shocking images of the Clutter family, each viciously gunned down where they lay, bound and gagged; the vast pool of blood drained from Herb Clutter's lacerated throat, his pajama-clad body lying on top of a cardboard box in the basement; and most significantly, two different boot prints—a distinctive Cat's Paw brand found in a patch of blood on the cardboard; and another bearing a diamond tread found in the dust on the cement basement floor.

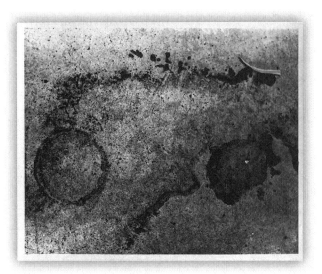

Figure 17. Perry Smith's bloody boot print
Photo © 1959 Richard Rohleder; Harold R. Nye Archives

Rohleder's keen discovery not only informed investigators they were dealing with more than one murderer, it was ultimately the only physical evidence authorities had tying any suspects to the crimes—provided the boots they were wearing at the time could still be found and matched.

After thirty years in law enforcement, Richard Rohleder retired in 1973, and in 1988, while tinkering in his home workshop, suffered a heart attack that ended his long and honorable life.

Jon Craig, an attorney in Garden City who knew Rohleder, said the former cop was proud of his work, but that "He wasn't interested in becoming famous. He was just doing his job."[96]

Richard Eugene Hickock

Figure 18. Richard Eugene Hickock
Photo © 1960 Jack Curtis, provided courtesy of the Curtis family

Raised by devoted parents on a farmstead near the village of
Edgerton, Kansas, "Dick" Hickock had every benefit of a good
middle-class childhood: a hard-working father, Walter, who built
the family home with his own hands on forty-four acres of rich
farm land; and Eunice, a deeply religious homemaker and doting
mother. Walter worked as an auto mechanic and body repairman

by day, and after hours would work the land with his family, yielding marketable crops of wheat, corn, hay, and strawberries, while their garden supplied an abundance of fresh fruits and vegetables for the family. According to Dick's younger brother, David, Walter and Eunice taught their sons "... the joy of living off the land, the beauty of nature, and the rewards of working and playing hard."[97]

All in stark contrast to the kind of life Perry Smith had.

But similar to Perry, two key incidents in Dick Hickock's youth put his life squarely on a calamitous path. In his book, Dick's brother David wrote that his brother had stolen a watch from a local drugstore. When discovered by his parents he readily admitted his guilt, made amends with the store, and no charges were filed.

Another more serious episode involved a car accident in 1950. At the time Hickock was on a date with his future wife, Carol, when he lost control of his car on a water-slicked highway. Dick was thrown from the vehicle into a water-filled ditch, in which he nearly drowned.[98]

Once a high-achieving, handsome and popular high school athlete, Dick was transfigured after the accident, both cosmetically and psychologically. His face was badly scarred, leaving his left eye skewed and out of proportion.

Almost overnight Dick's personality had changed from responsible, outgoing, and optimistic to "...more solemn, morose, and extremely reckless. He believed that he was able to do and say anything without any consequences.... His attitude continued to become more defiant and increasingly restless. His sporadic and irrational words left the rest of us wondering if the concussion he suffered in the accident had resulted in trauma to his brain."[99]

According to prison tests, Hickock had an IQ of 130, placing him in the second highest range: "Very Superior Intelligence," one level below Genius. Dick's car accident on its own, however, would appear unlikely as the sole agent of change, considering his theft of a drugstore wristwatch the year before. So, was the die cast early in his life, or did a head injury contribute to Dick's maladjusted and ultimately criminal activity?

Dr. James S. Walker, a specialist in severe trauma histories and one of only nine psychologists in the U.S. who are board-certified in both clinical neuropsychology and forensic psychology, reviewed Hickock's correspondence and known personal history, and offered this observation:

> From a nonscientific point of view, Dick Hickock was one who would have been called in his day and place "a man of low character." Examination of his personality from a modern forensic neuropsychology point of view reveal several characteristics that we now strongly associate with the concept of a "psychopath": superficial emotions, a glib style, lack of remorse, chronic irresponsibility, and callousness, to name a few. A very intriguing aspect of his case is his history of apparent severe traumatic brain injury. The motor vehicle accident that resulted in his facial disfigurement, with an extended loss of consciousness, is the sort that often results in frontal lobe dysfunction, a syndrome of impulsivity and poor behavior control known to at times result in violent criminality. In Hickock's case, his head injury can with certainty only be blamed for perhaps disinhibiting personality factors that were already present, as some criminal impulses were already evident prior to the crash.[100]

Dr. W. Mitchell Jones, the court-appointed psychiatrist who evaluated both Hickock and Smith in person, had asked each of them for biographical sketches in writing. In Hickock's, he confesses to a variety of crimes and misdemeanors, but one paragraph stands out: "There were other things I should have told you, but I'm afraid of my people finding them out. Because I

am more ashamed of them (these things I did) than
hanging...."[101]

Dr. Katherine Ramsland, a professor of forensic psychology
and distinguished author of several books on the science of crime
scene investigation and serial killers (including another Kansas
notable, Dennis Rader, the "BTK Killer"),[102] offered another
perspective on both men:

> Both Smith and Hickock were antisocial
> small-time offenders. Either might have
> resorted to killing if they had been seen or
> cornered, although I think that Hickock (an
> apparent narcissist), would more easily
> have killed a number of witnesses or
> pursuers than Smith would have.
>
> From how they present themselves
> (though not from a professional
> assessment), Hickock would probably have
> shown less remorse over taking a life than
> Smith. Neither demonstrated the collection
> of traits we usually see in extreme
> offenders—such as rampage mass
> murderers and predatory serial killers—so
> for these two to have committed such a
> crime, we must also include the
> circumstances in the calculation. Personality
> disorders alone would not explain what
> motivated them, individually or working
> together.[103]

Setting aside the fact that no one actually treated Hickock as a
psychotic patient—a basic precondition for rendering any
professional diagnosis—he does appear to fit the textbook
definition of a psychopath, and certainly that of a pathological
liar.

But liar or not, Hickock's most intriguing disclosures, in his
Death Row letters to Mack Nations, are in part corroborated by
Harold Nye's notes and official KBI reports—reports prepared

weeks before the killers had even been identified.

As readers will find in chapters to come, Hickock's elaborate retelling at least lends itself to a reconsideration of events.

Perry Edward Smith

Figure 19. Perry Edward Smith
Photo © 1960 Jack Curtis, provided courtesy of the Curtis family

Readers of *In Cold Blood* will already know much about Perry
Smith who was, in the words of prison chaplain James Post, "the
victim of an unfortunate childhood filled with adversity,"[104]
which included regular beatings at the hands of orphanage nuns;
the gas-poisoning suicides of his brother, Jimmy,[105] and Jimmy's
wife, Jean;[106] the loss of his sister Fern (also known as Joy), who
fell to her death from a fire escape; his promiscuous alcoholic
mother, Flo, and his abusive-when-not-absent father, Tex—both
erstwhile performers on the rodeo circuit when not engaged in
routine domestic violence. Hardly a setting for the American
dreams of any child. A lost soul who yearned for a life beyond the
hand that was dealt him, Smith constantly worked to improve
himself (and others), as his personal journals reveal in abundant
poetic detail.

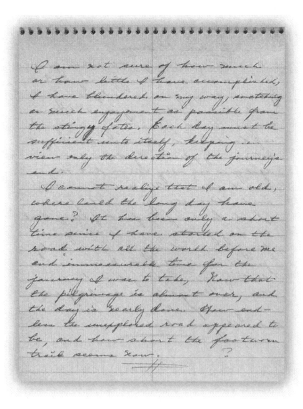

Figure 20. Perry Smith ponders life

Courtesy of Wendle & Josephine Meier Family

I am not sure of how much or how little I
have accomplished, I have blundered on my
way, snatching as much enjoyment as
possible from the stingy fates. Each day
must be sufficient unto itself, keeping in
view only the direction of the journey's end.
I cannot realize that I am old, where
could the long day have gone? It has been
only a short time since I have started on the
road with all the world before me and
immeasurable time for the journey I was to
take, now that the pilgrimage is almost over,
and the day is nearly done. How endless
the unexplored road appeared to be, and
how short the footworn trail seems now.

At age sixteen, Smith signed up for a two-year stint in the
Merchant Marine, and in 1948 enlisted in the U.S. Army,
serving a three-year tour of duty in the Asiatic–Pacific as a heavy
equipment operator with the 3rd Combat Engineer Battalion.
His last fifteen months of service were spent at the Bay of Inchon
during the Korean War, where he helped bridge the many rivers
needed to ensure troop mobility leading up to the Battle of
Inchon, where Smith was awarded the prestigious Bronze Star,
the Army's fourth-highest military decoration for valor—an
honor given only for heroic or meritorious achievement and
services in a combat zone.

Figure 21. Smith (right) with Army buddy; Inchon, Korea
Courtesy of Wendle & Josephine Meier Family

Smith's foreign service ended at sea on October 1, 1951, while crossing the Pacific on a troop ship sailing for home. Young Perry had the distinction of being the first man to set foot off the ship when it docked in Seattle, and was warmly greeted by high-ranking Army officials who had arranged a flight home for him to join his father in Trapper's Den, Alaska. Under the front-page headline *"Alaska Trapper Rotated Home from Battle; Cheered at Dock,"* a Fairbanks newspaper reported, "Troops aboard and crowds of welcomers cheered as the stocky, black-haired youth strode down the gangway, grinning."[107]

Perry spent his final months of unused furlough helping his father trap fur in Alaska, and while there he received his Honorable Discharge from the Army on June 9, 1952. Shortly thereafter he returned to Washington State, where two events occurred that would ultimately impact the lives of many people.

In September 1952 Perry suffered a motorcycle accident that nearly crippled him. The lasting damage was so severe that he walked with a noticeable limp on misshapen legs. The better part of the following year he spent recovering in the Cushman Indian Hospital in Tacoma.

Just four months before his accident, as we have recently learned, Perry fathered a son.[108] It's not clear who the mother was, nor whether Perry was actually aware of the boy's later birth. Now in his 60s, Jewell Praying Wolf James—raised in the Pacific Northwest by Perry's friend Joe James as his own son—is a master totem pole carver and prominent environmental activist for the Lummi tribe, the indigenous people of Washington's northern coast on the waters of the Puget Sound.[109]

In his book, Capote describes a nurse named "Cookie" who Perry met while hospitalized following his motorcycle accident, and with whom he had sexual relations. Cookie was the girl he almost married, whose name was tattooed on his upper right arm.

A small but relevant point can be made here that this, like many scenes that appear in *In Cold Blood*, is not true. Perry did have the name "Cookie" emblazoned on his right bicep, but that was long before the accident that brought him to the hospital in Tacoma, likely while he was serving in Korea, as revealed in this photograph taken around 1950 (with Perry in the upper left):

Figure 22. Perry (upper left) with "Cookie" tattoo, circa 1950
Photo courtesy of "Taro Leaf" 24th Infantry Division Association, February 1987
Photographer unknown.

Another thematic story point which Capote misconstrued about Perry was his heritage: he did not have a drop of Cherokee blood in him. Perry's mother, Florence Julia Buckskin, was in fact not a full-blooded Cherokee at all, but born of mixed Western Shoshone–Northern Paiute ancestry; his father, John "Tex" Smith, was Caucasian with Northern European streaks of Irish and Dutch.

That Capote identified Perry as Cherokee may have two possible explanations. First, people more easily recognize the three largest American tribal nations—Navajo, Cherokee, and Sioux—based largely (some would say tragically) on their storied roles in Western films.

Second, Perry's sister, Dorothy Marchant (interviewed by Capote and given the pseudonym "Barbara Johnson" in *In Cold Blood*), could have wanted to save face for her family's Shoshone–Paiute relations, sparing them association with the sins of her brother. The latter seems the more logical explanation.

As for the Clutter crimes, Perry seems to have just been along for the ride, literally. As *In Cold Blood* describes it, the only reason Smith was in Kansas at all was a hoped-for reunion with his "real and only friend," the prison chaplain's clerk "Willie-Jay," a pseudonym created by Capote for a young man whose real name was John McRell.

Figure 23. Chaplain's Clerk John McRell, aka "Willie-Jay"
Courtesy of Kansasmemory.org, Kansas State Historical Society.

McRell was a deeply religious soul who had spent most of his life in various penal institutions for such crimes as burglary and robbery. Prison records indicate that by age 30, around the time he met Perry Smith, McRell had already served five separate sentences in three penal institutions, and would continue this pattern well into his 80s, apparently drawn to a life of service behind bars until his death in January 2017 at age 87.

Though lacking much formal education, McRell was intelligent and acutely insightful, with a caring and positive influence on fellow inmates. Perry Smith, whose tragic childhood and lack of encouraging role models left him cautious and mistrustful of most people, found in his friend the type of man he truly wanted to be. In Perry's mind, McRell was the only person who really understood him.

Capote brilliantly laid the framework for Smith's emotional foundation when, like ships passing in the night, Perry and Willie-Jay missed reuniting within mere hours of each other, both having transited through the same Kansas City bus terminal, both now heading in different directions. That frustration, leaving Perry feeling angry and disappointed, combined with the predicament Hickock had handed him in "the perfect score," created the highly-charged "brain explosion"[110] scene, when on impulse he thrust a hunting knife into Mr. Clutter's throat. Though some controversy exists as to whether Smith's actions were spontaneous or premeditated, sufficient evidence would accept a coalition of both theories.

But here reality strikes again, for according to official prison records McRell was not even released from Kansas State Penitentiary until November 19—four days *after* the murders took place.[111] As Perry made clear in interviews and to his friend James Post, the prison chaplain, he had desperately wanted to reunite with McRell—his mentor, the manifestation of his conscientious ideals—but he would never see or speak with his friend again.

It also seems obvious that, in spite of Dick's arrogant bragging about leaving no witnesses, Perry had no such inclination, much less foreknowledge that Herb Clutter may have been the only target, with the lives of other family members taken as collateral damage.

Among other things, Perry was intent on buying black stockings to mask their faces, clearly presuming their robbery victims would be left alive to identify the intruders should their faces be seen. Evidently uncommon articles to come by at the time, Perry knew there was one place black stockings could easily be found—where there were nuns. En route to Holcomb, they stopped at St. Mary's Catholic hospital in Olathe. But that presented a new challenge.

When Perry was six years old, his mother—fed up with her husband and the rodeo circuit—took her children and moved to San Francisco where, not long after, she abandoned Perry to a California orphanage. It was there he suffered abominable episodes of abuse by Catholic nuns, "black widows" he called them, who beat him repeatedly with a flashlight for wetting his bed. Were it not for his fear of nuns (among his many omens of bad luck), Perry would have gone in and handled the task himself.

Instead he sent Dick, who only pretended to undertake the assignment and returned to the car empty-handed. If masking their identity was of so little importance to Hickock, it may argue that, at the onset at least, he had no intention of letting any of the Clutters live.

Jack Curtis, the Clutter family's longtime photographer, also took photos of Smith and Hickock after they were apprehended, and sometime later spent several hours interviewing Perry in his cell. In 1968, in a poignant and insightful article for the *Los Angeles Times*, Curtis wrote of that experience during which Perry revealed many things—including a clear admission that he alone killed all four Clutters.

> "You know," [Perry] said, "about that Clutter thing…" His body stiffened, and he leaned forward…. His hands, between his spread

knees, were opened wide, palms up. His big
brown eyes swept again from side to side;
his voice caught and dropped almost to a
whisper.

"I killed all four of them with these
hands!" he said. His eyes searched mine, a
feeling for some hint of understanding. I
have no idea what he saw there.
Unprepared for such a startling confession, I
just sat there. It was the first time I knew for
sure that he had done all the dirty work. I
don't remember what I said, but my eyes
must have shown something he wanted to
see. There was a long pause.

The hands dropped and his body wilted.
"I've cried my eyes out at night, but it
doesn't do any good!"[112]

This admission was also reaffirmed during Smith and
Hickock's final parole board clemency hearing on April 6, 1965,
one week before they would be executed, where Smith related
their actions in chilling detail, as depicted here in a portion of the
board's hearing summary [sic]:

It was then that Smith claims he loaded the
shot gun and while Hickcock held the
flashlight on Mr. Clutter, who was clutching
his injured throat, that Smith shot him in the
head, then went into the adjoining room and
shot the son. Then, Smith said, Hickcock
went around and picked up the ejected shell
cases, went upstairs and started outside.
He called to him and they went to the
second floor where Hickcock flashed the
light in the face each woman (Mother and
daughter) and he, Smith, shot each in the
head while they pleaded for mercy, after
which they picked up the shell cases and
left the house with some items of personal
property.[113]

Although *In Cold Blood* describes Perry apologizing for his actions[114] just before climbing the thirteen steps to his waiting noose, three journalists who witnessed the execution—Bill Brown, editor of the Garden City *Telegram*; Tony Jewell, a radio reporter for KIUL; and Art Wilson, a Garden City news director reporting for KAKE-TV Wichita—have flatly denied hearing Smith apologize, all having taken verbatim notes at the scene.

Charles McAtee, director of Kansas prisons, was also present at the execution. McAtee—a former Marine, FBI agent, and federal prosecutor—corresponded regularly with both Smith and Hickock over several years, developing an unusually compassionate view of both men in the exchange, especially Perry.

"Smith was an introspective man who tried to find peace through painting, reading and writing. [He] created biblical images in watercolors on [prison] bed sheets, [and] memorized a book, *"Thoreau on Man and Nature."*[115]

McAtee recalled Perry's last words to him. "Mr. McAtee, I would like to apologize to someone, but to whom? To them? To the relatives? To their friends and neighbors? To you? To the State of Kansas? But you know you can't undo what we did with an apology."[116]

Perry's own handwritten journals do reveal a measure of remorse not voiced while he was alive, written in the typical pedantic fashion he favored, and where in parts he seems to be having a one-way conversation with Capote:

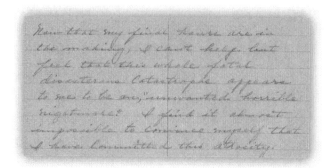

Figure 24. Perry Smith's "unwanted horrible nightmare"
Courtesy of Wendle & Josephine Meier Family

"Now that my final hours are in the making,"
Smith writes, "I can't help but feel that this
whole fatal disastrous catastrophe appears to
me to be an 'unwanted horrible nightmare.' I
find it almost impossible to convince myself
that I have committed this atrocity. But it has
happened and cannot be undone…. I am
powerless to make amends. The trouble with
me, Truman, is that I have the right aim in life
but the wrong ammunition."

Jack Curtis was so moved by his observations of Smith that
he closed his article on a distinctly melancholic note.

"It seems to me," he wrote, "that there is a real lesson to be
learned from Perry. All he had within him was dreams. He was
molded, in his weaknesses, by outside forces. He killed the
Clutters as an instrument of Dick Hickock…. His thirst for big
words, it seems to me, represented his desire for an education. He
was smarter than he knew. He was no hypocrite. His life was an
open book for those with eyes to see and ears to hear. It has
seemed to me ever since then that each of us has within us the
power to control our own destinies. If we don't exercise that
power, someone else will—with results that can be fatal. The pity
was that Perry didn't understand that any better than most of
us."[117]

"Judge Roland Tate and I were talking one
day about the murder trial, and the judge
said Perry wasn't a bad kid. He could have
been the kind of guy who would have gone
straight, if it weren't for Hickock. He was the
wild one."
   — *Keith Denchfield, former Deputy
Sheriff of Finney County, Kansas.*[118]

Among the many personal effects that Perry Smith left with
Undersheriff Wendle Meier and his wife Josie was this photo of
himself when he was sixteen, having just joined the Merchant
Marine.

Figure 25. Perry Smith at age 16

Along with other items Perry handed over to the Meiers, this note speaks to their close relationship:

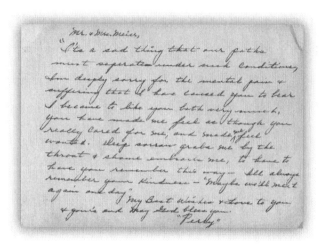

Figure 26. Perry Smith's note to the Meiers

Mr. and Mrs. Meier,
It's a sad thing that our paths must separate under such conditions, I'm deeply sorry for the mental pain and suffering that I have caused you to bear. I became to like you both very much, you have made me feel as though you really cared for me, and made me feel wanted. Deep sorrow grabs me by the throat and shame embraces me, to have to have you remember this way—I'll always remember your kindness—Maybe we'll meet again one day.

My best wishes & love to you & yours and may God bless you.

"Perry"

In a fascinating two-part article for *The New York Times Magazine* in 1978—successively titled "The Private World of Truman Capote" and "The Descent from the Heights,"—acclaimed author Anne Taylor Fleming laid out a cornucopia of insights into Capote's colorful life. Fleming's narrative includes a passage from the diary of Sandy Campbell, a close friend of Capote's who was also the fact-checker for *The New Yorker* magazine's publication of *In Cold Blood* months before the book came out in hardcover. In it, Campbell recounts a moving postscript of Truman's journey with Perry Smith, an affecting act not known by many people.

"When Perry was dead and taken away," Campbell wrote, "the warden came up to Truman and gave him an envelope. 'Mr. Smith wanted you to have this,' he said.

"It contained all the money Truman had sent Perry over the five years. Truman burst into tears."[119]

Who really killed the Clutters?

Who committed the actual killings is a question that still lingers in the minds of many, since responsibility was never resolved in Capote's book.

In his confession, Hickock alleged that Smith shot all four of the Clutters. In Perry's initial statement to investigators on the road trip from Las Vegas to Garden City, he claimed to have killed only the father and son, while Hickock killed the mother and daughter. Despite Perry's later changing his statement to confess that he shot all four, allegedly to save Dick's family further pain, Agent Alvin Dewey maintained his belief that each killed two. Prosecutor Duane West also believed each killed two, as did Bill Brown, editor of the *Garden City Telegram*, who knew the case intimately from start to finish. Capote, who had spent more time with both men than anyone else and had exchanged hundreds of letters with them over the years, was convinced that Perry himself had pulled the trigger all four times.

According to Perry himself, in his journals and elsewhere, he claims to have pulled the trigger on the entire family, one by one.

William Floyd Wells, Jr.

Figure 27. William Floyd Wells, Jr.
Courtesy of Kansasmemory.org, Kansas State Historical Society.

Local police and the KBI had accrued a slender body of evidence from the crime scene that, on its own, would have done little to offer up clues as to *who* was responsible for killing the Clutters. If it weren't for the sharp observations and photographic evidence taken by Officer Rich Rohleder, however, the KBI wouldn't have even had that.

But without the nearly untold story of one William Floyd Wells, Jr., an inmate in the Kansas State Penitentiary at Lansing, the fact is that the Clutter crimes would most likely have remained unsolved. The clues were that negligible, the evidence that scant. Without Wells there would have been nothing tying Smith and Hickock to the crimes except two prints from very popular boots. Assuming both men could have led otherwise clean lives, they could have easily gotten away with murder, since the overwhelming majority of U.S. homicides in the 1960 era, some ninety percent, were never solved.

Only Wells did report it. And his story is a curious one.

For such a pivotal character in the scheme of things, "Floyd" Wells was given remarkably short shrift in Capote's book. What little background information is available on the man is thinly disbursed and difficult to confirm, especially now, nearly fifty years after his death. But what details have been found are, much like Wells himself, puzzling and contradictory.

It's doubtful that Capote or Lee ever interviewed him, for despite two pages in the book describing Wells in some detail (much of it incorrect), no interview or background notes on him at all were found in the Capote Papers at the New York Public Library, nor in the Capote archives at the Library of Congress. The only time all three—Capote, Lee, and Wells—were even known to be in the presence of each other was in the packed courtroom during the trial.

Moreover, if there is any merit to a conspiracy in the larger story, that was not the book Capote wanted to write anyway, so there would have been little motivation to pursue it. One reliable source told me that Alvin Dewey actually prohibited anyone from visiting Floyd Wells in prison—even Truman Capote. Although I could find nothing conclusive to support this, neither could I find anything to disprove it. But since Capote already had Wells's statement to the KBI (grateful to "Foxy" Alvin Dewey for having provided it), why bite the hand that fed him?

Any detail of Wells that did make it into the book had appeared earlier in newspapers covering the trial and in (flawed, even perjured) testimony at the trial itself. What is revealed here is largely from a mash of military records, Harold Nye's notes, KBI documents, and vintage newspaper archives.

A native of Oswego, Kansas, born in 1927, Floyd Wells dropped out of high school without completing his second year, and at age eighteen enlisted in the U.S. Army, serving from 1946 until he was honorably discharged two years later at the rank of private first class.

In the summer of 1948, post-war America was flush with

economic opportunity and virtually no unemployment. Having few skills and no formal training, Wells at the time was working at W. J. Small's alfalfa mill in Holcomb, Kansas. With the approaching alfalfa harvest, a large spread just outside of town with the picturesque name of River Valley Farm was hiring, and in June, Wells found a job working as a ranch hand for Herbert Clutter, one of the most prominent farmers in the region.

Wells worked for the Clutters from June 1948 to January 1949,[120] and despite his claims ten years later that the family favored his work and the pleasure of his company (and he theirs), he left Clutter's employ after just seven months on the job. No records have been found for his performance or reasons why he left, and longtime Clutter employees, including ranch manager Gerald Van Vleet, had only a vague memory of him when questioned by authorities during the investigation.

Given his claimed mutual affection with the Clutters, and Herb Clutter's supposed extraordinary financial generosity to him, it's more than a little strange that Wells's tenure was so brief, especially for such a plum job many at the time would have fought to keep. Leaving of his own accord seems implausible; Clutter ran a year-round planting and harvesting operation, so there was constant work to be had and no reason for a motivated ranch hand to simply wander off like a stray heifer. After his departure, Wells apparently drifted from one garage to the next as a mechanic and "body and fender man."

Some ten years later, Wells, with no apparent job prospects at hand, hatched a scheme to start his own lawn mower rental business, which on its own would have been a laudable ambition if it weren't for one obvious problem: to get his venture started, he needed lawn mowers. Having no startup capital, Floyd embraced the wisdom of Sutton's Law—an axiom attributed to the famous American bank robber Willie Sutton, who, when asked by a reporter why he robbed banks, answered plainly: "Because that's where the money is."

So, Wells broke into an appliance store and, finding the equipment he needed to establish his legitimate venture, pilfered his new inventory. But he got caught in the act.

That bit of larceny in June 1959 earned Wells a prison sentence of five to ten years at Lansing,[121] where he was assigned to a two-bunk cell, half of which had just become available the week before, when its previous occupant, Perry Edward Smith, made parole and hightailed it to the West Coast, enjoined from ever showing his face in Kansas again, else hazard the prospect of reincarceration.

The other bunk in Wells's cell was occupied by a shrewd and talkative young Kansan named Dick Hickock. Hickock, also serving a five- to ten-year stretch for grand larceny, had been at KSP for just over a year, with a month or two remaining before he would be paroled.

In his effusive letters to Mack Nations, Hickock wrote of his dismay finding that he'd been assigned a new cellmate, preferring instead to serve out his remaining time alone now that Smith was gone.

But in those last few weeks Hickock found Wells to be quite the chatty fellow himself. Posing as a first-time offender, Floyd was itching with questions about life behind bars, and Hickock, having served multiple stints for various small-time misdeeds, gave his new companion the big picture of life in the big house.

(I say "posing" as a first-timer because Wells had actually served time before, "'about' three times" as he testified under cross examination during the trial.[122] He had been jailed for burglary, spent three months in the Army stockade for bad behavior, and was arrested for driving without a license. Why he professed rookie status to Hickock seems odd, though, as readers will find, it may have been a useful ruse.)

After about a week of small talk, Floyd got around to asking Dick what his plans were when he made parole. Hickock recalled the conversation [spelling and grammar are verbatim from his handwritten letters; emphasis added for discussion]:

> Wells asked me if I was going straight when
> I got out. I told him I was sick of doing time,
> that I had a job waiting for me when I got

> out.... **He told me that if he was getting out the first thing he would do, would be to take a little drive and pull the sweetest score he ever seen.** He went on to tell me about how he used to work for a guy in southwestern Kansas by the name of Herb Clutter....[123]

Assuming the reliability of Hickock's letters—and in multiple versions, including oral statements he gave to the KBI, his detailed narratives were invariably consistent—what we find here is an utterly new and startling claim: that Floyd Wells had intended to rob the Clutters himself. Nearly two years after committing the crimes about which he was writing, Hickock had nothing to gain by implicating Wells. There would be no point in making up such a detail.

But was Wells planning to do the deed himself, as he claimed? Or was this some kind of bait he was setting out for Hickock?

The letters go on, with Wells providing Hickock unusually intimate details about Herb Clutter, his family, the "new home," and the business dealings of a successful farmer:

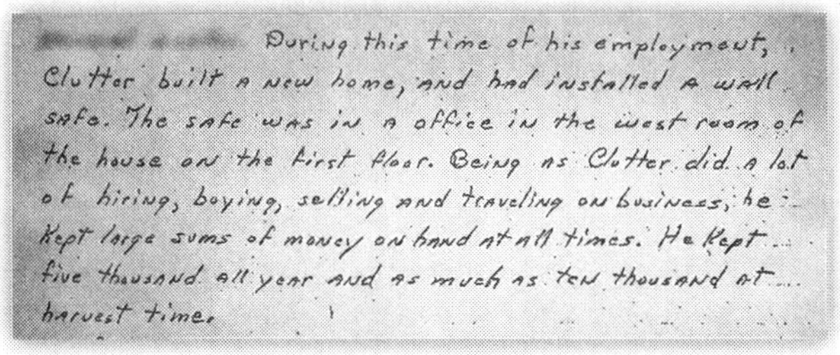

Figure 28. Hickock on the safe as told to him by Wells
Author's archives

> ...This guy was a big rancher and done a lot of seasonal hiring. Especially at harvest time. He went on to elaborate how he worked for Clutter in 1954, (I think) [*ed. it*

was actually 1948] and had worked for him several months. During this time of his employment, Clutter built a new home, and had installed a wall safe. The safe was in a office in the west room of the house on the first floor.] Being as Clutter did a lot of hiring, buying, selling and traveling on business, he kept large sums of money on hand at all times. He kept five thousand all year and as much as ten thousand at harvest time.[124]

Despite his assertion that he became close to the family, what follows next would seem to be at odds with Wells's reciprocating the Clutters' generosity. As Hickock described it [emphasis added; sic]:

During the time Wells is telling me this, I'm thinking to myself, "Another one of these cinches I've heard so much about. Probably doesn't keep his safe locked or some crap like that." I made up my mind not to go for it, but Well's next statement made me do a lot of thinking. Wells told me that he knew what he was talking about and the deal is a "cinch." He said he would set me up on it, if I promised to send him a thousand bucks for doing it.

I got to thinking that this isn't free information like all the rest I've heard. I've had a dozen guys tell me of easy scores, but they didn't want nothing out of them, and that made them a lie. But this is different I thought. I told Wells that I might be interested, and for him to tell me the set up. He said, "Oh no, not unless you promise me to send me a grand ... if I don't get a grand at least out of it, I'll pull it my self when I get out." I told him, "If I pull it, I'll send you a grand." *Wells asked me, "Will you tell anybody else?" I told him, No."*[125]

Now, by demanding a share of the heist in exchange for critical information, Wells is clearly implicated as an accomplice in the scheme. Yet the mere suggestion of Wells's complicity was roundly dismissed by the KBI, who claimed Wells was simply an "innocent bystander" in the affair.

But Wells's last question—*"Will you tell anybody else?"*—sheds a different light on the exchange, given the possibility that he was setting Hickock up with darker intentions in mind.

Hickock continues:

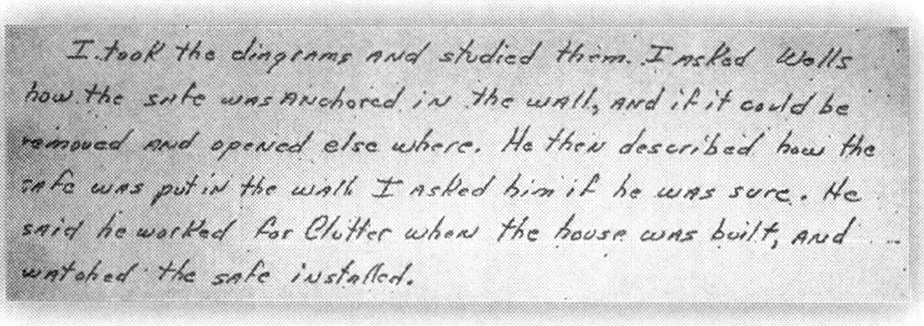

I took the diagrams and studied them. I asked Wells
how the safe was anchored in the wall, and if it could be
removed and opened else where. He then described how the
safe was put in the wall I asked him if he was sure. He
said he worked for Clutter when the house was built, and
watched the safe installed.

Figure 29. Wells claims he watched the safe being installed
Author's archives

> I took the diagrams and studied them. I asked Wells how the safe was anchored in the wall, and if it could be removed and opened else where. He then described how the safe was put in the wall. I asked him if he was sure. He said he worked for Clutter when the house was built, and watched the safe installed.[126]

Like a spawning salmon leaping into the jaws of a patient grizzly, Hickock couldn't turn back now. His eagerness laid bare, he challenged Wells over and over, trying to find cracks in his story:

> For the next two weeks, when ever I thought of it, I asked him to repeat the Clutter deal.

His story never changed. I believed him. But
before I left for home I told him, "If things
don't go right for me in the free world and I
ever decide to knock off this safe, I'll send
you a grand." He said, "It's a deal." And we
shook hands on it.[127]

Savoring the prospect of a "sweet score," Hickock could not
have known that most of what he had just heard was a lie, a fact
confirmed by Wells's testimony at the trial, where he denied ever
discussing a safe:

The conversations we had were more
lengthy than I have written, because I
questioned him a lot as to the safe and each
and every other detail he had related to me.
His story never varied, and I might add that
he was a convincing lier. Wells testified at
the trial that he never told me Clutter had a
safe, but he emphatically insisted that he
did, and would not tell me the whole thing
unless I promised to send him one thousand
dollars. *He had a ulterior motive for
telling me what he did, and I wish I knew
what it was. It may have been just what
happened. Wells may have had a grudge
against Herb Clutter and was hoping
some physical harm might come to him.*
But this is just a conjecture on my part, as I
have no proof.[128]

As *In Cold Blood* describes, Wells first heard about the
Clutter murders while listening to the radio in his cell, two days
after the crime had occurred. Wells made no immediate mention
of what he knew about it to anyone, presumably fearing that
time-honored prison axiom "snitches get stitches."

But three weeks later, burning with a desire to share what he
knew, he claimed he did mention it to a fellow inmate at KSP.

In fact, at least two others were aware of Wells's story:

inmates of no particular account named John Sabol and Frank Harper, and if they knew, others knew as well. But KBI agent Alvin Dewey and county prosecutor Duane West shrugged off any significance of others having knowledge of Clutter's supposed cash trove.

Don Kendall, one of the more persevering reporters who covered the Clutter murder trial for the *Hutchinson News*, filed some of the most detailed stories on the case from Garden City, providing keen insights unobtainable from other sources.

On March 30, 1960, the case went to the jury. That evening's edition of the *Hutchinson News* featured several columns by Kendall, each laying out key elements of the proceedings. Among those was a piece headlined "*'Smoke Screens' Set by Hickock*,"[129] in which the reporter relates an absorbing account of testimony regarding knowledge of the plot by other inmates. In it the prosecution team offered conflicting observations on the issue:

> **Al Dewey** – "Wells is the only one we heard about." He said he hadn't heard the names, Sabol and Harper.
> **County Atty. Duane West** – "We had heard there were others that have heard of this talk and planning." But, West added, the plan probably circulated in the prison "like a lot of talk does."
> **Harold Nye** – Asked if he had heard about Sabol and Harper, Nye replied quickly: "No." Asked if anyone else was thought to have heard of Hickock's scheme in the prison, Nye replied: "Oh yeah, there were several in there that knew."

As to the contention that Wells was in for a cut if Hickock went through with the robbery, Kendall writes:

> Consensus among KBI and Finney County

officials was that Wells, through "normal" prison boredom and conversation, paved the way for Hickock's plan by inadvertently mentioning he had once worked for a "rich farmer out west." This, officials said, doesn't imply complicity in the crime that Wells will be charged as an accessory. However, this opinion was voiced by the authorities before the trial was over.[130]

So, consider for a moment that if Wells were casting a wide net for the right person to execute a more duplicitous plan, he may have just been trying out his story until that individual emerged. Then he crossed paths with Dick Hickock, a man bragging of sociopathic exploits and with a history of seeking a quick buck, especially one that could be a "cinch" to pull off. An easy score. If Floyd Wells had hoped for this outcome, he couldn't have chosen a better, if unwitting, fall guy than Dick Hickock.

This theory acquires a bit more heft in light of Wells's unabashed lies to the KBI under oath, not to mention the KBI's passive endorsement of them when presented to the jury. Wells was allowed to spin a shockingly contradictory tale of denial, also while under oath, with the KBI failing to inform the Court that the witness was perjuring himself.

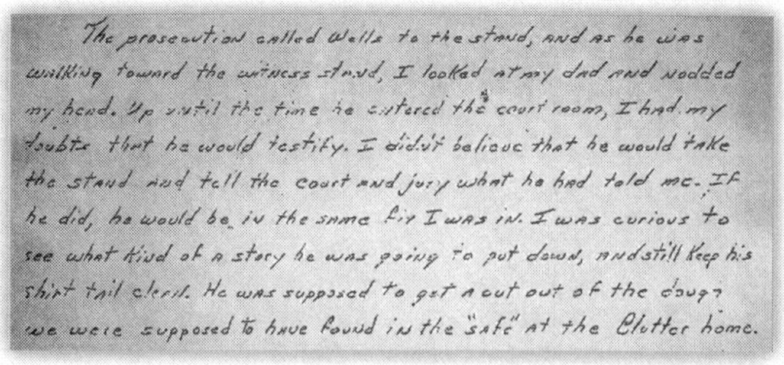

The prosecution called Wells to the stand, and as he was walking toward the witness stand, I looked at my dad and nodded my head. Up until the time he entered the court room, I had my doubts that he would testify. I didn't believe that he would take the stand and tell the court and jury what he had told me. If he did, he would be in the same fix I was in. I was curious to see what kind of a story he was going to put down, and still keep his shirt tail clean. He was supposed to get a out out of the dough we were supposed to have found in the "safe" at the Clutter home.

Figure 30. Hickock writes about Wells taking the stand
Author's archives

> The prosecution called Wells to the stand,
> and as he was walking toward the witness
> stand, I looked at my dad and nodded my
> head. Up until the time he entered the court
> room, I had my doubts that he would testify.
> I didn't believe that he would take the stand
> and tell the court and jury what he had told
> me. If he did, he would be in the same fix I
> was in. I was curious to see what kind of a
> story he was going to put down, and still
> keep his shirt tail clean. He was supposed
> to get a cut of the dough we were supposed
> to have found in the "safe" at the Clutter
> home.[131]

During the trial Hickock grew furious as he listened to Floyd Wells spin lies on the witness stand, telling a factually different story than the one he weaved in their cell at Lansing; one that also conflicted with the statement Wells gave under oath to KBI Agent Wayne Owens. His anger mounting, it was all Hickock could do to remain seated in the courtroom, later telling Capote in an interview that he almost jumped Wells right there during the trial, but he had friends in Oklahoma who could take care of Mr. Wells if need be.[132]

Given this new information, several things are clear:

> ❧ Floyd Wells contrived a sufficiently
> attractive story for the benefit of Dick
> Hickock, a man obsessed with making a big
> score, and who bragged that he would leave
> no witnesses;
>
> ❧ Wells lied under oath to the KBI that

Herb Clutter had a safe containing $10,000.
There was no safe, and there was no
money. The KBI knew this and yet still used
Wells testimony as evidence in court;[133]

✎ Wells could not have drawn the map of
the Clutters' new house, simply because he
had never been inside it. By his own
admission, supported by press reports at
the time, Wells left Clutter's employ before
the home had even been completed—and
before the family had moved in.[134] Even in
his testimony at trial he was quoted as
saying he "had made no maps or drawings
for Hickock."[135]

Presented with Wells's request for early clemency, Kansas
Governor George Docking wasn't convinced that Wells hadn't
been an actual accomplice to the crimes, since he reportedly
expected a thousand-dollar bounty from Hickock in return for
laying out the heist. "I'm not sure this man didn't plant the idea
in the first place,"[136] the governor said. Consequently, Docking
denied clemency for Wells.

But Wells did win release from prison a mere two months
after the March 1960 trial, despite the fact that, according to
prison records, the earliest parole he was eligible for was July
1962. Though everyone denied it, including Wells and the KBI,
there had to have been a plea deal by the State for his testimony.
Wells was immediately transferred from the prison in Lansing to
the Kansas State Industrial Reformatory in Hutchinson, where
inmates were eligible for parole after serving 10 months—an
expedient way to get around the governor's denial of clemency.
Wells didn't even serve that minimum, however. He was released
after just five weeks.

Retired federal probation officer Sally J. Keglovits, an expert on the Clutter case,[137] put it more bluntly. "From my experience, Kansas authorities would be disingenuous claiming there was no quid pro quo involved in the early release of Floyd Wells," she said in an interview. "Under usual circumstances, an inmate in Kansas in this time period would not become eligible for parole until he had served the minimum sentence—and for Wells that was five years—minus whatever "good time" had accrued. Prisons didn't face the same pressures they do now, so over-crowding was not a big issue. There was no need to grant an early parole to Wells, but there may have been reasons to reward him."[138]

Having gained a swift reprieve from his original five- to ten-year sentence, and walking away with a $1,000 reward to boot, the "informer" who was undeniably complicit in the Clutter murders was paid off handsomely, earning both money and his freedom in the bargain.

And then... he disappeared.

As might well be imagined, the pressure was overwhelming to find those responsible for killing the Clutter family and put an end to the "*If it can happen there, it can happen here*" state of mind that gripped Kansas, the Midwest, and beyond. The attraction of such a singularly notorious crime had drawn journalists from across the country to, as one *Wichita Eagle* reporter described it, "this rural outpost on the Kansas prairie." The political burden on local authorities to solve a mass murder that had fostered such fear in a bucolic town unaccustomed to that sort of infamy would have been punishing. By choosing to ignore Wells's perjury, the KBI was employing a self-serving strategy to expedite the trial at any cost. To conclude otherwise is irrational.

All of which leaves us with some of the more enigmatic questions central to this story:

- Why did Wells so brazenly lie to the KBI in his

interview after informing on Hickock and Smith, having much more to lose than gain by doing so?

- What was the justification for allowing Wells to perjure himself in court, when the KBI was clearly aware he was doing so?

- Who really drew that detailed layout of the Clutter's new home, even identifying who slept in which bedroom?

- Was Wells planning to pull off the robbery himself, as Hickock claimed? Or was he merely setting out a trail of bread crumbs, one he expected would be impossible for an ambitious schemer like Hickock to ignore?

- And what forces are capable of making a five- to ten-year prison sentence vanish, resulting in Wells going free after serving just ten months in two institutions having disparate parole conditions? Did somebody want him unavailable or out of reach?

Following a 1961 arrest in Oklahoma for burglary, larceny, and interstate transportation of a stolen vehicle, Floyd Wells seems to have all but vanished. Nine years later, however, he was reported to have been imprisoned again, this time for an armed robbery conviction in Tishomingo County, Mississippi, for which he was sentenced to thirty years at the maximum-security prison in Parchman.

The oldest prison in Mississippi, Parchman is a sprawling 28-square mile prison farm with an environment "so inhospitable for escape that prisoners working in the fields are not chained to one another, and one overseer supervises each gang. A potential escapee could wander for days without leaving the property."[139] Situated on flat farmland of the Mississippi Delta, the outer edge of the prison's vast property had no fencing and virtually no trees.

But despite the odds and obstacles, on the morning of Friday, April 3, 1970, Wells is reported to have attempted a brazen but unhurried escape—on a tractor. He was on duty in the prison mess hall, and with the help of two other inmates stole the tractor and—though their absence wasn't discovered until two hours after they had taken flight—made it only two miles north of the prison when they found themselves cornered in a wooded area by a posse of armed prison guards and highway patrol officers.

Wielding kitchen knives as their only weapons against a small army with guns, two inmates surrendered without a struggle, but Wells is reported to have refused giving himself up and was shot by prison guards. He died on the way to the hospital. At least that was the official story as told to the press.

Starling Mack Nations

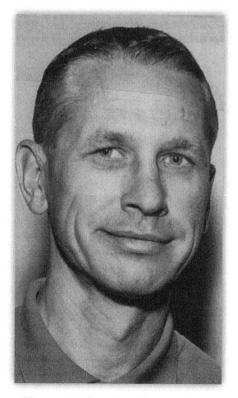

Figure 31. Starling Mack Nations
Courtesy of Kansasmemory.org, Kansas State Historical Society.
Used with permission.

"Who?" you may ask. One of the sidelined principals of this story never even appeared in *In Cold Blood*. Yet without his fervent efforts and influence, none of the many unresolved questions now posed would have ever surfaced.

During the 1954 Kansas gubernatorial campaign, Lieutenant Governor Fred Hall, in his run for the state's top job, hired as his political advertising director a seasoned newspaper veteran by the memorable name of Starling Mack Nations, the scion of a small family newspaper published in Kansas since the

1930s.

Nations' father, Hobart, had owned and published *The Greensburg News*, where young "Mack," not even 20 years old yet, earned his chops in the newspaper business before and after school. After Hobart died of tuberculosis in 1933, Starling dropped out of school for a while to work at the paper full-time.

Two months before the Japanese attacked Pearl Harbor on December 7, 1941, Nations enlisted in the United States Navy, serving until September 1945, a month after the Japanese surrendered, winding down World War II.

Newly married and with a family on the way, Nations went back into publishing, starting his own first newspaper in 1946, *The Chase Index*. A year later he bought the *Kingman Journal* in partnership with some local businessmen, and after a few years sold that newspaper and bought up several others in various small Kansas towns, notably the *Kinsley Mercury*. It was during his time at the *Mercury* that Nations met future Kansas governor Fred Hall.

Every newspaper publisher since ink was invented has had to contend with political forces in their community, and Mack Nations had to learn to balance unsparing reporting of candidates and officeholders throughout Kansas and Missouri with the need to generate sufficient ad revenues that kept his newspapers thriving.

That particular fusion of experience was good enough for then-Lieutenant Governor Fred Hall to choose Nations to manage his political advertising. Nations accepted the position and became the new governor's executive secretary when Hall won the election in November. As executive secretary (otherwise known as chief of staff), Mack Nations was now the gatekeeper to the governor.

It wasn't a particularly long tenure for either man, however, since at the time Kansas chief executives only enjoyed a two-year term, and Hall would not win reelection in 1956. Mack Nations held his job for even less time, just ten months.

A rather strange event took place in 1962, when Nations

was arrested for income tax evasion by the Internal Revenue Service. The claims made by the IRS, years after the alleged tax evasion took place, stemmed from a charge that Nations had received a $10,000 cash bribe—presumably on behalf of Governor Hall—as an inducement to obtain a pardon or parole for Mrs. Annas Brown, a jailed abortionist whose family had made arrangements for the payoff.

As reported in *The Wall Street Journal*,[140] Mack's son Michael remains convinced that his father's arrest was instigated by Kansas officials in efforts to derail his book project with Richard Hickock, while facilitating Capote's work on *In Cold Blood*. While a bold claim, there is documentation to support such efforts. Indeed, Alvin Dewey himself informed his friend Truman of the indictment against Nations, and Capote was so delighted by the news he wrote to his publisher, Bennett Cerf, exclaiming his apparent delight in Nations's arrest.[141]

Nations pleaded innocent and was ultimately acquitted of the charges, but the ordeal took an enormous toll on his life, his family, and his reputation. He returned to the newspaper business as a legislative reporter in Topeka for the *Wichita Eagle*.

In 1961, while on assignment for the *Eagle*, Mack Nations interviewed several Death Row prisoners at the Kansas State Penitentiary in Lansing, where he met Richard Hickock and Perry Smith, both with executions pending while the Kansas Supreme Court was hearing their appeals.

Truman Capote was well into the work of writing *In Cold Blood* by this time, and although he spent a good deal of time with both killers, it's clear the author had a more nuanced interest in Perry Smith, in whose life Capote found, as author Ralph Voss astutely described, "many parallels to his own: childhood abandonment, the need to be loved and appreciated, a flair for and interest in language and the arts.... This affection for Smith undoubtedly affected Capote's treatment of *In Cold Blood*."[142]

Hickock was single-mindedly focused on mounting an

appeal to his conviction, a task on which, according to prison records, he'd spent a good deal of time preparing. But to take it further he knew he needed money to hire an attorney. The opportunity presented by Mack Nations provided the logical, if not the only, avenue for such funds. And if he begrudged Capote's focus on Smith, it also gave him a chance to tell his own side of the story. So Hickock proposed that he and Nations collaborate on Hickock's "side of the story." Nations agreed and both signed a contract for the project, the genesis of the Hickock letters destined for a book that would eventually be titled *High Road to Hell*.

Nations and Hickock were able to meet in prison and corresponded regularly over the next several months, during which time Hickock produced at least 200 handwritten pages of remarkably detailed storytelling. Some of it was in response to specific questions Nations had posed, but most of it was a rambling opus memorializing hideous details of the Clutter crimes, the killers' cross-country capers after the murders, their adventures in Mexico, and rants on a variety of perceived offenses during their flight from justice, including such things as Floyd Wells's testimony on the stand, whether Smith intended to kill Hickock, or whether Hickock himself should have killed Smith.

Many scenes Hickock described to Nations are consistent with corroborated accounts, while some appear to be embellishment of known facts. Still others (we might assume) were simply imagined by Hickock to garnish the book the reporter wanted to write. Regardless, what grips the reader is the elaborate added material Hickock infuses into a narrative we thought we already knew. And to what we do know, he instills a fascinating level of vivid detail, typical of those with eidetic memory (which Hickock clearly did possess).

The constant requests by reporters to interview Smith and Hickock—the brass ring of front-page sensationalism following the Clutter murders—became such a concern to prison officials that the state's director of penal institutions, Colonel Guy

Rexroad, issued a directive prohibiting reporters from further access to prison inmates, including personal visits and correspondence by mail.

Though by this time Nations had acquired sufficient material for his book, the prohibition meant that Hickock could no longer track or influence the progress of the book, nor could Nations reach Hickock for any follow-up.

The prohibition also barred (or should have barred) Truman Capote from having similar access to Smith and Hickock. But when Capote discovered he had a competitor in Mack Nations—news delivered by the obliging hand of Alvin Dewey[143]—his lawyers, from the Garden City law firm Hope, Haag, Saffels & Hope, took an unusual and very high level action to persuade prison officials to make special accommodations allowing Capote, "a writer of very high stature," not "of the 'pulp magazine' variety..."[144] to interview Hickock and Smith in person.

Capote had chosen no ordinary Kansas law firm. Its managing partner, Clifford Hope Sr., was a former U.S. Congressman, and his son, Clifford Jr., had been, by no small coincidence, Herbert Clutter's attorney. Indeed, the younger Hope and his wife Dolores, who was city editor at the *Garden City Telegram*, became lifelong friends to Capote and even entertained him and Harper Lee at their home on numerous occasions, making introductions to fellow Garden Citians that much easier.

Another of the firm's partners, Dale E. Saffels, wrote a fulsome letter to Col. Rexroad making the case for exempting Capote from the new prison rule barring journalists. At the time Saffels was also minority leader in the Kansas House of Representatives and a powerful figure in state politics.

After five long-winded paragraphs dedicated solely to validating his client's need for unfettered access to Smith and Hickock, Saffels concludes with a baffling non sequitur. In his sixth and final paragraph, Saffels writes: "Col. Rexroad, I am, of course, very much interested in the situation at Hutchinson reformatory and sincerely hope that at the completion of the investigation there that it will be determined that many of the accusations and much of the publicity which has occurred are not based on fact. / Yours very truly, Dale E. Saffels."[145]

What Saffels makes reference to was a deep and embarrassing investigation by the KBI into "irregularities" at the Kansas State Industrial Reformatory, including prolific use of narcotics, reports of homosexuality and mistreatment of prisoners, and theft of state property. Rexroad was in no position to suffer the implied consequences of non-compliance given Saffels's threat.

As Capote's biographer, Gerald Clarke, reported in his book, "...Finally, in desperation, he [Capote] bribed his way in...paying a powerful political figure to pull the right strings. 'If I hadn't got what I wanted, I would have had to abandon everything. I had to have access to those two boys. So I went for broke and asked for an interview with this behind-the-scenes figure, who was a man of great distinction and renown in that state. "I'll give you ten thousand dollars if you can arrange this..."' ."[146]

Thirteen days later Saffels received Rexroad's response, but the wait was worth it: "...Although it is believed that the rule prohibiting interviews between inmates and reporters is a necessary one, I believe that in fairness to Mr. Capote and other writers who have been preparing materials on this case, consideration should be given to waving [sic] the rule in this instance. It is requested that either you or Mr. Capote notify this office of the date the interview is desired."[147]

On November 3, just two days after Rexroad granted Saffels's request, Attorney General William Ferguson declared that, "Kansas State Industrial Reformatory is well managed and efficiently operated," citing "only minor irregularities in operation of the Hutchinson institution," thus ending the investigation.[148]

Incensed that Capote would now have direct communications with Hickock, potentially undermining his own work, Mack

Nations (who was not extended the same courtesy) fired off a
letter to the warden threatening Hickock with forfeiture of his
half of any royalties generated by the book should he allow
Capote to interview him.[149]

Any worries Capote might have had about Nations,
however, faded after reading, as he put it, "that extraordinarily
vulgar magazine containing the preposterous Hickcock Nations
contribution," [sic] which was sent to him in Switzerland by
Alvin Dewey and his wife Marie. In the same letter thanking
them, Capote also expressed his desire to see the original
manuscript.[150]

Capote did, in fact, try to buy the manuscript from Nations
in a phone call made to the reporter's *Wichita Eagle* office.
Nations was unequivocal in his response: *"Hell, no!"* he said,
according to Shirley Wise, a reporter for the *Eagle* and Nations's
girlfriend at the time. Ms. Wise also reported that Nations
believed "there was something fishy about the Clutter case. But
he wouldn't say what."[151]

Mack Nations never found a book publisher for *High Road
to Hell*, the full account of Richard Hickock's version of the
story. The only ink it earned appeared as a condensed excerpt in
the December 1961 issue of *Male*, an obscure men's pulp
adventure magazine—the one referred to by Capote as
"extraordinarily vulgar."[152]

Figure 32. Male *article by Mack Nations, December 1961*
Author's archives

As with most prisons at the time, correspondence to and from inmates was censored, and Hickock's unrestrained letters to Mack Nations ultimately found their way to Warden Tracy Hand, who then passed the letters on to Kansas Assistant Attorney General Robert Hoffman. Hoffman, who personally argued for the State against appeals by the killers, was deeply concerned that the U.S. Supreme Court might reverse Smith's and Hickock's convictions on some technicality. With Hickock's letters in hand he now possessed an elaborate unsolicited confession which he believed would be useful in the event of a retrial argument.

That the attorney general intended to rely on certain of Hickock's letters in arguments before the U.S. Supreme Court bears the presumption that *all* the letters were credible. One can't simply cherry pick which elements to believe and which to cast aside if one is depending on their wholesale veracity in a court of law. By the AG's own actions, then, the letters were deemed to have had legitimate standing.

Accordingly, Hoffman prepared a certified copy of the letters for the AG's files and, as discovered in unpublished documents,[153] made a set of "personal" copies for himself, which (presumably attesting to their value) he attentively encased in a leather-bound folder. Copies of that set were graciously sent to me by *Wall Street Journal* reporter Kevin Helliker (who obtained them from one of his sources), and which provided years of spirited discussion as each of us worked on our respective projects.

Why did Hoffman go to the extraordinary step of making a personal copy of the letters, which he then took home for safekeeping? Did he have doubts that the attorney general's certified copy on file might not be sufficient? Or, in a state well known for its secrecy, did he suspect the letters might one day go missing?

On Christmas Eve 1968 Starling Mack Nations was killed while driving home in rural Colorado when his car struck a concrete barrier. The only copy of the full bound manuscript of his book, *High Road to Hell*, containing content not seen by anyone else but last observed sitting on his office desk, mysteriously disappeared that night and has never been found.

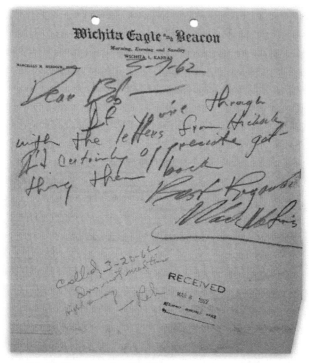

Figure 33. Nations asks Hoffman to return Hickock letters
Author's archives

3-7-62

Dear Bob—

If you're through with the letters from Hickock I'd certainly appreciate getting them back.

Best regards,
Mack Nations

[*Hoffman's appended note reads:* "Called 3-20-62; does not need these right away; —REH"]

Privileged Communications

"The moment a man sets his thoughts
down on paper, however secretly, he is in a
sense writing for publication."

— Raymond Chandler

Polygraph

On discovering its first apparently solid lead three weeks after the murders, the KBI dispatched Special Agent Wayne Owens to the Kansas State Penitentiary at Lansing to interview inmate Floyd Wells.

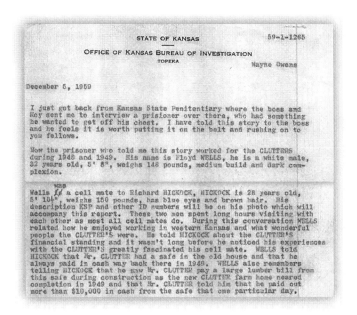

Figure 34. KBI interview of Floyd Wells at KSP
Author's archives

Wayne Owens
December 5, 1959

I just got back from Kansas State Penitentiary where the boss and Roy sent me to interview a prisoner over there, who had something he wanted to get off his chest. I have told this story to the boss and he feels it is worth putting it on the belt and rushing on to you fellows.

Now the prisoner who told me this story
worked for the CLUTTERS during 1948 and
1949. His name is Floyd WELLS, he is a
white male, 32 years old, 5' 8", weighs 148
pounds, medium build and dark complexion.

Wells was a cell mate to Richard HICKOCK,
HICKOCK is 28 years old, 5' 10", weighs
150 pounds, has blue eyes and brown hair.
His description KSP and other ID numbers
will be on his photo which will accompany
this report. These two men spent long hours
visiting with each other as most all cell
mates do. During this conversation WELLS
related how he enjoyed working in western
Kansas and what wonderful people the
CLUTTER'S were. He told HICKOCK about
the CLUTTER'S financial standing and it
wasn't long before he noticed his
experiences with the CLUTTER'S greatly
fascinated his cell mate. WELLS told
HICKOCK that Mr. CLUTTER had a safe in
the old house and that he always paid in
cash way back there in 1949. WELLS also
remembers telling HICKOCK that he saw
Mr. CLUTTER pay a large lumber bill from
this safe during construction as the new
CLUTTER farm home neared completion in
1949 and that Mr. CLUTTER told him that
he paid out more than $10,000 in cash from
the safe that one particular day....

In his own signed statement under oath, Wells recounted a
scene of pastoral contentment working for Herb Clutter and
claimed that he enjoyed a surprisingly close relationship with the
family:

The Clutters were all good to me and Mr.

Clutter, who was a very "well-to-do man"
financially was very generous to me, the
other help too but he was always giving me
a "bonus" when the work was extra heavy or
the hours extra long. I was very close to Mr.
Clutter and liked to visit with him Sundays,
evenings and other times when we weren't
working. I spent considerable time with him
in his den or office where he had a desk and
I believe a safe—this was in the old house
where the Clutter's lived in 1949. I
remember just a short time before I left the
Clutters, I was with Mr. Clutter in his den,
this was just about the time the new house
was completed, Mr. Clutter was sitting at his
desk and men were coming in for their pay.
I distinctly remember Mr. Clutter paying a
large lumber bill and I thought he paid in
cash with money from the safe. The reason
I remember is because Mr. Clutter made the
remark to me that evening when we left his
den that he paid out more than $10,000 that
day.[154]

Of course, Herb Clutter had no safe. He also never made a
practice of paying out large amounts in cash for purchases, but
relied on bank checks for nearly all transactions, even those for
just a few dollars. In 1949, $10,000 was the equivalent of around
$100,000 today, so the very thought of Clutter having such an
amount of cash on hand is inconceivable. On that score alone,
it's difficult to imagine Wells having credibility.

Wayne Owens pushed back rigorously on Wells to verify
everything, especially the safe. In an *"Off the Record Supplement"*
that Owens appended to Wells's signed statement, he noted:

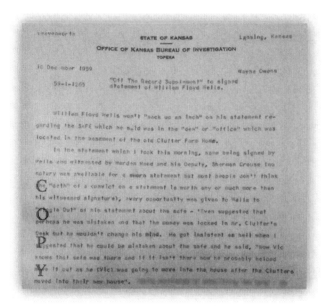

Figure 35. Agent Owens pushed Wells hard on the safe
Author's archives

"Off the Record Supplement" to signed Statement by William Floyd Wells.

William Floyd Wells won't "back up an inch" on his statement regarding the SAFE which he said was in the "den" or "office" which was located in the basement of the old Clutter Farm Home.

In the statement which I took this morning, same being signed by Wells and witnessed by Warden Hand and his Deputy, Sherman Crouse (no notary was available for a sworn statement but most people don't think the "oath" of a convict in a statement is worth any or much more than his witnessed signature), every opportunity was given to Wells to "Wiggle Out" of his statement about the safe – Even suggested that perhaps he was mistaken and that the money was locked in Mr. Clutter's Desk but he wouldn't change his mind. He got insistent as hell when I suggested that he could be mistaken about the safe and he said, "Now Vic [Vic Irsik, a hand on Cutter's farm] knows that safe was there and if it isn't there now he probably helped move it out as he (Vic) was going to move into the house after the Clutters moved into their new house."

Wells also provided the KBI with a meticulously detailed description of Clutter's safe—the safe that never existed:

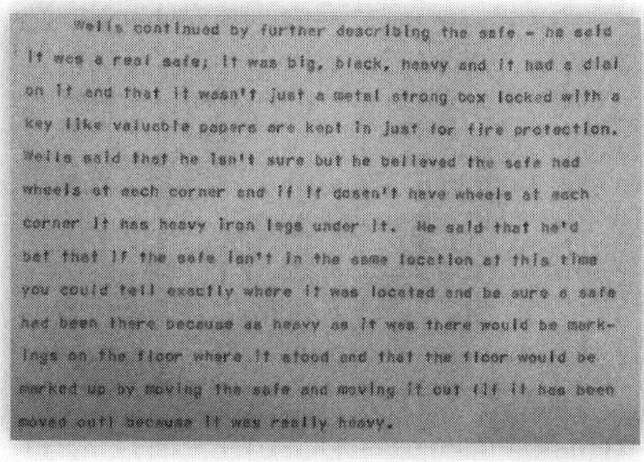

Figure 36. Wells describes "the safe" in precise detail
Author's archives

Wells continued by further describing the safe—he said it was a real safe; it was big, black, heavy and it had a dial on it and that it wasn't just a metal strongbox locked with a key like valuable papers are kept in just for fire protection. Wells said that he isn't sure but he believed the safe had wheels at each corner and if it doesn't have wheels at each corner it has heavy iron legs under it. He said that he bet that if the safe isn't in the same location at this time you could tell exactly where it was located and be sure a safe had been there because as heavy as it was there would be markings on the floor where it stood and that the floor would be marked up by moving the safe and moving it out (if it has been moved out) because it was really heavy.[155]

As noted, Wells worked only seven months at River Valley Farm, until January 1949, when he was 20 years old. Yet what stands out here is the extraordinarily personal access which he claims Herb Clutter had granted him. That a prominent and successful man, one hardly known for boasting, might disclose to a young and relatively unknown farm hand such extraordinary financial details would be foolish and irrational. And Mr. Clutter was anything but foolish and irrational.

Longtime River Valley Farm hands Vic Irsik and Alfred Stoecklein, both of whom worked for Clutter at the time Wells left and were still there up until the murders, remembered hardly anything of Wells.[156] And that was the last time anyone had seen him on the farm.

In a 1960 interview with reporter Ted Blankenship of the *Hutchinson News*, Wells denied ever telling Hickock about a safe, and that he knew "nothing at all" about the new home:

> Wells said he told Hickock that the Clutters had a safe when he worked for the family, but they were building a new home when he left their employ. He said **he told Hickock that he knew of no safe in the new home. He said that he knew nothing at all about the new home.**[157]

In interviews with town locals, the *Garden City Telegram* also confirmed that Wells had never seen the Clutter's new home: "[Wells] worked for Clutter in 1948. **That was when the Clutters lived northwest of Holcomb, and before they** constructed the fine, new home in which they were slain."[158]

This admission, and official records contradicting it, presents fundamental problems, both factually in terms of the known story and, as a consequence, legally as it pertained to Wells being the key witness at the trial.

If Wells had never seen *"the fine, new home in which they were slain,"* then the pivotal question persists: *Who* drew the map that Wells gave Hickock at KSP? And who provided Wells with such intimate details as the room in which each family member slept, and that Herb Clutter had his own bedroom apart from Bonnie, downstairs next to his office?

Given this crucial new fact, it's highly probable that someone else familiar with the home's layout and the family's habits provided Wells with a diagram of the new house or described it to him in such detail that he could later render it himself for Hickock. That "someone" had to be close enough to the family to possess such intimate information, in turn suggesting it was someone in the local community.

The interview and signed statement Floyd Wells gave to the KBI under oath—later perjuring himself by contradicting it in court—is among the most inexplicable problems of the Clutter murder investigation. Having this fresh and verifiable perspective, Floyd Wells was a significantly more central character than previously assumed.

Confession

The letters Hickock wrote to Nations are effusively detailed, energized by Hickock's uncommon ability to visualize scenes and images with near-perfect clarity, despite his reflexive prattle and boasting. And while I am neither qualified to analyze his psychopathy nor is that the goal here, we must take into account Dr. W. Mitchell Jones's diagnosis of Hickock's "psychopathic and sociopathic" tendencies[159] when considering his correspondence with Mack Nations. (In the 1960s, psychiatric interviews of offenders were scarcely comparable to the full diagnostic work-ups of today. Psychiatrists at the time lacked diagnostic instruments with the degree of sophistication, validity, and reliability that they have now; even the terms *psychopath* and *sociopath* have evolved.)

The bulk of Hickock's writings—most neatly printed in block letters, many in surprisingly graceful cursive—conform to the story as it's currently known. But he divulges a number of puzzling details that, to some, amount to little more than the ramblings of a pathological liar. Others, however, feel that certain of Hickock's revelations cannot be easily dismissed, especially since they are corroborated, at least in part, by official police reports.

That these letters have until now remained largely unknown is a curiosity on its own. We know the originals were intercepted by censors at KSP in 1962, which were then forwarded by Warden Tracy Hand to Assistant AG Robert Hoffman, whose certified copies presumably still exist in the files of the attorney general's office. We also know that Hoffman made copies for himself before sending the originals on to Mack Nations— originals that vanished after Nations's death, along with the full manuscript of his book *High Road to Hell*.

What we have yet to find evidence of, however, is any investigation into Hickock's incriminating assertions. The Kansas attorney general was relying on those same letters to discredit Hickock's appeal before the U.S. Supreme Court, if it came to that. What are we to make of all this, then, sixty years after the fact?

One dramatic scene in *In Cold Blood* differs significantly from how Hickock elaborately described it in his letters to Mack Nations, and it's worth mentioning here not only as historical remedy to the facts, but as an exercise in the curious synchronicity of events.

Two days before 1960 ushered in a new decade beneath the dazzling casino lights and boisterous celebrations of Las Vegas, Nevada, Perry was behind the wheel as he and Dick cruised the Strip in their stolen black-and-white 1956 Chevrolet. It was just after sunset, and the first order of business was to stop at the main post office before it closed to pick up Perry's box of "junk," the package he had shipped from Mexico. With that accomplished, the second task was to find a generator, since the one in their stolen car had gone bad.[160]

Rather than buy a new generator, Hickock decided to steal one, a simple ten-minute job if he could find the right car. As Perry pulled into a parking lot off the Strip, Dick spotted the perfect candidate: a 1957 Chevy whose generator he knew would be identical. The lot didn't have many lights on it, so they sat in the car until it got darker, so as not to be seen.

After about fifteen minutes of waiting, Hickock heard footsteps on the gravel behind the vehicle. Turning to look he saw a heavyset policeman holding a .38 special approach the car on one side, with another officer coming up on them from the other side, his weapon also drawn.

"Judas Priest," Dick wrote. "...Believe it or not, I felt relieved for the first time in two months. I thought, Well, it's over."[161]

Two vigilant Las Vegas police patrolmen had spotted the vehicle and license matching the FBI's nationwide pickup order. After securing Dick and Perry in their squad car, they searched the stolen vehicle, discovering Perry's box containing, among his other things, both pairs of boots the killers had worn while slaughtering the Clutter family: Perry's Cat's Paw and Hickock's diamond-patterned soles, the only evidence that would cinch their presence at the crime scene thanks to Rich Rohleder's keen eye for discovering both boot prints in Herb Clutter's dried blood stains.

"The one thing that I worried about," prosecutor Duane West said, "was the fact that our evidence was footprints on the mattress box cover where Mr. Clutter was killed.... I was fearful that they might be arrested but we wouldn't be able to recover those boots."[162]

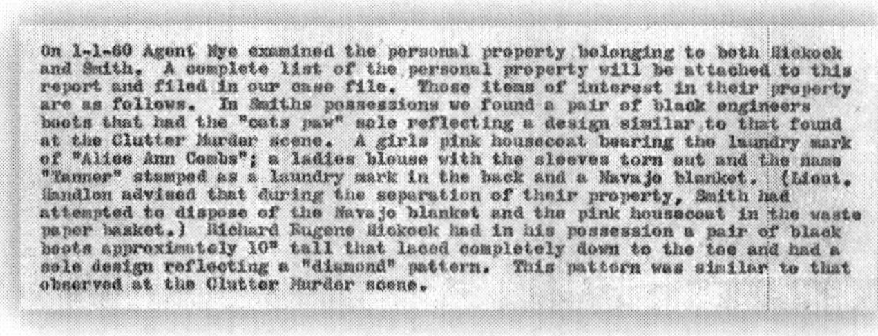

On 1-1-60 Agent Nye examined the personal property belonging to both Hickock and Smith. A complete list of the personal property will be attached to this report and filed in our case file. Those items of interest in their property are as follows. In Smiths possessions we found a pair of black engineers boots that had the "cats paw" sole reflecting a design similar to that found at the Clutter Murder scene. A girls pink housecoat bearing the laundry mark of "Alice Ann Combs"; a ladies blouse with the sleeves torn out and the name "Tanner" stamped as a laundry mark in the back and a Navajo blanket. (Lieut. Handlon advised that during the separation of their property, Smith had attempted to dispose of the Navajo blanket and the pink housecoat in the waste paper basket.) Richard Eugene Hickock had in his possession a pair of black boots approximately 10" tall that laced completely down to the toe and had a sole design reflecting a "diamond" pattern. This pattern was similar to that observed at the Clutter Murder scene.

Figure 37. Nye's report on evidence in the stolen car

Author's archives

On 1-1-60 Agent Nye examined the personal property belonging to both Hickock and Smith. A complete list of the personal property will be attached to this report and filed in our case file. Those items of interest in their property are as follows. In Smiths possessions we found a pair of black engineers boots that had the "cats paw" sole reflecting a design similar to that found at the Clutter Murder scene. A girls pink housecoat bearing the laundry mark of "Alice Ann Combs"; a ladies blouse with the sleeves torn out and the name "Tanner" stamped as a laundry mark in the back and a Navajo blanket. (Lieut. Handlon advised that during the separation of their property Smith had attempted to dispose of the Navajo blanket and the pink housecoat in the waste paper basket.) Richard Eugene Hickock had in his possession a pair of black boots approximately 10" tall that laced completely down to the toe and had a sole design reflecting a "diamond" pattern. This pattern was similar to that observed at the Clutter Murder scene.

Had officers Pigford and Macauley picked up the killers just a short while earlier, before they had stopped at the post office, it's entirely probable there would have been no evidence at all tying the killers to the crimes apart from Wells's testimony. Perry's box of treasures, including the only physical evidence tying them to the crimes,[163] would have ended up in the postal service's Dead Letter Office where, after one year, its beggarly contents would have been auctioned off or donated to charity.

NB: One observation of note in Nye's report (above) is Perry Smith's curious attempt to dispose of two articles found in the car: the Navajo blanket and the girl's pink housecoat.

In the official (and publicly accessible) investigation files of the Clifford Walker family murders—the December 1959 Florida cold case in which Perry Smith and Richard Hickock have been considered prime suspects—is a letter from Alvin Dewey to Sarasota County Sheriff Ross Boyer, dated January 19, 1960. In it, Dewey cites a detailed timeline of the activities of Smith and Hickock while they were in Florida, based on their interrogations. Two paragraphs describe some of the unusual items in their possession:

> At the time of their arrest in Las Vegas, they had in their possession a size 9 girl's housecoat, pink with a flower design, containing the name "Anna Combs" or "Alice Combs", also a baby's undershirt, honeysuckle brand, size 4, for a child between 29-38 lbs., 100% cotton and fairly new, found under the front seat of their car. They claim these came from a Salvation Army post and there is a discrepancy in their stories as to whether these were stolen or given to them.
>
> In regard to the two dolls given by the

> subjects to Rev. John Gibson...on 12/24/59,
> they also stated these were obtained from
> the Salvation Army in Jackson, Miss., and
> again there is a discrepancy in their stories
> as to whether these were stolen or given to
> them.

As of this writing, the Walker family murders remain an unsolved case, although Sarasota County detectives remain convinced that, despite having passed a 1960 polygraph test about their involvement in the crimes, Smith and Hickock are still the prime suspects. In 2013 Florida authorities had their bodies exhumed for DNA testing, the results of which were deemed "inconclusive."[164]

With chilling objectivity, Hickock's letters reveal a callous emotional detachment as he recites the most gruesome events.

In a letter to Mack Nations dated June 12, 1961, Hickock signed off with his assurance of fidelity to the facts: [Spelling, grammar, and punctuation are shown as they appear in the original letters; missing off-margin words have been supplemented as presumed for continuity; emphasis added for discussion]:

> Mr. Nations:
> I found as I was writing the prior material
> that my memory became quite vivid. I
> rewrote it three times before I felt I had it all
> in…. I hope I haven't outdone myself on
> this, but I can connect the emotions with the
> same ones or type that I had at the Clutter
> house. I never made the connection before,
> and when I started writing this, they seemed

to fall in, or fit in, I don't know quite how to describe it. I know you were wanting emotional feelings, and I hope I have adequately described it for you. My lack of a sufficient vocabulary is a great hindrance to my writing, but this particular one, seems to me, to be some of the best I have written. I may have got carried away with it, but as I wrote, I actually relived the event.... I realize it tends to make me look worse than ever, but I wasn't going to polish it up to make me look better. I explained to you before that I would tell you the facts, regardless what they were.

Figure 38. Richard E. Hickock - Prisoner #14746
Author's archives

Following are key excerpts of Hickock's letters to Mack Nations relevant to the matter at hand.

In an early letter, Hickock describes how he and Smith entered the Clutter home through an unlocked door off the kitchen. His remarks here also suggest that this was an act of premeditation—and that he was being paid for it:

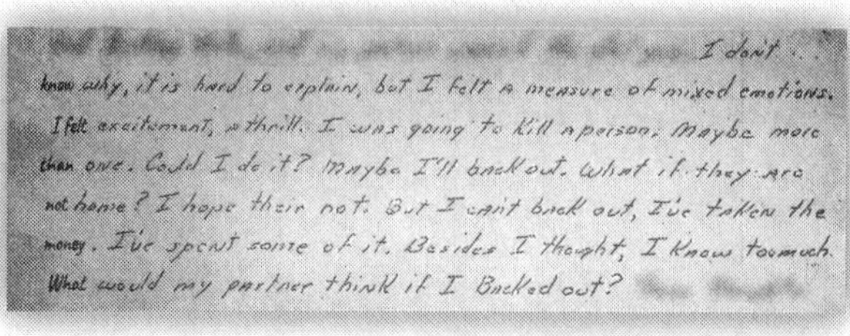

Figure 39. Hickock implies premeditation; paid for the job
Author's archives [missing off-margin words; supplemented as presumed]

I gently pushed the door open and entered the house. It was dark. The only light visible was coming in around the blinds at the windows. I turned the light on in the kitchen and the sudden beam of light was frightening. I shut it off. It was really dark then. We moved forward as quickly as possible, but no matter how hard I tried I couldn't stop the floor from squeeking. They hear it, I thought, I know they do. I've got to hurry....

I don't know why, it is hard to explain, but I felt a measure of mixed emotions. I felt excitement, a thrill. ***I was going to kill a person. Maybe more than one.*** Could I do it? Maybe I'll back out. What if they are not home? I hope their not. ***But I can't back out, I've taken the money. I've spent some of it. Besides I thought, I know too much.*** What would my partner think if I backed out?

Here Hickock appears to define the limits of his objective: "*I was going to kill a person. **Maybe** more than one.*"

Why would he single out just one life ("*kill a person*"), adding the possibility of killing more almost as an afterthought? He also used first person singular, "I"—"*I've taken the money. I've spent some of it*"—not "we," implying that his intentions and rewards may not have been shared or even known by Perry

Smith. It could be an important distinction, helping to understand why Smith never spoke of such a conspiracy.

For the first time anywhere, Hickock reveals he had actually received money for the job, some of which he had already spent. And what was it he knew "too much" about?

Of the hundreds of pages that likely comprised Mack Nations's original book manuscript, only a single torn page has survived. In it, Hickock describes a visit to the Finney County jail by his father Walter and brother David soon after the crimes, during which his father asked him one notable question:

> I was taken to the top floor of the court house, where the jail is located, and locked in a cell away from the rest of the prisoners. I didn't know what to expect from the crowd outside. I had heard of incidents where men were taken from a jail and hung to the closest tree. But the night proved uneventful, as far as we were concerned.
>
> But I decided to wait a while, and see what developed. I had a visit by my dad and my brother.
>
> I had been at Garden City about two or three weeks, when they came to see me. One of the first questions my dad asked me, was, if I was paid for it. I told him no, that it wasn't anything like that. He then proceeded to tell me, how he had been questioned as to the possibility of me having any large sum of money. He told me how three different men had asked him the same thing.

Figure 40. Hickock's father asks if Dick got paid for murders
Courtesy of Michael Nations[165]

I was taken to the top floor of the court house, where the jail is located, and locked

> in a cell away from the rest of the prisoners.
> I didn't know what to expect from the
> crowds outside. I had heard of incidents
> where men were taken from a jail and hung
> to the closest tree. But the night proved
> uneventful, as far as we were concerned.
>
> But I decided to wait a while, and see
> what developed. I had a visit by my dad and
> brother.
>
> I had been at Garden City about two or
> three weeks, when they came to see me.
> One of the first questions my dad asked me,
> was, if I was paid for it. I told him no, that it
> wasn't anything like that. He then
> proceeded to tell me, how he had been
> questioned as to the possibility of me having
> any large sum of money. He told me how
> three different men had asked him the same
> thing.

Assuming the *"three different men"* who questioned Hickock's father about *"a large sum of money"* were law enforcement officers (the most reasonable deduction, since they were in the jailhouse), each must have had good reason to pursue that line of inquiry, especially tied to the prospect of a large sum of money.

One wonders what the basis might have been for even asking the question. Undoubtedly, Hickock's reply to his father's question starkly contradicts what he wrote in his letters to Mack Nations.

But the scene takes an even more interesting turn. In his 2010 memoir, David Hickock spoke openly about having agonized for years over his brother's actions, tortured over his own role in having innocently bought Dick the shotgun that was used to murder the Clutter family.

Describing that first jailhouse meeting, numbed with shock at what he was hearing, David relates how he and his father listened as his older brother dispassionately recounted gruesome details of the crime he had just freely confessed to masterminding, adding Dick's curious assertion about "other details" [emphasis added]:

> When I finally asked Dick if all the stories on television were true, he shrugged and simply said, "Not all of them." According to Dick, the story of that fateful night had many of the same components that we heard on television, **but he knew other details that only appeared in his version of the story.**[166]

Shouldering the guilt for being an unwitting accomplice in the crimes weighed heavily on David for the rest of his life. His memoir, a form of atonement for Dick's crimes 40 years earlier, sought to rationalize the actions of a brother he loved, but in whom he found unsettling flaws:

> It is so strange when I think about my part in buying the gun and the fact that no one ever questioned me about it. I do not even know if law enforcement officials ever checked out the fact that I had bought the gun used in the murders…. A more thorough investigation would have been done and I would have been interrogated. I do not understand why they did not investigate certain aspects of the crime.[167]

In what appears to be another example of rushing the investigation, the KBI never interviewed David Hickock nor traced the origins of the weapon, a compulsory protocol that would have been thoroughly probed even in those days. That such a lead was overlooked fits with other lapses previously noted.

In the following passages from his letters, Hickock makes what may be his most intriguing statements: that someone identified simply as "Roberts" had provided the diagram of the Clutter home. Hickock also lays out what can only be described as setting the scene for a "staged" robbery, premeditating Mr. Clutter's singular fate:

> ***Just like the diagram Roberts had given me showed***, a hallway led off to the left, and on the left of this was the bed room. I flashed the light in the bedroom and the beam fell across the bed. A man sat up and said "who is it"? I told him, "Take it easy pop." I thought to myself, where is the rest of the family? ***We can't let him have it until we know where the rest of them are***. My partner told him, "Come on get up." I asked him "You got a safe?" I hadn't seen it when I had the light on in the west room. Of course it didn't look good. We escorted Clutter into the west room, and figured we just as well get all we can. ***Besides, we had to make it look like a robbery***.

Apart from the hotel guest registers shown earlier, "Roberts" is a name that appears in no other document I've seen—not in Harold Nye's notes, not in accessible police or KBI reports, not in Capote's or Lee's notes, nor on the pages of *In Cold Blood* or any other book related to the Clutter case. Nowhere. It's hard to imagine Hickock simply invented the name, or that it was just a mistake.

As we know the story, at least Capote's version, it was Floyd Wells who purportedly drew that diagram when he and Hickock celled together at KSP, as well as the map leading to River Valley Farm and all the details of the Clutter family, including their ages and where each family member slept.

The problem with accepting Capote's rendering, as noted earlier, is that Floyd Wells could not possibly have known anything about the new house. By his own testimony in court, and the factual timeline supporting it, Wells said *he had never been in the new house*; that he left Clutter's employ before the house was even finished and the family had moved in. He also confirmed that he "had made no maps or drawings for Hickock."[168]

The next phrase is of unusual importance: *"We can't let him have it until we know where the rest of them are."* This presupposes that there was a plan to kill Herb Clutter regardless of any money that might be found in the non-existent safe. It suggests, in other words, that the crime was premeditated, as does the statement, *"we had to make it look like a robbery."* If the motive *was* robbery, why would they need to make it *look* like a robbery? Finally, why would Hickock have to wait to *"let him have it"* until the whereabouts of the rest of the family was known?

Even assuming Hickock was juicing the story to provide a livelier rendition of the crimes for the book on which he and Mack Nations were working, why didn't he stick with the well-known facts, adding the dramatic nuance his collaborator had expected? How could such wildly divergent yet precise details possibly be construed as anything but fantasy? For such a shrewd and calculating person, it makes no sense.

Unless, of course, he was telling the truth as he knew it.

In another passage, Hickock further alludes to making the crime *appear* to be a robbery:

> ... back from fixing the phones, we went into Clutter's bed room. I told him to give me his wallet, which he did. It contained about thirty dollars and some travel checks. I left the wallet laying on the bed. I wanted it to be found empty. My partner found a couple other articles that were likely to be missed, and these he took to the car. ...

Figure 41. Hickock wanted Clutter's wallet found empty
Author's archives [missing off-margin words; supplemented as presumed]

... after listening to Clutter talk, I knew there was no safe....[illegible]...back from fixing the phones, we went into Clutter's bed room. I told him to give me his wallet, which he did. It contained about thirty dollars and some travel checks. ***I left the wallet lying on the bed. <u>I wanted it to be found empty</u>. My partner found a couple other <u>articles that were likely to be missed</u>, and these he took to the car.***

"I left the wallet lying on the bed. I wanted it to be found empty..." (?) "Articles that were likely to be missed..." (?)

The unambiguous actions Hickock describes here are too deliberate to be pointless. In the aggregate, they shape a much different narrative. Despite his flaws, Hickock was a very smart guy; he studied legal reference books for years while on Death Row. He wrote these letters when he was in the process of appealing his conviction. Surely, he knew that the radical differences between his sworn testimony and the events described in the letters could scuttle all hope of an appeal.

Hickock continues, adding more provocative details, further fueling the theory that the murders were carried out with conspired premeditation. He also divulges more about his relationship with the mysterious "Roberts," confirming an arranged meeting with Roberts for what can only be construed as a payoff [shown before; reinserted here for continuity]:

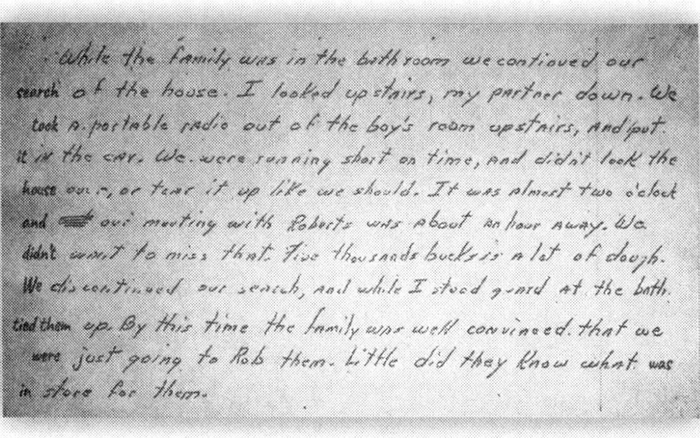
While the family was in the bathroom we continued our search of the house. I looked upstairs, my partner down. We took a portable radio out of the boy's room upstairs, and put it in the car. We were running short on time, and didn't look the house over, or tear it up like we should. It was almost two o'clock and our meeting with Roberts was about an hour away. We didn't want to miss that. Five thousands bucks is a lot of dough. We discontinued our search, and while I stood guard at the bath. tied them up. By this time the family was well convinced that we were just going to Rob them. Little did they know what was in store for them.

Figure 42. "... meeting with Roberts about an hour away"

Author's archives [missing off-margin words; supplemented as presumed]

> While the family was in the bathroom we continued our search of the house. I looked upstairs, my partner down. We took a portable radio out of the boy's room upstairs, and put it in the car. We were running short on time, and didn't look the house over, or tear it up like we should. ***It was almost two o'clock and our meeting with Roberts was about an hour away. We didn't want to miss that. Five thousand bucks is a lot of dough....*** By this time the family was well convinced that we were just going to rob them. Little did they know what was in store for them.

The identity of "Roberts," if he did exist, remains for now an unsettled mystery. Hickock could hardly have confused his name with "William Floyd Wells," whom he well knew (and who was still in prison at the time). If he had only mentioned the name once, we might dismiss it as a mistake. But he has referred to "Roberts" twice now, both in key performance roles—as having provided the map and house diagram, and in an arranged meeting to collect *"five thousand bucks."*

And as we now know, Wells could not have drawn that diagram of the new Clutter home.

But someone did. Someone who knew the inside of the home and where each family member slept.

As before, and here with gruesome repugnance, Hickock casually ponders the baffling option of leaving the family alive after killing Mr. Clutter—if only they weren't witnesses to the crime:

> My partner and I, while the family was still in the bathroom, had discussed what should be done. If we killed the old man and left the rest of them alive, we were leaving a bunch of witnesses. So we decided that we would tie them up in separate rooms, and, cut their throats. That way, no member would know what was going on till their throat was cut. There wouldn't be any ruckus that way. We also had to tie them up, because if we didn't we would have to shoot them, and one of them might make it out doors. Besides it was too noisey that way, with all the screaming and shooting going on.

Figure 43. "If we killed the old man and left the rest alive..."
Author's archives [missing off-margin words; supplemented as presumed]

My partner and I, while the family was still in the bathroom, had discussed what should be done. ***If we killed the old man and left the rest of them alive, we were leaving a bunch of witnesses.*** So we decided that we would tie them up in separate rooms, and, cut their throats. That way, no member would know what was going on till their throat was cut. There wouldn't be any

ruckus that way. We also had to tie them
up, because if we didn't we would have to
shoot them, and one of them might make it
out doors. Besides it was too noisey that
way, with all the screaming and shooting
going on.

Once more, Hickock speaks of Herb Clutter in the singular
context of his fate being pre-determined, with separate regard for
the rest of the family. The emphasis here isn't so much on the *"if"*
of Clutter's demise, but rather on the fact that leaving the body
downstairs after the killers fled, with the family able to come
down and find it, necessitated tying the others up—in which case
the killers would be seen.

And that, he writes, simply *"wouldn't do."*

We were going to have to do something about the rest
of the family. If we were to cut Clutter's throat and leave
him down stairs, the family would come down as soon as we left
them, and the heat would be on. We had to at least tie them up. But,
then, I thought, they would see us, and that wouldn't do. Oh well, I
would cross that bridge when I come to it.

Figure 44. "... do something with the rest of the family."
Author's archives [missing off-margin words; supplemented as presumed]

We were going to have to do something
about the rest of the family. If we were to cut
Clutter's throat and leave him downstairs,
the family would come down as soon as we
left and the heat would be on. We had to at
least tie them up. But, I thought, they would
see us and that wouldn't do.

The decision made, Hickock describes in chilling detail, and with pathological clarity, his eagerness as the climactic moment approaches. He is frenzied with anticipation to finally prove his worth to those who have misjudged his abilities and accomplishments. Being an excellent student and star athlete wasn't enough; he "was going to show everybody."

Then, leaving no room for misinterpretation, Hickock proudly claims "And I'm getting paid for it too."

> Mr. Clutter was the first to be tied, then the boy, then Mrs. Clutter, and last of all the girl. When I went to the basement with my partner, where Clutter and the boy was tied, I though to myself time is getting close. My heart was pounding and I broke out in a sweat. My hands were trembling with excitement. I was going to show them. I was going to show everybody. All my life I had heard I wasn't ever going to do anything that amounted to much. But wait till they find these people, then they will know. And I'm getting paid for it too.

Figure 45. Hickock boasts of getting paid for the job
Author's archives [missing off-margin words; supplemented as presumed]

Mr. Clutter was the first to be tied, then the boy, then Mrs. Clutter, and last of all the girl. When I went to the basement with my partner, where Clutter and the boy was tied, I though[t] to myself time is getting close. My heart was pounding and I broke out in a sweat. My hands were trembling with excitement. I was going to show them. I was going to show everybody. All my life I heard I wasn't ever going to do anything that amounted to much. ***But wait till they find these people, then they will know. And I'm getting paid for it too.***

A word of caution: The next two letter segments may be difficult reading for some. In one, Hickock matter-of-factly describes the disturbed and conflicting emotions facing him as Perry, having just cut Mr. Clutter's throat, handed the knife to Dick so that he would "feel better;" how Dick was heart-broken and infuriated, even on the verge of tears—because he hadn't been the one to kill Clutter.

> It was during the time, which I have related to you, that I hit Clutter, Smith pushed the knife toward me and told me to stick him. At first I didn't pay any attention to him, because if I remember correctly, and, if I am right in stating this, I was really heart broken and infuriated, because I wasn't the one to cut Clutter's throat. As I look back on the incident and try to remember, I believe I was actually on the verge of tears. Smith then said that I would feel better if I done it. I don't remember if I grabbed the knife in a rough manner or not, but I think I did. I know I thought there was no use of me doing anything to Clutter, because Smith had already done it. But I walked to the head of Clutter and knelt down behind him. I thought that I should use the knife on Smith, but I raised the knife and drove it into Clutter's throat. It went in real easy, and it surprised me. I pulled it out and looked at Smith. I noticed he had the shotgun and I knew what was coming next. I told Smith to shoot him. I think I have told you the rest. How I kept from getting any blood on me I don't know. I did get some on my right hand glove. These gloves were thrown away somewhere along the road.
>
> — Richard E. Hickock

Figure 46. Hickock describes killing Mr. Clutter
Author's archives[169]

It was during the time, which I have related to you [Mack Nations], that I hit Clutter, Smith pushed the knife toward me and told me to stick him. At first I didn't pay any attention to him, because if I remember correctly, and if I am right in stating this, I was really heart broken and infuriated because I wasn't the one to cut Clutter's throat. As I look back on the incident and try to remember, I believe I was actually on the verge of tears. Smith then said that I would feel better if I done it. I don't remember if I grabbed the knife in a rough manner or not, but I think I did. I know I thought there was no use of me doing anything to Clutter, because Smith had already done it. But I walked to the head of Clutter and knelt down behind him. I thought that I should use the knife on Smith, but I raised the knife and drove it into Clutter's throat. It went in real easy, and it surprised me. I pulled it out and looked at Smith. I noticed he had the shotgun and I knew what was coming next. I told Smith to shoot him. I think I have told you the rest. How I kept from getting any blood on me I don't know. I did get some on my right hand glove. These gloves were threw away somewhere along the road.

Richard E. Hickock

In the next, he reflects boastfully on how much "fun" the killings were, bizarrely envisioning the same fate for his ex-wife's parents:

> As I think about it now, I realize it was fun. Nobody was telling us what to do. We were boss in that house. It felt good to be able to do as I damn well pleased. No orders no bosses no nothing. I got to thinking how much fun it would be to do this to my in-laws. I heard a lot of guys say they would like to, but they were cowards. It took guts to do what we were doing, but it was so simple I was really surprised.

Figure 47. "We were the boss in that house."

Author's archives [missing off-margin words; supplemented as presumed]

As I think about it now, I realize it was fun. Nobody was telling us what to do. We were boss in that house. It felt good to be able to do as I damn well pleased. No orders no bosses no nothing. I got to thinking how much fun it would be to do this to my in-laws. I heard a lot of guys say they would like to, but they were cowards. It took guts to do what we were doing, but it was so simple I was really surprised.

Their work completed, the killers fled. The Chevy raced out through the long majestic row of Chinese elms lining the road to River Valley Farm. Juggling emotions from resentment to jubilation, Hickock had one thing on his mind:

> I was hungry. Boy was I hungry.

Figure 48. "I was hungry. Boy was I hungry."

Author's archives

Dr. James Walker, the forensic neuropsychologist, found this particularly revealing:

> Hickock's letters reflect narcissistic characteristics to an extreme. In his presence on that fateful day were terrified, living human beings. Yet there is not a word of empathy for their horrifying experience or their fate. Instead his mind was filled with excitement that he was going to "have the guts" to do what others wouldn't, and take their lives, followed by disappointment that his partner took the initiative in killing Mr. Clutter before he did. Afterward, his primary thought was apparently finding a meal to eat. His self-absorption was extreme. Whether it was the extreme self-absorption of a pure psychopath, or the disordered mind of a man with severe brain damage incapable of reflection and judgment, cannot be determined with precision at this point.[170]

On June 10, 1964, expecting his appeal before the 10th Circuit Court would be declined, Hickock decided to seek executive clemency from Kansas governor John Anderson, based on his continued assertions that he was not guilty and had nothing to do with the actual killing of the Clutter family; that Perry Smith was fully to blame.

In advance of his application, Hickock was interviewed by Charles D. McAtee, director of Kansas state prisons, who gathered necessary information the governor might need to consider the merits of granting or denying clemency.

When McAtee asked Hickock why he would have allowed Mack Nations to publish such a detailed story about his role in the crimes if, as he was now alleging, he hadn't participated in them, Hickock gave McAtee a surprising but logical explanation:

> I let him write that story to get money to hire a lawyer. I would have let him write anything for that. I wrote two stories, that one—**and then one that was the truth**. The Attorney General's Office has the one that he published and now they are going to use it against me. I wonder if they have **the other story**?[171]

Despite its economy of words, the context here is significant and indisputable. Recall that the Kansas attorney general's office has copies of every letter Hickock wrote that passed through the prison censor's office.

The first story, which Hickock referred to above as *"...that one,"* was undoubtedly the basis for Mack Nations's article that appeared in *Male* magazine; the one largely consistent with the story most readers know today thanks to *In Cold Blood*.

But *"...and then one that was the truth"* can only mean those pages that Nations chose not to include—or perhaps pages he never even received after prison censors read them—among which the most provocative excerpts appear here. Why Nations selected which passages he did for publication remains unknown.

If we are to believe that anything Hickock says here has some basis in truth—and the Kansas attorney general most certainly relied on that assumption in preparation for a possible Supreme Court appeal—then these highly charged excerpts from Hickock's letters suggest four conclusions: that robbery was not the primary motive of the crime; that Herbert Clutter was the intended target; that the rest of the family's fate was discretionary; and finally, that money may have changed hands for getting the job done.

This chapter, *Privileged Communications,* would not be complete without mentioning the existence of information we do not or cannot know about the Clutter murder investigation.

Among other collections, the Kansas Historical Society is the ultimate repository for official government documents, including those from the Kansas state prison system. In the online abstract describing the contents of the Smith and Hickock files available for research, a curious notation appears at the very end:

> **Restricted: KSA 45-221(a)(29)**
> Action note: One folder of "Hickock & Smith Correspondence" removed from this series to Governor William H. Avery's records.[172]

Governor Avery's two-year term started in January 1965, three months before Smith and Hickock were executed. That it contains the entirety of Hickock's correspondence with Mack Nations is entirely plausible, since all letters passed through the censors and the warden at KSP and on to the attorney general's office in 1962.

But that would suggest that the Clutter investigation file taken from the KBI by Attorney General Curt Schneider in 1974 contains something more—information that authorities *beyond* the KBI still felt would be too "unprotected" even to remain in the bureau's custody.

What sort of information is so sensitive as to merit such exceptional security measures over half a century after the crime?

ACCESS TO EVIDENCE ROOM

As an exclusive bonus to readers of this book, you are invited to access the confidential Evidence Room, where you'll find a curated selection of original pages from the Nye notebooks, official investigation reports, Richard Hickock's Death Row letters to Mack Nations, select crime scene photos, and a reimagined map of the killers' journey based on the new information revealed here. Access the Evidence Room and register as an authorized user at: www.garymcavoy.com/evidence-room/.

Once you have registered and created your personal password, login to the Evidence Room using this secret password: **StreckfusPersons** (case sensitive). _Please do not share or post this password_. Access to exclusive content is governed by the restrictive terms and conditions posted on the website.

Suspicion

While one might question, as many have, Capote's account of events in *In Cold Blood*, his raw unedited notes archived in the New York Public Library attest to the potent talent he possessed for interviewing people. (*NB:* Shortly after Capote's death in 1984, George Plimpton famously quipped, "Truman used to talk about how he never used a tape recorder or notes or anything doing that book. But sometimes he said he had 96 percent total recall, and sometimes he said he had 94 percent total recall. He could recall everything, but he could never remember what percentage recall he had.")[173]

In the earliest interviews, taken in the first weeks following the murders, Capote and Lee each made note of numerous doubts and suspicions voiced by many people from Garden City and beyond. Few believed robbery was the sole motive; but that so many people who knew the Clutters well presumed that a darker purpose was afoot is startling. One of those doubters was Alvin Dewey, the KBI agent coordinating the investigation and a close friend of Herb Clutter.

Alvin Dewey

Agent Alvin Dewey was working on a bombing case in Wichita when he got a call from Sheriff Earl Robinson regarding the murders. Dewey wrote: "Mrs. Clutter's recent emotional illness flashed through my mind. 'Any possibility of murder-suicide, Earl?' I ventured."[174] The sheriff's response, that all victims had been bound hand and foot, excluded that possibility.

Dewey was a seasoned former FBI man and his instinctive response is noteworthy. He maintained his suspicions that the crime was more than a robbery even after hearing Floyd Wells's story about Hickock and Smith.

County prosecutor Duane West, who did a great deal more in the overall investigation than he has been given credit for, confirmed that "Alvin Dewey didn't think the testimony of Kansas Penitentiary prisoner Floyd Wells would break the case; he was pursuing a "grudge killing" theory and did not go to Lansing to talk to Wells, sending other Kansas Bureau of Investigation (KBI) agents instead."[175]

Harold Nye

According to *In Cold Blood,* Harold Nye also left open the possibility for motives other than robbery: "Nobody would kill four people for fifty bucks... Sure, maybe the killer did take the money—but just to try and mislead us, make us think robbery was the reason."[176]

Remarkably, Capote quoted Nye voicing suspicions which were later confirmed by Richard Hickock in his letters: *"Besides, we had to make it look like a robbery."*

Another on Nye's short list of possible motives turned out to have been prescient: "I thought the answer might be another woman—a triangle. Well, consider: Mr. Clutter was a fairly young, very healthy man, but his wife, she was a semi-invalid, she slept in a separate bedroom...."[177]

During the investigation, and even some forty years after it, Harold Nye was steadfast in maintaining there was more to the Clutter case than had been described in *In Cold Blood*, one reason for his now well-known gesture of throwing the book across the room angrily, calling it "a fiction," and, when the film was released in 1967, marching out of the movie theater after the first fifteen minutes.

Ron Nye is convinced his father knew a great deal more, the reason Harold had desperately wanted his son to help him lay out the truth in his own book, which never came to pass.

As author Ralph Voss confirmed, "Nye was deeply troubled about the case, both during the investigation and after it was resolved. He and other agents worked eighteen to twenty hours each day, and he did not believe Capote dealt with him and others honestly in getting the story. Nor did he believe Capote was honest in telling the story once he got it."[178]

Nye was also distressed by Dewey's failure to abide by the bureau's investigative standards and practices, having done so with impunity in the glare of publicity for the KBI following the murders. But at the time he was just a fellow agent, and not one to blow the whistle on a colleague. By the time he later became assistant director, it was pointless to take any meaningful action.

Duane West

The young Finney County attorney who served as chief prosecutor for the case, Duane West, was as central to the investigation as anyone at the time. Capote didn't much care for Mr. West, and the feeling was mutual.

That resentment carried over into *In Cold Blood,* where Truman gave far more credit to Logan Green, an assistant West brought in to consult on the trial, than to the chief prosecutor himself—even attributing West's own closing argument in the trial to Green.

As recently as November 2017, in an interview with the *Wichita Eagle*, West maintained that "Dewey didn't believe that story [of a robbery], and he pooh-poohed the whole thing, and so that's why he wasn't sent up there [the prison] to visit with Wells. And then even after that, they still didn't think that was the thing; he still thought it was a grudge thing."[179]

Earl Robinson & Logan Sanford

On November 16, 1959, the day after the murders, *The Kansas City Star* reported that Finney County Sheriff Earl Robinson doubted that robbery was a motive, as did Logan Sanford, director of the Kansas Bureau of Investigation.[180] In fairness, law enforcement had few clues so early in the investigation, apart from the discovery that "A diamond ring and church pledge envelope, containing several dollars, lay on a bureau in the girl's bedroom."[181]

Jack Curtis

Among the unsourced contributors to the *In Cold Blood* story was an otherwise well-known Garden City photographer and writer named Jack Curtis. An honors graduate of Kansas State University's School of Journalism, Curtis's articles and photographs appeared in such prestigious publications as *Time*, *Life*, and *People* magazines, and he was a regular contributor to the UPI News Features syndicate.

Curtis had long been close with the Clutters and was, in fact, the family's "official" photographer. He took nearly all photos of the Clutter family that are widely seen today, including the famous scene of happier times depicting the whole family gathered around the fireplace at Christmas.

Figure 49. Clutter family circa 1950
Photo © 1950 Jack Curtis; provided courtesy of the Curtis family

Curtis also photographed Perry Smith and Richard Hickock while they were at the Finney County jail. Photos of the menacing eyes of each killer from the mug shots taken by Curtis were used in Capote's book without credit or compensation. As Curtis's youngest son Ken recounts, his father was so furious with Capote that he destroyed all remaining photos he had taken of the Clutters, including the negatives.[182]

Figure 50. Richard Hickock and Perry Smith
Photos © 1960 Jack Curtis; provided courtesy of the Curtis family

In a separate interview Curtis's eldest son, Jack, maintained that his father "always said there was someone else, not just Smith and Hickock" involved in the crimes.[183] Whether he held that view based on firsthand knowledge or was told by someone in a position to know, Jack's father neither elaborated on the matter nor revealed his source before he died in 2008.

Arthur Clutter

Two days following the murders, Herb Clutter's own brother Arthur, in Garden City with his wife for the funeral, was unequivocal in his assessment of the murders. As *Time* magazine reported, "'When this is cleared up,' said Clutter's brother, 'I'll wager it was someone from within ten miles of where we now stand.'"[184]

Reverend Leonard Cowan

On Sunday, January 10, 1960, eight weeks after the murders and with the suspects having just been identified, the Reverend Leonard Cowan, pastor of the Clutter's First Methodist Church, was asked by a reporter what he would say to his congregation in that Sunday's sermon.

Rumors about the motive behind killing such a prominent family had spread through town like a field of wheat ablaze in a drought. Rev. Cowan felt an obligation to douse the flames and put his flock at ease.

In another example of Kansas authorities controlling the message, Cowan's placating sermon to his parishioners was telling. "The solving of the case has cleared up a lot of false rumors about Mr. Clutter's character that were circulating," he said. "I knew these were false because KBI agents told me they found no basis for them."[185]

Dr. Austin J. Adams

In a KBI interview, Mrs. Clutter's own psychiatrist, Dr. Austin J. Adams—under whose care she had been from 1951 to 1959—stated that "it was the work of someone in the immediate vicinity, with a deep hatred for the whole family."[186]

Larry Hendricks

Larry Hendricks, a young Holcomb High School English teacher who accompanied Sheriff Earl Robinson to the scene of the crime, was later interviewed by Capote. Hendricks's first thoughts centered, curiously, on Bonnie Clutter, asserting that she may have hired killers in some scheme involving blackmail or "dope." But he was convinced that nobody in town believed robbery was the motive. [187]

Describing the tension that gripped the town, Hendricks later recalled: "... no one visited anyone else in Holcomb. If approaching a house at night, after knocking on the door, the visitor stepped back to the edge of the porch and waited. If the visitor was unknown, they would face a gun barrel. The town was armed, he said."[188]

[NB: Sharp observers may recall that "Larry Hendricks" was also the name of the presiding judge in our litigation with Kansas. It should be noted they are different individuals.]

Preston Burtis

One of the most intriguing paragraphs in *In Cold Blood*—especially when viewed now, with new perspective—alludes to an unnamed former employee of Clutter's whose identity Truman Capote would later come to find was actually Floyd Wells. Capote writes [emphasis added]:

"Of the many stories circulating, the most nearly accurate was contributed by a prominent car dealer (*who refused to disclose its source*): 'Seems there was a man who worked for Herb way back yonder around '47 or '48. Ordinary ranch hand. Seems he went to prison, state prison, and while he was there he got to thinking what a rich man Herb was. So about a month ago, when they let him loose, the first thing he did was come on out here to rob and kill those people.'"[189]

It reads as a passing but nonetheless prescient anecdote. Capote was too smart a writer to drop in such a big clue to foreshadow the revelation to come, and he never underestimated his audience. So why employ such a leading statement at all if it weren't true?

Though Capote chose not to identify this "prominent car dealer" in the book, his notes give a clue as to who it was— Preston A. Burtis, owner of Burtis Motors, the Ford dealership in Garden City that he bought from Lester McCoy. Burtis not only sold cars to Herb Clutter over the years, he had loaned a vehicle to Capote while he and Harper Lee were going about their research in town. (In his papers, Capote made a note to include "Mr. P. A. Burtis, for car"[190] in the book's acknowledgments, though few acknowledgments, including this one, actually made it into the published work.)

If we are to presume, then, that such a prophetic statement was accurately provided *before* Wells had been identified, then we must also assume that someone knew details about the murders that even the authorities were not yet aware of. This single verifiable fact alone is simply breathtaking, leaving little room for ambiguity.

Decades later, in an interview given a few years before he died, Preston Burtis reasserted his position. Burtis recalled meeting Capote, Lee, and celebrity fashion photographer Richard Avedon at a party he hosted in his home.

"He was an interesting little duck," Burtis says of Capote, "and created quite a tidal wave in town; he was more of a character than we were used to...." "But, oh, those murders rattled everybody," Burtis adds. "They were *supposedly* killed for their money, and I don't know if Herb had $50."[191] [Emphasis added.]

When Burtis said this in 2001, the crimes had been solved for decades. Yet the person to whom Capote attributed that prophetic "rumor" still had doubts many years later.

That so many people who knew Herbert W. Clutter well would

so hastily attribute the murders to someone local, someone with a grudge, ought to have merited deeper investigation. Instead, authorities were politically motivated to put this case behind them posthaste. The swift trial and convictions of Hickock and Smith, from capture to sentencing, all occurred in less than three months, with an execution date set for six weeks later, on May 13, 1960,[192] surprising even local law enforcement veterans at the hastiness of events:

> "[Undersheriff] Wendle [Meier] and I both thought it was odd that the KBI was rushing things to get a conviction, but we didn't know why. Cases like that usually took ten years with appeals before punishment was administered. For whatever reasons, somebody wanted all this to end quickly." [193]
> — *Keith Denchfield, former Deputy Sheriff of Finney County, Kansas.*

According to Bill Brown, editor of the *Garden City Telegram*, there was even widespread belief that Arthur Fleming and Harrison Smith, the killers' defense attorneys, were appointed *not* to mount a vigorous defense, but to make certain Smith and Hickock were found guilty.[194]

Obstruction

"Truth is confirmed by inspection and
delay; falsehood by haste
and uncertainty."

— Tacitus, Historian of the Roman Empire

Pinched

When writing about a crime, especially one that has taken on almost mythical stature, the logical first step is to review the official record. After all, the Clutter murders and the arrest and trial of Richard Hickock and Perry Smith have been subject to creative interpretation for more than fifty years. The criminal trial resulting in a sentence of capital punishment, and ultimately the executions of Hickock and Smith, underwent numerous appellate reviews. Surely, one would think, original source material, specifically the official transcript of what is arguably the most famous criminal case in Kansas history, has been preserved and is easily available.

This is where our story takes another curious turn.

Over a period of several months starting in February 2015, I made numerous attempts to obtain the original 1960 trial transcript. I was originally directed by the court clerk to contact Philip C. Vieux, *chief judge* of the Finney County District Court. Not by email, but by phone, personally.

Unable to reach the judge, we tried his office again and were advised that inquiries should instead be directed back to the clerk's office—where we were informed that Finney County is not in possession of the transcript! An assistant in the clerk's office explained that it "may be in a vault" but access would be difficult after so many years. Strangely, we were told to contact the Calihan Law Office in Garden City, Kansas.

It seems that a court reporter with some relationship to the Calihan firm was known to collect memorabilia related to the case and in all likelihood had the transcript. A Calihan staff member advised us that their office did not, in fact, have the transcript, but the (now retired) court reporter was the best person to contact regarding our request. We were given the telephone number of the court reporter's residence in Arizona. After numerous failed attempts using the number given, we again contacted the Calihan Law Office and were told that was the only contact information they had. Having other things to deal with at the time, I set the task aside.

Then, in March 2017, we again contacted the Finney County Clerk's Office, this time via email. Their prompt reply informed us that our email had been forwarded to the Calihan Law Office with a request that they get in touch with us regarding the transcript.

Months passed until we received a phone call from a relative of the court reporter, *a private citizen*, who confirmed that, yes, they did have the transcript—a copy of which we could acquire for the price of $600. (The issue wasn't price, but accessibility to "public" documents.)

"What is Kansas trying to hide?"

While transcripts of Smith's and Hickock's later appeals can be found online quite easily, as of this writing that oddly elusive original transcript—which it appears many others were able to acquire in the years following the trial—remains publicly inaccessible. What would compel a state government to make it so difficult to gain access to historically significant public documents?

One need only turn to the Pulitzer Prize-winning Center for Public Integrity for one answer, when in 2015 they awarded Kansas a score of "F" for public access to information,[195] an evaluation based on research by determined advocates of transparency in government. One can only imagine what else is being shielded from the citizens of Kansas in the name of good public governance.

But things get even murkier when elected leaders take it upon themselves to decide what "good" means.

In a "preposterous opinion," Kansas Attorney General Derek Schmidt "created an opportunity for each and every state employee to operate behind a curtain of secrecy," by permitting state agencies' staff to use their private email accounts to transact public business, immune from public disclosure. This veil of privacy came in the wake of Governor Sam Brownback's budget director using his own private Yahoo email account to give sneak previews of the 2016 budget to influential lobbyists before it was sent to legislators. In a scathing editorial, *The Kansas City Star* excoriated the policy, which allowed state officials to "enlist special interests in shaping the public's business...outside the public eye."[196]

Two years later, following months of investigation detailed in a November 2017 article beneath the headline "One of the most secretive, dark states: What is Kansas trying to hide?," *The Kansas City Star* exposed a multitude of covert activities and executive decisions shielded by the State from public view, revealing an obsessive pattern of secrecy that goes back decades, declaring: "Kansas runs one of the most secretive state governments in the nation, and its secrecy permeates nearly every aspect of service.... [With] examples [that], when stitched together, form a quilt of secrecy that envelops much of state government...."[197]

Fingerprints

In his book, Capote gives only the briefest account of how Agent Alvin Dewey brushed off KSP inmate Floyd Wells's claim that Richard Hickock and Perry Smith were responsible for the Clutter murders. This was an especially peculiar brevity since Wells turned out to be key to solving the case. In fact, since the day *In Cold Blood* was first published, both Dewey, and the KBI by way of official statements, have characterized the book as factually accurate.

While critics have long taken issue with Capote's dramatized efficiency of the KBI, many have wondered if some kind of informal pact may have been part of the deal, in which the KBI's shortcomings would either be downplayed, generously modified, or even disregarded, in exchange for the bureau's not

only vigorously applauding Capote's effort, but permitting its
agents (Dewey in particular) to appear at book signings and,
years later, publish a series of intimately-detailed newspaper
columns about the murders and the investigation—all in service
to fortifying the heroic mythology.

Further evidence of its long-standing pride over the Clutter
case has been deeply etched inside the bureau, whose
headquarters in Topeka boasts an elaborate glass-encased display
of the actual instruments of murder involved in the Clutter
crimes. Among the collage of photographs and press clippings
visitors will discover the adhesive tape and nylon cord used by
the killers to bind the mouths, hands, and feet of their victims;
the very knife that ripped through Herbert Clutter's throat; a
Cat's Paw boot worn by Perry Smith that was once caked with
Mr. Clutter's blood; and Richard Hickock's Savage 12-gauge
pump-action shotgun that blasted open the heads of each of the
four Clutter victims. Mounted prominently above the shotgun is
a hardcover copy of *In Cold Blood*.

Figure 51. KBI display of Clutter murder memorabilia
Photo courtesy of and © 2018 Mali Sastri.

In a news release announcing the state's intention to press a
lawsuit against us to prevent this book's publication, Attorney

General Derek Schmidt proclaimed, "It is important for these materials to be returned to the State of Kansas for the protection of the integrity of the records and out of respect for the Clutter family."[198] The sensational exhibit at the KBI's headquarters belies these lofty sentiments. The State's hypocritical claims of sheltering the surviving Clutter family from further emotional burdens clearly extended no further than its desire to thwart our efforts out of intramural pride.

While the court ultimately affirmed our right to publish Harold Nye's archived materials, Ron and I, for reasons discussed, decided not to release or even display the most disturbing photographs here. Yet up until their lawsuit made public the State's deep concern for display of these images, many of the same grisly crime scene photos found in Nye's files had long been publicly posted on, among other official places, the Garden City police department's website.[199] Given the viral nature of the internet, they now appear on websites around the world. Many have aired in programs on A&E and SundanceTV channels and elsewhere around the world—all done with the approval and eager assistance of the State of Kansas, its impulses for compassion firmly in check.

In July 1997 KBI Director Larry Welch issued an internal memorandum to all KBI employees announcing the bureau's cooperation with several television productions for various cases. Among those mentioned was A&E Network, which was planning a retrospective documentary on the Clutter murders for their award-winning series "American Justice."

In December 1997, A&E Networks aired the compelling documentary, *American Justice: Murder 'In Cold Blood'*, featuring many of the principals involved with the investigation, notably Harold Nye, who by that time had been long retired.

However, Alvin Dewey's name was not mentioned even once, which rankled the KBI, who had graciously extended bureau resources to the production team.

After viewing the program, Director Welch sent a scathing letter to the producers:[200]

> Before I viewed A&E's television revisit of the Clutter case, I thought it impossible to discuss those historical murders for fifteen minutes, let alone one hour, without, at least, the mention of the name, Al Dewey.
>
> After watching your production, I am persuaded more than ever that presumption is true.
>
> The bad news is that you permitted *one*, who always refused to acknowledge Dewey's leading role in that tragic case to dominate the narrative. [*Ed.* The "one" being Harold Nye.]
>
> The good news is you have reinforced my original belief that I must never again cooperate with any movie or television KBI-related production without demanding that a KBI technical advisor be utilized.

In one of several conspicuous examples of dubious intent, Welch's letter succinctly corroborated our belief, and thus our legal standing, that the State's strident opposition to our project was based, in part, on the KBI's desire to protect and perpetuate myths about the Clutter murder investigation that were developed in close alliance between Alvin Dewey and Truman Capote.

Undoubtedly the most successful recent adaptation of the *In Cold Blood* story was achieved in Bennett Miller's 2005 Oscar-nominated film *Capote*, for which the late Philip Seymour Hoffman received an Academy Award for his performance in the leading role.

As with many productions before it, the producers of *Capote* reached out to the KBI for assistance. But in the wake of their "renegade" experience with A&E, the KBI flatly denied the request.

In its letter of censure, while acknowledging the KBI's cooperation with previous productions, the Kansas attorney general's office referred producers to a Kansas statute citing "... [the State] shall not be required to disclose...public records containing information of a personal nature where the public disclosure thereof would constitute a clearly unwarranted invasion of personal privacy."[201]

An odd rationale, given that any previous "invasion of privacy" concerns were waived for other films. The letter goes on:

> ... we did make an exception to [two production companies] who made a film about the murders. In both cases, we stipulated our conditions for cooperation and the importance of preserving an accurate portrayal of the facts and of the KBI's involvement in this case.
>
> Unfortunately, promises that were made were not honored by both companies and facts were not presented accurately. We regretted very much giving our cooperation in both instances. Therefore, we will not make any further exceptions to your company or other movie companies in the future.[202]

That Kansas continues to press for constraint over its own "approved" version of the Clutter murders, consistent with Capote's book, should be of concern to anyone who values free speech and creative control. It certainly was for us—and the Court agreed when it lifted the State's "*Confidential*" designation on these KBI letters and granted us permission to publish their correspondence.

Whether or not he was aware of the influence or value of his contributions, it has been well established that KBI Agent Alvin Dewey was intimately involved in the evolution of Capote's bestselling book. And for those services, willing or incidental, Dewey and his wife Marie were generously rewarded for years to come.

Dozens of Capote's letters to the Deweys, laid out chronologically in Gerald Clarke's splendid anthology *Too Brief a Treat: The Letters of Truman Capote*,[203] exhibit the warm and genuine friendship that developed between them over the many years following Capote's first visit to Kansas. Interspersed between the greetings and the gossip, however, numerous examples of Dewey's having obliged Capote's appeals for access are laid bare: Truman asking "Poppy" (Capote's nickname for Alvin) for particular details of the investigation, with Alvin only too willing to oblige the many requests of "Coach" (Dewey's nickname for Truman).

Denoting one of many such instances, Capote wrote to William Shawn, his editor at *The New Yorker*, while working on the book in Spain. In the letter Capote delights in his good fortune having acquired confidential details—the entire FBI file containing all interviews connected with the Clutter case— which was clearly provided by Dewey.[204]

The Deweys benefitted quite handsomely for their services, including parties with Hollywood celebrities like David Selznick, Jennifer Jones, and Irving Lazar; all-expense paid trips to San Francisco and Los Angeles; parties in Palm Springs, Washington D.C., and New York city, with dinners at the homes of Washington Post publisher Katharine Graham and socialite Gloria Vanderbilt; and, of course, that hottest ticket of all—to Capote's famed Black and White Masked Ball at Manhattan's Plaza Hotel in 1966.

The most indulgent perk, however, was enjoyed by Marie Dewey, who fetched a generous contract with Columbia Pictures as a "technical consultant" on the 1967 film version of *In Cold Blood*. For her participation Marie was paid $10,000—the equivalent of about $80,000 today—according to the terms of a 1965 contract in which Capote sold the book's film rights to Columbia for $15,000.[205]

When questioned about accommodating Capote and Lee with their research, Alvin Dewey's protestations were emphatic. "I never treated Truman any differently than I did any of the other news media after the case was solved... as far as showing him any favoritism or giving him any information, absolutely not."[206] But the record shows otherwise.

On Monday, January 11, 1960, barely a week after perp walking the killers up the steps of the Garden City courthouse, and despite his earlier proclamation to the press that interviews with the suspects were forbidden, Dewey permitted Smith and Hickock to be secretly interviewed in his own office, individually, by Capote and Lee. After the killers had been taken back to their cells, Dewey shared with his special guests the full transcript of Smith's interrogation in Las Vegas.

As author Ralph Voss observed, "The KBI rules were clear to Nye; no one should share specific details about an investigation with the media, and Alvin Dewey did so with impunity."[207]

To be fair, Harold Nye himself fell victim to Nelle's charms, providing her with a list of items he had recovered from the stolen vehicle in which the killers were apprehended in Las Vegas. And in a 1962 letter to Capote, Nye related his activities tracking down Perry Smith's sister in California and his father in Alaska, Reno, and elsewhere. But this was long after the killers had been convicted, and Capote—seeking just such details to flesh out his story—had persuaded Nye that, since he would figure so prominently in the book, this kind of richness was essential to ensure the factual narrative he was composing.

There is no doubt that the KBI's guiding hand, in the person of Alvin Dewey, gave up the most to shape the story that ultimately emerged. In a recent *Wall Street Journal* article, Mack Nations's son, Michael, who has studied this topic deeply over many years, held firm to that opinion, saying, "'Capote was telling the story that Kansas authorities wanted told, and Mack Nations was telling a story that they wanted to silence."[208]

Harold Nye fostered lasting bonds with many of his colleagues in law enforcement, but none were closer to him than his KBI partner and best friend David E. Johnson, who himself served as director of the bureau from 1987 to 1989. That mutual bond was also shared by both men's wives, Joyce Nye and Peggy Sue Johnson.

Alvin Dewey passed away in November 1987. The following month KBI staff assembled for their annual Christmas party. According to Peggy Johnson, who attended the event with her husband, KBI Director David Johnson—Marie Dewey, though still mourning her husband, felt compelled to make an appearance at the gathering, and asked if she could have the microphone to address her husband's fellow agents. Choking back tears, Marie shocked many by apologizing to everyone in the room, saying she was "very sorry for what Alvin and she had done, and asked for their forgiveness."[209]

Mrs. Dewey did not go into detail (nor did she need to, for her husband's actions were by that time widely known). Harold Nye's wife, Joyce, believed that Dewey had asked his wife to clear the air with his fellow KBI agents for lines he may have crossed while helping their friend Truman with *In Cold Blood*. Despite his many public denials of any impropriety, apart from evidence to the contrary, many expressed disappointment, even anger, at the access Dewey had given the author, seduced by Truman's fame and the many generosities he allowed the couple. According to prosecutor Duane West, even Logan Sanford, head of the KBI during the investigation, "thought that Dewey was a better agent before the Clutter case."[210]

Stakeout

As with any government agency, law enforcement is hardly immune from the reach of political influence. Logan Sanford, the KBI's second director who served from 1957 to 1969—and an ardent champion of Nye's loyal service—noted, in a 1988 interview reviewing his accomplishments as director, that he was fairly free from political pressures himself, one reason the KBI grew stronger and progressed as far as it did during his tenure. When Sanford was offered the post by then Attorney General John Anderson, the AG simply said, "You take over, you run it, if I have any objections, I'll let you know."[211]

In that same interview, nearly two decades after his retirement, "Sanford noted that politics did not play a role during his time with the KBI, and *until after he had left* there was never a hint of political involvement in hiring practices or direction of the Bureau"[212]—clearly implying that political forces had already influenced official KBI affairs.

But Harold Nye, the director succeeding Sanford, was loath to bend to the will of politicians, and that intractability eventually put his head on the line.

With the election of Vern Miller as Kansas attorney general—and his taking office in 1971, two years into Harold Nye's tenure as KBI director—the bureau's immunity to political influence was about to expire.

Miller, a flamboyant "super cop" as colleagues and the press dubbed him,[213] had promised in his election campaign to combat the possession of marijuana and amphetamines and "leap into the drug-ridden hippie communes of Lawrence [Kansas] with both feet."[214] And leap he did, quite literally, to the chagrin of many in Kansas law enforcement, though much to the amusement of the media.

Imagine, if you will, the most senior law enforcement official in the state hiding in the trunk of an undercover agent's car at the scene of a "major" drug bust in Wichita. Once Miller whispered the signal by radio to reinforcements surrounding the area, he popped out of the trunk and leaped into action. Officers rushed to the scene, where they found the AG holding a suspect at gunpoint.

But the night was young, so Miller got back into the trunk for another raid in another section of town, where—after lying in wait for half an hour, still in the trunk—he again popped out on signal, surprising the suspect who fled the scene with Miller in hot pursuit for two blocks, where the attorney general finally tackled the perp, and sat on him until arresting officers arrived to take him away. Fortunately for all, the press had been staged nearby to memorialize the events.

In an unmistakable sign validating Logan Sanford's chagrin over politics impacting KBI affairs, Vern Miller made it clear he wanted his own man installed as director of the bureau—the position currently held by Harold Nye—whose occupant serves solely at the pleasure of the attorney general. And by all accounts, this attorney general had little pleasure for by-the-book traditionalists he couldn't control.

On the very day he took office, January 11, 1971, Miller abruptly replaced Nye as KBI director, preferring instead someone who would be "responsive to the attorney general's office and its role."[215] Someone unlike Harold Nye, whose contempt for the bootlicking side of politics—especially the "go along to get along" attitude many powerful politicians expect from those in their orbit—put him at odds with the new AG, who instead picked Sergeant Fred Howard, an old friend of Miller's from the Kansas Highway Patrol, to replace Nye as head of the bureau.

Under the state's civil service statutes, however, Miller could not fire Nye without cause, a man whose performance was first-rate. A fifteen-year veteran of the KBI, Harold Nye was well-liked and widely respected within and beyond the bureau, so Miller needed to find some solution that would ease internal resentments and avoid a mass exodus of seasoned agents loyal to Nye.

Unfortunately, mired in a situation over which he had little control, Nye gave the AG the opportunity he needed to make his move. Harold's son Ron tells the tale:

> Between January and June of 1971 Dad was working with FBI agents out of Kansas City on a major undercover operation, one not coordinated with other KBI personnel or even the attorney general. For whatever reasons the feds made it clear that my dad couldn't bring anyone else into this, it was a big deal, something about organized crime syndicates, I think, and the FBI may have suspected there was corruption higher up, where a strict "need to know" basis had to be enforced. The FBI trusted my dad, he'd worked with them for years, and being an independent sort Dad had no issues with discretion; the less he had to deal with higher-ups, the better. But by this time Miller was out to get him, and actually had Dad followed, searching for any reason to fire him.
>
> I used to race hot rods on the weekend, and one night Dad showed up at my house terribly agitated. He said he'd been working a covert operation out of town with his FBI buddies, but told the boss he was in

Topeka. While the operation was underway Dad noticed he was being tailed by someone, and since he couldn't use his state car, he needed a "getaway," and asked if my gasser "Godzilla" was here. I said *"Yes,"* and he said, *"Let's go!"*

Without another word, I grabbed my keys and we jumped into Godzilla and took off. We hauled out of the driveway, headlights off, and I pushed that gasser as hard as it would go. Whoever was in that vehicle following us never got close enough to see my license tag.

Speeding down Topeka Boulevard I took a highway on-ramp heading west. My car easily hit 150 mph and I never saw the headlights of our tail even once. Certain we had lost them, I took the next exit off and Dad, seeing a pay phone, asked me to pull over. As I sat there with the engine off, I was able to hear his conversation; he'd called an FBI agent in Kansas City and was explaining his situation about the AG. Dad asked the agent if he would come into the office with him and explain what they were working on, but the agent said *No*, he was not going to take on the AG and "blow up" their undercover work. And that was that.

On the ride back home Dad was pretty upset, grousing about the predicament he was in now. He couldn't reveal his activities to the AG, which was the only way he could explain why he was not where he said he was. It didn't take long for Miller to take Dad down on some non-existent "morals" violation. Unable to defend himself, Dad was fired on the spot.

But when the AG learned that he had no legal grounds to fire him, the only thing he could do was reduce Dad to the lowest possible rank, Agent 1, and exiled him to the boonies of western Kansas, where he could run a backwater division there and keep his mouth shut.

No one knew the true reason behind Miller's decision to fire Harold Nye. But Ron is convinced his father knew something of sufficient gravity that higher ups did not want made public. Whatever this knowledge might have been, Ron believes it was related to the Clutter investigation, the one case that had bothered his dad ever since it was officially closed in 1960.

Closing Argument

"Cui bono?"
("Who stood to gain?")

— Cicero, Roman philosopher

Patterns

Readers must bear in mind that nearly everything we knew about the Clutter murder investigation before now was derived from a *novel* (not my description; Capote took great care in choosing it himself). By definition, a novel is fictitious prose narrative, which—when merged with details of the crime that Capote was either given or came by on his own—allowed him to create such a realistic and stimulating account.

As a consequence, however, in a way we're dealing with fictional characterizations of real people, thanks to Capote's dramatic treatment of them to suit his story. Few people alive know more than what the author has told us, which nearly everyone continues to cite as fact because that's all they were given. The compelling nature of his story has become the stuff of legend, reshaped time and again in print and on film. And since others long before now have already exposed many of Capote's embellishments, who's to say Hickock and Smith really were faithfully depicted on the pages of his "novel"?

As literary detectives, then, we're not so much working with facts as we are with Capote's rendition of them. When I consider Smith or Hickock or Wells—or anyone in the book, for that matter—I must set aside Capote's interpretations and rely, to a larger extent, on what I have in hand: Harold Nye's personal field notebooks; "most" of the official KBI and FBI reports; interrogation transcripts; Capote's and Lee's firsthand notes; recorded interviews with townspeople; reliable press coverage and reputable published biographies; and yes, even Hickock's own letters and Smith's effusive journals.

As objective analysts after the fact, we must resist the lure of being taken in by Capote's novelistic approach, simply because it's suspect as an impartial assessment of reality, and we are only now beginning to understand by what measure.

Considering the rough-and-tumble political stakes of the
burgeoning post-war agricultural industry, the very public
acrimony between Secretary of Agriculture Ezra Taft Benson
and Herb Clutter over pricing parity for farmers could have led
to enormous consequences for either side, not to mention the
country at large. If Clutter were some average farmer, the issue
might have been insignificant. But he was far from that, with
more power and political prestige than was revealed in the pages
of *In Cold Blood*, including personal influence with the President
of the United States, Dwight D. Eisenhower.

In a recent disclosure of Benson's FBI file, "[Benson] argued
to [FBI director] Hoover, whom he viewed as a friend and fellow
fighter of communism, that Eisenhower helped communism's
spread more than he hurt it... [and that] because freedom was
threatened by soft stands against communism, [Benson]
pondered making public such feelings 'even at the risk of
destroying the influence of men who are widely respected and
loved'—including Eisenhower."[216]

One undersecretary of state even advised the FBI that "the
president is a little 'teed off' with Secretary of Agriculture
Benson" because he "has not been successful in quieting the
farmers, cattlemen, dairymen and Capitol Hill."

But it wasn't just ranchers and their cowed Congressmen
who were disquieted. Governors of sixteen Midwestern states,
led by Nebraska's Ralph Brooks, were up in arms over the "grave
and tragic situation confronting the farmers of the Midwest."
Brooks cited an "explosive feature" of Benson's new farm
program that would remove government controls on wheat and
fix price supports to a moving average market, resulting in
abandonment of market quotas and price parity for farmers.

In economic terms, that meant farmers were facing a
proposed loss of $1 billion dollars in expected farm income for
1961 (roughly $8 billion today). Given that the 1959 production
value for all U.S. wheat crops was just $1.8 billion, the
devastation would have been considerable. "Benson's proposal,"
Brooks said, "is a move to kill the wheat program as he already
has done for corn."[217]

High stakes indeed. By the time Benson was finally called to task, however, Herb Clutter had been dead for two months, no longer able to protect the industry he helped shape. Benson left government service a year later, eventually becoming the thirteenth president of the Mormon Church.

As for the elusive "Roberts" referred to by Hickock, exhaustive research yielded little more than those separate hotel guest registers listing two Robertses. If they were, in fact, two different men, their concurrent departures the day before the murders seem oddly coincidental.

Assuming Roberts did exist, he may have been an intermediary acting on behalf of someone else, someone who wanted to see Herbert Clutter dead. In any event, time is the adversary in getting any sensible answer now. With half a century gone by, few principals of that period are still alive, and records—those that may be potentially worthwhile anyway—appear to be inaccessible, sheltered by a state having, for whatever reasons, strong motives for secrecy and self-protection.

String Theory

You've seen them on TV, the evidence boards or "crazy walls" police use for making connections between loose bits of information picked up during an investigation, each bit linked to others by string and pushpins, a process loosely known as "string theory" (with apologies to theoretical physicists).

An excess of nagging details and peculiar observations came to light during the many years of researching this book—in official documents and personal letters; public and private archives; historical newspapers and magazines; during interviews and email correspondence—most of which were simply too peripheral or detached from the themes laid out here. Yet they remain notable.

What follows are the loose bits that string theory couldn't resolve—discoveries that seem to have importance but didn't fit anywhere else—along with some lingering questions.

- During his interrogation Richard Hickock drew a diagram of each room of the house, by memory, six weeks after the fact—a house they were inside for only one hour, after midnight, and which was completely dark except for their flashlights.

- The map Floyd Wells supposedly provided Hickock in their prison cell was never recovered. It seems to have not even been considered worth finding by investigators, nor was it mentioned as being among the evidence Smith and Hickock burned at a roadside rest stop after the murders.

- Of all the reports the KBI produced, none bothered to consider a murder-for-hire conspiracy, implying only three possible reasons:
    1. There was gross negligence or incompetence;
    2. They decided (or were instructed) not to investigate further, despite an abundance of compelling detail;
    3. There was further investigation, but those records have been expunged from the file.

- What might be found in that Clutter file taken from the KBI by Attorney General Curt Schneider "to lock up and protect?" Could it be the same mysteriously inaccessible "Hickock & Smith Correspondence" folder retained by Governor Avery's office? Might it contain the complete set of Hickock Letters intercepted by prison censors? And if so, what else do they contain?

- How to explain the curious and oddly timed

disappearance of Mack Nations's final full manuscript of his book *High Road to Hell* shortly after he was killed? Who removed it from his desk in an obscure newspaper office in tiny Huerfano, Colorado—and where might it be today?

- To his dying day, Capote maintained that his book was immaculately factual—which to his thinking would have been true if the KBI had provided cherry-picked details to the author, reinforcing the story they wanted to be told.

In a 1966 interview with George Plimpton, Capote revealed a now newly-compelling detail he obtained in his interviews with the killers but omitted from *In Cold Blood*:

> They had two other murders planned that aren't mentioned in the book. Neither of them came off. One "victim"... was a man they never even knew – like the Clutters. He was a banker in a small Kansas town. Dick kept telling Perry that sure, they might have failed with the Clutter score, but this Kansas banker job was absolutely for certain. They were going to kidnap him and ask for ransom, though the plan was, as you might imagine, to murder him right away.[218]

These jobs, as Truman said, were never carried out. But could this intended banker have been Kenneth Lyon, the spouse of Mr. Clutter's presumed paramour, Mildred? Having planted the seed that resulted in Herb Clutter's death, could Floyd Wells have been a willing conspirator, assigned with the demise of both men? Again, who would have gained by such an arrangement?

Wells certainly could have met Lyon since their paths would at some point have crossed in both business and personal settings—on the ranch, where Wells worked, and of which Lyon was a partner at the time; and in the very busy social milieu of the

Clutter home, since Wells claimed to have had such a close relationship to the family.

As for the reported presence of spermatozoa on Bonnie Clutter's nightgown, the coroner's autopsy report revealed no evidence of intercourse. The nightgown had been sent to the FBI Forensics Lab in Quantico, Virginia, for examination, resulting in a report of findings returned personally by Director J. Edgar Hoover himself, confirming the presence of semen.[219]

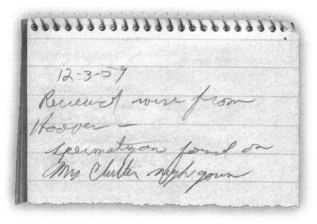

Figure 52. FBI Confirmation of Spermatozoa on Nightgown
Nye Notebook 1-73 – Harold R. Nye Archives

12-3-59
Received wire from
Hoover —
spermatozoa found on
Mrs Clutter night gown

So how did it get there? Hickock, with an acknowledged history of pedophilia, did admit his intention to rape Nancy Clutter, and was only prevented from doing so by Smith. But the two were not together the entire time in the house.

DNA analysis technologies were not available at the time, and though we filed a Freedom of Information Act request with the FBI for any documents related to the Clutter case, the bureau's official response, surprisingly, advised that such records had been destroyed, and no copies were retained.

Another perplexing discovery was found on closer inspection of one of the crime scene photographs. Several publications are laid out on the coffee table next to Kenyon Clutter's body on the sofa in the basement—a lurid selection of pulp romance magazines, surprisingly incongruous given the rigid Methodist sexual mores of both the family and the era.

Figure 53. Lurid magazines next to Kenyon Clutter's body
Photo © 1959 Richard Rohleder; Harold R. Nye Archives

Thinking this rather unorthodox for a man of Clutter's rigorous prohibitions, I turned to an expert in Methodist practices of that era, Dr. Ashley B. Dreff, author of *Entangled: A History of American Methodism, Politics, and Sexuality.*[220]

"Given Mr. Clutter's position against the use of alcohol and cigarettes," Dr. Dreff noted, "one could classify him as a socially conservative Methodist. As such, it is quite surprising and out of character that pulp magazines such as this, which advocate sex outside of marriage, would be found in his home, especially out in the open."[221]

Reasonable Doubt

So, in the end, what have we learned?

There is no question that Richard Hickock and Perry Smith committed the crimes. Ample evidence suggests that *motive* may have involved much more than mere robbery. That fact alone makes as little sense today as it did to so many other people in 1959—people who knew both the Clutter family and their killers.

I think a clear case can be made that Herb Clutter—a good and decent but flawed human being, like the rest of us—may have found himself at a point in life where he had, in the eyes of some, overstepped boundaries. As we have seen in the most public of present-day examples, powerful and successful men often have appetites that outstrip their achievements, and many have paid a dear price for the expectations of position and entitlement.

Cui bono, an archaic Latin phrase used in the process of identifying criminal suspects, expresses the view that crimes usually benefit their perpetrators. Who actually benefits from a crime may not be obvious, but blame often falls to a scapegoat. And if this story shows us anything, neither Richard Hickock nor Perry Smith earned any great reward for their efforts. Quite the contrary. Only Floyd Wells came out of it unscathed and actually compensated—both by the fishy circumstances of his parole and the payment of a reward for "breaking" the case.

So, to whom was it a benefit that Herbert Clutter should die? *Cui bono?*

According to official records, Mr. Clutter had many enemies in his local farming community, some who had even made specific threats against him for multiple offenses. At a time when others were losing their farms, as former USDA policy expert Dr. Keith Collins suggested, Clutter's success "may have bred enemies through the methods he used to build his business or jealousy at his economic success." For a man so deeply involved in shaping public policy on one of America's principal agricultural crops— wheat, "the staff of life"—Clutter could have made even more powerful adversaries in Washington D.C.—as he did with Agriculture Secretary Ezra Taft Benson and perhaps others loyal to Benson's anti-socialist causes in the waning days of McCarthyism. All it took to cause the death of Thomas Becket, the venerated Archbishop of Canterbury in twelfth-century England, was for King Henry II to complain to his court, *"Will no one rid me of this meddlesome priest?"* prompting four servile knights to carry out what they presumed were the king's wishes. Days later Becket was dead, yet no specific order had been issued.

Then there's the romantic angle, one of the first suspicions voiced by Harold Nye. If Herb Clutter was having an *affaire de coeur* outside of his marriage (as Dewey's suppressed evidence makes the case for), it's fairly obvious what would have been at stake should such a transgression become widely known. Public antipathy—socially and politically, especially in the mid-1950s— would be unforgiving for a highly respected community leader whose wife was virtually bedridden. Perhaps this is why, in his final days, Mr. Clutter had become uncharacteristically anxious, had taken to smoking cigarettes, and finally procured that long-planned life insurance policy.

Perhaps his paramour might have felt threatened as well, since Mildred Lyon was married to a prominent banker also at the height of his career. Women of position have been known to kill for fear of vulnerability or the prospective loss of financial security, not to mention jealousy (of which anyone is capable). Taking assumptions further, we also have the cuckolded husband, Kenneth Lyon, whose finances and business relationships intertwined with Clutter's for years, and into whose hands responsibility for Clutter's estate passed as its administrative trustee.

As to why neither Smith nor Hickock tried to save themselves from paying the ultimate price on the gallows, we may never know. Why did neither attest to a conspiracy when it mattered most? Personally, if in fact there was such a conspiracy, I would contend that Perry Smith knew nothing about it. His acceptance of full blame as the sole executioner, and his later but sincere regret at the "whole fatal disastrous catastrophe," speaks more to someone caught in the line of fire than it does a shrewd schemer.

Richard Hickock's actions present a more complex puzzle. His unmistakable hints at being paid by a third party ("Roberts") and the abundance of intriguing circumstantial evidence, corroborated in part by law enforcement reports of that Western Cafe meeting, certainly makes the case for a contract killing. But given what we now know, and the high stakes involved—be they position, power, money, emotions, or some combination—if this was a murder-for-hire plot, it could not have been carried out less professionally. Despite Hickock's intelligence, his reckless pathological impulses for money and recognition would have made him a classic candidate as a pawn in someone else's larger game.

Which brings us back to where it all started—the enigmatic Floyd Wells. So little is known of him, yet he was the key figure where it mattered most: feeding Hickock's head with visions of an "easy" score; not pushing back when Hickock spoke of leaving no witnesses, while happily providing crucial logistical details in exchange for a cut of the prize (including the diagram of the Clutters' new home which Wells, by his own admission, could not possibly have produced himself); lying to the KBI, and then perjuring himself in court testimony (to which the KBI turned a blind eye); and most disturbingly, his being granted, a mere two months after the murder trial ended, an inexplicable amnesty that dramatically reduced his five-to-ten-year sentence, liberating him three years earlier than even the statutory minimum term would demand.

From my perspective—having invested serious scholarship in

this matter over the past six years—the whole business reeks of institutional culpability. But which institution and for what reasons, I cannot surmise. One cannot dismiss the possible actions of individuals—even through one or more intermediaries acting on their behalf, which could account for "Roberts"—but applying Carl Sagan's aphorism that "extraordinary claims require extraordinary evidence," I'm afraid I've exhausted further pursuits in that direction. A good friend kept cautioning me about the dangers of going down rabbit holes, but for a naturally curious fellow like myself, it was all I could do to draw the line somewhere. And that line (for the time being) ends here.

In addition to the many new and surprising facts of the case, I do believe proof does exist somewhere, perhaps hidden in the dark recesses of some long-forgotten archive, much like that final scene in *Raiders of the Lost Ark*, where just one more artifact is stowed away in some cavernous, nondescript warehouse containing thousands more, secreted away from public view.

But if I've learned anything in my many years of seeking out and acquiring rare and valuable manuscripts from around the world, eventually anything once tucked away in the pages of history can surface at the most unexpected times.

Harold Nye's cache of case files in the attic comes to mind. And look what has come of that discovery.

Closure

"Publicity is justly commended as a remedy for social and industrial diseases. Sunlight is said to be the best of disinfectants; electric light the most efficient policeman."

— Louis Brandeis, Associate Justice of the United States Supreme Court

Due Process & the First Amendment

The sheer weight of the State's efforts to beat us down at any cost—including brazenly reshaping legal statutes expecting we might overlook such mundanities—did nothing to douse our speculation as to their overriding motivating factors. To that point, the questions posed throughout this book—*Why would the State go to such lengths, even taking such obvious legal risks?*—must now be obvious.

For readers drawn to legal machinations, following is a slightly more elaborate account of how Kansas attempted to suppress our constitutional rights to publish Harold Nye's personal archives of the Clutter murder investigation.

On September 27, 2012, Kansas Attorney General Derek Schmidt paved the way for the adventures to come by filing an ex parte restraining order that prevented Ron Nye and his family, along with me and my company, Vintage Memorabilia, from selling, replicating, or publishing any portion of the personal journals or copies of Harold Nye's case files. The State claimed that everything in the Nye archives were "highly confidential criminal investigation files" that Nye had "misappropriated," and that Ron and I were engaged in a civil "conspiracy" involving his father's personal records. According to the State, a preliminary injunction was essential to protect the State's paramount interest in the "confidentiality" of its "criminal investigation files" and the "privacy of the victims and their surviving family members."

Then, in an unprecedented and extraordinarily aggressive defense of its gag order, Kansas refused our obviously relevant discovery requests and shamelessly claimed that (a) because the Nye journals were misappropriated "criminal investigation" files, none of our constitutional arguments were valid; (b) the Clutter murder investigation records were off-limits because the investigation had been reopened (for exhumation of the killers' bodies in Florida's Walker murder cold case); (c) the requirements of the Kansas Open Records Act trumped civil discovery rules; (d) the preliminary injunction was proper; (e) the preliminary injunction was the law of the case; (f) our motion to vacate was premature; (g) our motion to vacate was an impermissible attempt to introduce impermissible evidence; and (h) our motion to vacate was an improper attempt to secure prompt appellate review of the preliminary injunction.

Feeling at times like marks in a game of three-card monte, Kansas persistently blustered its way through the very legal process it initiated. But after two years of contentious, time-consuming and expensive discovery—including legal briefings and oral arguments that gave the Court an eye-opening view of the State's shenanigans—the Court ordered Kansas to provide all discovery it had objected to on the basis of the Kansas Open Records Act, and awarded a discovery sanction against Kansas, and Derek Schmidt personally, in the amount of $3,986.80.

Then, on November 26, 2014, in an extensive Memorandum Decision and Order, Kansas District Court presiding Judge Larry Hendricks delivered a thorough, well-reasoned opinion in his final ruling on our First Amendment rights, one firmly grounded in the facts of our case as well as controlling U.S. and Kansas Supreme Court decisions, declaring that the legal and factual premises of the State's preliminary injunction request were misleading. It vacated the preliminary injunction and granted summary judgment against the permanent injunction Kansas had requested:

> The Court finds that the restraint in this case is, on its face, neither content or speaker neutral. It unconditionally enjoins four private citizens by name from publishing precisely identified material. Any prior restraint or constitutionally protected speech bears a heavy presumption of unconstitutionality. Prior restraints on

speech and publication are considered "the most serious and the least tolerable infringements on First Amendment Rights." Here, the plaintiff has sought and received an injunction prohibiting speech prior to its publication and this court finds the state did not meet its burden of showing that as a result of the publication both great and certain harm will result.

The court is sensitive to the plaintiff's concern about publicity and its effect on the Clutters. However, publicity continues to follow this case even fifty-five years after its occurrence. Also, [s]peech remains protected even when it may 'stir people to action,' 'move them to tears,' or inflict great pain.

The court finds the stated government interests supporting prior restraint against publication do not satisfy the constitutional standards set out above. The confidentiality of criminal investigative records, The Kansas Historical Society's mission to preserve government records of enduring value, and the Clutter family's privacy interests do not support the prior restraint of the defendants' First Amendment rights to publish the Nye Material as outlined above.

The Court finds that its prior grant of Injunctive Relief was in Error. After further review the Court finds there is no substantial likelihood of eventual success on the merits on this issue, the State will not suffer irreparable harm and the threat of suffering injury does not outweigh whatever damage the proposed injunction may cause the opposing party.

The Court finds the Nye journals are essentially a collection of facts and personal impressions, observations, conjecture, action plans, lists of suspects, and to-do-lists concerning Harold Nye's investigation of the Clutter murders. "The creation and dissemination of information are speech within the meaning of the First Amendment."[222] "The defendants wish to publish information contained in the Nye Journals and because the plaintiff believes that the material belongs to the State this Court initially issued a Temporary Injunction. However, the two issues are not linked together as the plaintiff led the Court to believe.

Even material that is stolen may be subject to First Amendment prohibition against prior restraint. [223] In this case there is no evidence to show that the Nye materials were stolen. At worst Harold Nye maintained material that at the time may or may not have been prohibited by the KBI. The defendants however, are under no such prohibition. Ronald Nye received the material by permission of his mother when she threw them away. He now wishes to use this material in a book to highlight differences in his father's notes to prior publications and statements. There is no doubt that public interest is high in this murder investigation. There is also no doubt that the case has been closed since the execution of Hickock and Smith almost 50 years ago. The State's position that a Florida investigation somehow reopens the file is unpersuasive. At best information is

being provided to the Florida authorities, but
an investigation into the Clutter murders
cannot be reopened when the killers have
been captured, tried, convicted and
executed. [224]

By affirming our First Amendment rights to publish, the
Court handed us a major victory in the main battle. The only
remaining issue was to determine who actually owned the
material. So, while Ron and I savored our triumphant win, the
lawyers geared up for the next skirmish.

Concealment

On a routine discovery visit to examine materials which might be
useful in our ownership defense, our intrepid Kansas lawyer Tai
Vokins met with Assistant AG Ward Loyd in the belly of the
beast, the KBI archives. Tai's notes of the meeting paint an
intriguing picture:

> They had...put about a dozen boxes of
> various KBI files and two boxes of Clutter
> files on a long table. Ward was with me in
> the room and I went through each file, one
> at a time, making notes.... The last thing I
> looked at was the Clutter file. There were
> numerous documents in the file [and] three
> discs...with Sharpie writing [on them].
>   One was a digital copy of the Clutter file.
> I think the two other discs just said "Hickock
> and Smith." I was interested in what was on
> the discs, and Ward said it was audio
> recordings of [the killers'] conversations
> made without their knowledge, while in the
> Garden City Jail. I had my MacBook, but
> they would not let me [listen to] the disc on

> my computer. They made me use their
> computer. It was a real piece of
> ["surprisingly old equipment"], probably ten
> years outdated and barely worked…. I told
> him I wanted copies. He implied I would get
> copies (which we never received). They did
> not "play" anything audible when I tried in
> their ["shoddy"] computer.[225]

Rather than risk being found in contempt of court (once again) by having to deny us access to that material, the State chose to fold its hand—and in doing so, escaped having to disclose whatever remained unseen and unheard. That secretly taped recording of Hickock and Smith in Garden City would be of particular interest.

Case Dismissed

Following additional wrangling over the terms of the State's voluntary request for dismissal of its case against us, on October 18, 2017, the Court dismissed the case and awarded substantial fees and costs to defendants. Tellingly, this is how the Court described the multi-year litigation:

> [T]his case was novel and difficult. The
> questions involved required significant time
> and skill to perform the requisite services
> properly…. The result involved was
> exceptional, especially considering the
> Court's initial ruling. Numerous hours were
> involved in difficult research to provide the
> Court with information not provided by
> plaintiff in its initial pleadings.[226]

After five-plus years in court, one can only imagine the cost to Kansas taxpayers for taking on such a draconian venture. Our

defense alone ran well into the high six-figures. Knowing the
number of Kansas state lawyers and KBI agents who dealt with
our case, their costs had to be at least comparable.

For that matter, putting things in ironic perspective, the
State could have just as easily purchased the entire lot for
$20,000 and been done with it.

But, as we ultimately came to realize, that may not have
been the point at all.

Redemption

Reflections by Ronald Nye

Figure 54. Harold Nye
Photo © 2003 Harold Nye; courtesy of Ronald R. Nye

In the months leading up to his retirement in 1975, my dad drove back and forth between Kansas and Oklahoma on weekends, testing for and passing his real estate licensing exam. As soon as his retirement party was over, he left for Oklahoma City to find and buy a house for his family, away from Kansas, no longer wanting to live in the state he had faithfully served over a forty-year career; one that turned its back on him in the shadow of political vengeance.

My dad was never the same afterwards. He was never able to share one word about what had happened to him, or what else he might have known, but the whole family felt his pain. He never again carried himself quite the same way, with the proud bearing of a KBI agent who served not just his state, but his country. He lived out the balance of his life a broken man and passed away in 2003.

When you work around people every day and see the things that happen to them, as I have—situations that would make most people sick to their stomach or be stricken with grief—you learn to suppress your instinctive response and just do what needs to be done.

For me, twenty years of working in a hospital filled up all the spaces inside me where I stored those feelings. My dad did the same thing for almost forty years. That should tell you what kind of amazing man he was.

As he grew older, though, his life experiences had finally filled all the space he had, and he found it nearly impossible to repress his emotions. He would cry when hearing anything despondent on the news, or even while watching a "sad" movie on TV. He simply had no place left inside where he could push his feelings to. My dad was a brave man who did the hard things that life threw at him in the face of danger and violence, but he never once turned his back when it came to serving the people he had taken an oath to protect.

Figure 55. Joyce Nye
Photo © 2003 Harold Nye; courtesy of Ronald R. Nye

My mother, ever the faithful and supportive wife, loved Kansas
with all her heart. She was born in the small town of Oakley, and
never really adapted to life in Oklahoma. Kansas was her home.

Sometime after Dad died my mother suffered a heart attack.
She was so frail when she finally left the hospital that I couldn't
let her live alone, all on her own, so I set her up in an assisted-
living center near my home where we could visit often.

When the State of Kansas sued us over my father's personal
journals, we were shocked to find that my mother and sister were
also named as defendants, two people who had nothing at all to
do with it. But Kansas, in a final stroke of injustice to my father's
career, chose to round up whoever they could in the first of
countless intimidation tactics.

Because my mother was named as a defendant, I had to read
her the essence of the complaint. Reciting the State's terrible
accusations against me and my father, I watched my mom's eyes
glisten with tears, seeing in them confirmation of the suspicions

she'd always harbored about the KBI. Sobbing with grief, she said, "But I don't understand. I had all those boxes shredded years ago. Why are they doing this?"

When I told her of the State's specious accusations that Dad's journals had been "stolen" and that both he and I were "liars," her spirit simply folded. Once a strong and proud woman, she no longer had the will to defend herself or her family. She could not get the fact of being sued out of her mind, and had great difficulty resting at night. Unable to sleep, she would pace the halls of the center all night long, wearing out two pairs of shoes a month. As time passed and things did not get resolved, she slept fewer and fewer hours each day.

Early one morning the nurse went in to give Mom her medication and found that she had died in her sleep. Her heart had just given out.

My mother literally died a heartbroken woman, without ever knowing that her husband had done nothing wrong. The State of Kansas, whose judicial system ultimately ruled convincingly in our favor, had cleared Harold Nye's good name.

It was just too late.

Legacy

Thanks to Truman Capote, the tragic murders of the Clutter family have been memorialized as one of America's earliest and most enduring true crime stories, achieving a pinnacle in world literature. Against long odds, the successful solving of a multiple murder, at least as we know it from *In Cold Blood*, remains a case study in law enforcement, social psychology, and capital punishment.

The countless books, articles, and film treatments that have spun out of Capote's work all relied on public access to historical materials, a great many of which have been archived in the Truman Capote Papers of The New York Public Library and are available in perpetuity to scholars seeking to shed new light on an old but still popular event and its aftermath.

We believe Harold Nye's personal journals and his archive of official reports relating to the Clutter murder investigation add significantly to the historical record. For that reason, Ron and I have chosen to donate his father's collection to the Manuscripts and Archives Division of The New York Public Library, allowing future scholars the opportunity to research this valuable collection, perhaps with renewed understanding based, hopefully, on revelations yet to come.

Despite the costs and intangible toll this has taken on both Ron Nye and me, it has been one of the great privileges of my life to have met and worked with Ron on this project. In the end, I hope this narrative brings some relief to him and his family, and to the memory of his father, Harold Nye.

As for what might remain of the rest of the story, I invite anyone in possession of reliable, previously unrevealed information on the Clutter murders or its investigation to come forward. Qualified individuals may do so using our secure confidential submission system at **www.AndEveryWordIsTrue.com**. Anonymity will be assured for all legitimate sources.

Finally, we challenge the State of Kansas to release all "protected" files from the Clutter investigation held by any of its state agencies or repositories, including that elusive audiotape of Richard Hickock and Perry Smith's private conversation, one recorded without their knowledge. The answers to many of the lingering questions posed in this book may depend on the content of that recording, and possibly other yet-to-be found materials, being made publicly available.

As the Court determined in our case, the State's assertions of confidentiality were baseless, since *"... the killers have been captured, tried, convicted and executed."* Logically, then, there is no justifiable reason for the State of Kansas to keep buried the bones of such a high-profile literary mystery, one that may carry with it potentially explosive political implications.

Or is there?

Index

Bibliography

Capote, Truman. *In Cold Blood: A True Account of a Multiple Murder and Its Consequences*. New York: Random House, 1966.

Capote, Truman. *Selected Writings of Truman Capote*. New York: Random House, 1963.

Capote, Truman. *Too Brief a Treat: The Letters of Truman Capote*. Edited by Gerald Clarke. New York: Vintage International, 2012.

Clarke, Gerald. *Capote: A Biography*. New York: Simon & Schuster, 1988.

Dreff, Ashley B. *Entangled: A History of American Methodism, Politics, and Sexuality*. Nashville: New Room Books, 2018.

Fersch, Ellsworth Lapham. *Thinking About Psychopaths and Psychopathy: Answers to Frequently Asked Questions with Case Examples*. Bloomington, IN: iUniverse, 2006.

Friedan, Betty. *The Feminine Mystique*. New York: W.W. Norton, 1963.

Hickock, David and Linda LeBert-Corbello. *In the Shadow of My Brother's Cold Blood*. iUniverse, 2010.

Hunter, J.T. *In Colder Blood: True Story of the Walker Family Murder as depicted in Truman Capote's In Cold Blood*. RJ Parker Publishing, 2016.

Kansas Bureau of Investigation: 1939–1989. Topeka: Jostens, 1990.

Madden, Kerry. *Up Close: Harper Lee*. New York: Viking/Penguin Group, 2009.

Voss, Ralph F. *Truman Capote and the Legacy of "In Cold Blood,"* Tuscaloosa: University Alabama Press, 2011.

Malin, Irving. *Truman Capote's 'In Cold Blood': A Critical Handbook*. Belmont, CA: Wadsworth Publishing Co., 1968.

Plimpton, George. *Truman Capote: In Which Various Friends, Enemies, Acquaintances, and Detractors Recall His Turbulent Career*. New York: Nan A. Talese, Doubleday, 1997.

Ramsland, Katherine. *Confession of a Serial Killer: The Untold Story of Dennis Rader, the BTK Killer*. Lebanon, NH: ForeEdge, 2016.

Rubin, Richard. *Confederacy of Silence: A True Tale of the New Old South*. New York: Atria Books, 2002.

Shields, Charles J. *Mockingbird: A Portrait of Harper Lee*. New York: Henry Holt, 2006.

Welch, Larry. *Beyond Cold Blood: The KBI from Ma Barker to BTK*. Lawrence: University Press of Kansas, 2012.

Williams, Tennessee, *The Selected Letters of Tennessee Williams*. Edited by Albert J. Devlin and Nancy Marie Patterson Tischler. New York: New Directions Pub, 2000.

Endnotes

[1] Phillip K. Tompkins, "In Cold Fact," *Esquire*, June 1966, 58.

[2] Truman Capote. *In Cold Blood: A True Account of a Multiple Murder and Its Consequences.* (New York: Random House, 1966).

[3] Truman Capote. *Selected Writings of Truman Capote.* (New York: Random House, 1963).

[4] Ralph F. Voss, *Truman Capote and the Legacy of "In Cold Blood,"* (Tuscaloosa: University Alabama Press, 2011).

[5] Gerald Clarke, *Capote: A Biography*, (New York: Simon & Schuster, 1988).

[6] George Plimpton. *Truman Capote: In Which Various Friends, Enemies, Acquaintances, and Detractors Recall His Turbulent Career.* (New York: Nan A. Talese, Doubleday, 1997).

[7] Charles J. Shields. *Mockingbird: A Portrait of Harper Lee.* (New York: Henry Holt, 2006).

[8] George Plimpton. "The Story Behind a Nonfiction Novel." *The New York Times*, January 16, 1966.

[9] Jack De Bellis. "Vision and Revisions: Truman Capote's *In Cold Blood*," *DISCovering Authors*. Detroit: Gale, 2003. Student Resources in Context. Web. Accessed May 11, 2015.

[10] "Deep Throat" was the pseudonym given to the confidential informant (later revealed to be FBI Associate Director Mark Felt) who provided information in 1972 to *Washington Post* reporter Bob Woodward. Deep Throat provided key details about the involvement of U.S.

President Richard Nixon's administration in what came to be known as the Watergate scandal.

[11] *The New York Times*, November 16, 1959, 39.

[12] *Great Moments*. San Francisco Film Festival. History.sffs.org (published May 4, 2006). 1974. Retrieved July 30, 2018.

[13] Ralph F. Voss. *Truman Capote and the Legacy of In Cold Blood*. (Tuscaloosa: University of Alabama Press, 2011).

[14] *In Cold Blood* paints a more dramatic (but fictitious) scene that occurs on December 4, five days prior to the actual visit, in which Harold Nye, alone at the Hickock farm, spies the murder weapons but does not confiscate them.

[15] As readers will later discover in detail, Wells plainly perjured himself, and despite the KBI being aware of it, they allowed Wells's sworn testimony to stand—a fact Capote was likely unaware of when he wrote *In Cold Blood*.

[16] Clarifying the record, it was Finney County Attorney Duane West who questioned Wells on the stand, not assistant prosecutor Logan Green, as identified by Capote in his book.

[17] Don Kendall, "Cellmate Tells Hickock Plan," *The Hutchinson News*, Hutchinson, KS, March 24, 1960, 21.

[18] Although never mentioned in his book's omniscient narrative, Capote's presence is noted here for historical accuracy.

[19] Interview with the author.

[20] Interview with the author.

[21] Interview with the author.

[22] Interview with the author.

[23] *Cold Blooded: The Clutter Family Murders*. Written and directed by Joe Berlinger. SundanceTV, November 2017.

[24] A "one-down position" is an intervention technique in which the therapist avoids gaining advantage over a patient, so as not to trigger feelings of inferiority.

[25] Interview with the author.

26 *Topeka Journal*, 1969 (full citation not available).

27 Internal KBI email messages, July/August 2012.

28 The Kansas Supreme Court has interpreted that State's eavesdropping and privacy statutes to allow one-party consent for taping of conversations, and has ruled that as long as one party consents to the conversation, the other party cannot challenge the eavesdropping in court. In other states, both parties to the phone conversation must consent to the recording.

29 Referring to Larry Welch, author of *Beyond Cold Blood: The KBI from Ma Barker to BTK*. (Lawrence: University Press of Kansas, 2012), in a discussion with *The Wall Street Journal* reporter Kevin Helliker.

30 David and Albert Maysles. *"USA: The Novel: A Visit with Truman Capote;* later titled *With Love from Truman*. (1966; New York: Maysles Films, Inc.), TV.

31 Irving Malin. *Truman Capote's 'In Cold Blood': A Critical Handbook*. (Belmont, CA: Wadsworth Publishing Co., 1968)

32 Originally published in *Esquire* magazine, June 1966.

33 George Plimpton. "The Story Behind a Nonfiction Novel." *The New York Times*, January 16, 1966.

34 Phillip K. Tompkins. "In Cold Fact." *Esquire*, June 1966.

35 As related to the author in a January 2018 phone interview with Keith Denchfield, the Meier's son-in-law.

36 George Plimpton. "The Story Behind a Nonfiction Novel." *The New York Times*, January 16, 1966.

37 Kevin Helliker. "Capote Classic *'In Cold Blood'* Tainted by Long-Lost Files." *The Wall Street Journal*, February 8, 2013.

38 *Kansas Bureau of Investigation: 1939–1989*. (Topeka: Jostens, 1990).

39 Sheriff Jim Kramer, email correspondence with the author, December 8, 2017.

40 David Hickock and Linda LeBert-Corbello. *In the Shadow of My Brother's Cold Blood*. (iUniverse, 2010)

41 David Hickock and Linda LeBert-Corbello. *In the*

Shadow of My Brother's Cold Blood. (iUniverse, 2010). Kindle Edition, location 341.

[42] Truman Capote. *In Cold Blood: A True Account of a Multiple Murder and Its Consequences.* (New York: Random House, 1966), 170.

[43] Gerald Clarke. *Capote: A Biography.* (New York: Simon and Schuster, 1988), 319.

[44] Tennessee Williams, Albert J. Devlin, and Nancy Marie Patterson Tischler. *The Selected Letters of Tennessee Williams.* (New York: New Directions Pub, 2000). 368.

[45] As one example: T. Madison Peschock, *What was Harper Lee's role in writing 'In Cold Blood?'* AL.com, accessed March 8, 2016, https://www.al.com/opinion/index.ssf/2016/03/what_was_harper_lees_role_in_w.html

[46] Kerry Madden, *Up Close: Harper Lee*, (New York: Viking/Penguin Group, 2009), 120.

[47] Charles J. Shields. *I Am Scout: The Biography of Harper Lee.* (New York: Henry Holt and Co., 2008), 107.

[48] Nelle Harper Lee, "Dewey Had Important Part In Solving Brutal Murders," *The Grapevine*, March 1960, 8.

[49] Charles J. Shields. *Mockingbird: A Portrait of Harper Lee.* (New York: Henry Holt and Co., 2006), 239-240.

[50] Truman Capote. *In Cold Blood: A True Account of a Multiple Murder and Its Consequences.* (New York: Random House, 1966), 84.

[51] C.B. Palmer. "A Farmer Looks at Farming '54." *The New York Times*, August 1, 1954, SM8.

[52] Alvin A. Dewey. (November 27, 1959). *Memorandum for the File.* Garden City, KS. Kansas Bureau of Investigation.

[53] Alvin A. Dewey (1959). *Memorandum for the File: Interview with [redacted].* Garden City, KS. Kansas Bureau of Investigation.

[54] Truman Capote papers. Manuscripts and Archives Division. The New York Public Library. Astor, Lenox, and Tilden Foundations, Box 7, Folders 1-14.

[55] Alvin A. Dewey (1959). *Memorandum for the File:*

Interview with Kenneth Lyon. Garden City, KS. Kansas Bureau of Investigation.

[56] Wendell Cowan (1959). *Memorandum for the File: Interview with Dr. V. A. Leopold.* Garden City, KS. Kansas Bureau of Investigation.

[57] Wendell Cowan (1959). *Memorandum for the File: Interview with Dr. V. A. Leopold.* Garden City, KS. Kansas Bureau of Investigation.

[58] Nelle Harper Lee. Research Notes dated December 27, 1959. Truman Capote papers. Manuscripts and Archives Division. The New York Public Library. Astor, Lenox, and Tilden Foundations.

[59] Truman Capote. Research Notes, undated. Truman Capote papers. Manuscripts and Archives Division. The New York Public Library. Astor, Lenox, and Tilden Foundations.

[60] Dr. Keith Collins, email to the author, December 27, 2017.

[61] Alvin A. Dewey (November 27, 1959). *Memorandum for the File: Interview with Kenneth Lyon.* Garden City, KS. Kansas Bureau of Investigation.

[62] Librium, released in 1960, and Valium, 1963, also fell into this category.

[63] C. B. Palmer. "A Farmer Looks at Farming '54." *The New York Times*, August 1, 1954, SM8.

[64] Betty Friedan. *The Feminine Mystique.* (New York: W.W. Norton, 1963)

[65] Horwitz, Allan V. "How an Age of Anxiety Became an Age of Depression." *The Milbank Quarterly* 88.1 (2010): 112–138. PMC. Web. 26 Dec. 2017.

[66] Truman Capote. *In Cold Blood: A True Account of a Multiple Murder and Its Consequences.* (New York: Random House, 1966), 30.

[67] Nelle Harper Lee. Research Notes, 1959. Truman Capote papers. Manuscripts and Archives Division. The New York Public Library. Astor, Lenox, and Tilden Foundations, Box 7, Reel 7, Folders 11-14. Used with permission of the Capote Trust.

[68] Alvin A. Dewey (November 27, 1959).

Memorandum for the File: Interview with Kenneth Lyon.
Garden City, KS. Kansas Bureau of Investigation.

[69] Larry Welch to Andrew Holland, December 29, 1997.

[70] *Kansas Bureau of Investigation: 1939–1989.* (Topeka: Jostens, 1990).

[71] Larry Welch. *Beyond Cold Blood: The KBI from Ma Barker to BTK.* (Lawrence: University Press of Kansas, 2012).

[72] Email to KBI staff, July 21, 2012.

[73] Kansas v. Nye, McAvoy et al. District Court of Shawnee County, KS. 26 Nov. 2014. Print.

[74] *Kansas Bureau of Investigation: 1939–1989.* (Topeka: Jostens, 1990), 77.

[75] Today the NCIC database is available to every cop in every car on every beat; it's the computer being checked, for example, while your car has been pulled over for an observed offense.

[76] With one exception: Kevin Helliker's reporting in *The Wall Street Journal* on new discoveries in the Clutter investigation were based in part on information contained in Nye's notebooks (February 2013).

[77] Details which do not appear in the Capote Archives at either the New York Public Library or the Library of Congress.

[78] George Plimpton. *Truman Capote: In Which Various Friends, Enemies, Acquaintances, and Detractors Recall His Turbulent Career.* (New York: Nan A. Talese, Doubleday, 1997), 170

[79] Plimpton, *Truman Capote*, 170.

[80] Interview with Ronald Nye.

[81] Gene Smith. "Topekan disputes lurid tale of Capote." *Topeka-Capital Journal* (Topeka, KS), December 14, 1997. Web.

[82] Charles Ferruzza. "Killer Queen." *The Pitch.* December 1, 2005. Web.

[83] George Plimpton. *Truman Capote: In Which Various Friends, Enemies, Acquaintances, and Detractors Recall His Turbulent Career.* (New York: Nan A. Talese,

Doubleday, 1997), 170.

[84] According to Stuart Hinds, Assistant Dean for Special Collections & Archives at the University of Missouri, Kansas City, Capote most likely visited the Colony Club.

[85] Plimpton, 170.

[86] Interview with Ronald Nye.

[87] Email interview with the author, September 23, 2018

[88] Charles J. Shields. "See NL's Notes." In *Mockingbird: A Portrait of Harper Lee.* (New York: Henry Holt, 2007). Kindle edition, 173

[89] Dolores Hope. "The Clutter Case: 25 Years Later KBI Agent Recounts Holcomb Tragedy." *Garden City Telegram* (Garden City, KS), November 10, 1984, 11A.

[90] Michael Bruntz. "Technology might have helped solve crime faster." LJWorld.com, April 5, 2005.

[91] Alvin A. Dewey (November 23, 1959). "Memorandum for the File." Garden City, KS. Kansas Bureau of Investigation.

[92] Kevin Helliker. "Capote Classic 'In Cold Blood' Tainted by Long-Lost Files." *The Wall Street Journal*, February 8, 2013.

[93] Email interview with the author, January 18, 2018.

[94] Patrick Smith, "Garden City officer forgotten in Capote's book," *Lawrence Journal-World*, April 5, 2005, www2.ljworld.com/news/2005/apr/05/garden_city_officer/)

[95] Smith.

[96] Smith.

[97] David Hickock and Linda LeBert-Corbello. *In the Shadow of My Brother's Cold Blood.* (iUniverse, 2010). Kindle Edition, locations 286-287.

[98] Hickock, 362-370.

[99] Hickock, 409-411.

[100] Author's email interview with Dr. James S. Walker, December 2018.

[101] Truman Capote. *In Cold Blood: A True Account of a Multiple Murder and Its Consequences.* (New York: Random House, 1966), 279.

[102] Katherine Ramsland PhD. *Confession of a Serial Killer: The Untold Story of Dennis Rader, the BTK Killer.* (Lebanon, NH: ForeEdge, 2016).

[103] Author's email interview with Dr. Katherine Ramsland, December 2017.

[104] James E Post. (1960). Special Progress Report. Kansas State Penitentiary. Lansing, KS.

[105] At age 25, Perry's brother James "Tex" Smith took his life not by shotgun, as described by Capote, but by gassing himself in the kitchen, desolate over his wife's own suicide the same way two days earlier.

[106] UPI, "Husband, 25, Follows Wife in Death Act," *Daily Capital Journal* (Salem, OR). November 19, 1949.

[107] Associated Press, "Alaska Trapper Rotated Home from Battle; Cheered at Dock," *Fairbanks Daily News-Miner*, October 2, 1951, 1.

[108] As revealed by Smith's son, Jewell James, in *Cold Blooded: The Clutter Family Murders.* Directed by Joe Berlinger. SundanceTV, November 18, 2017.

[109] http://www.lummi-nsn.org/

[110] As later described by Capote in an interview with George Plimpton, "The Story Behind a Nonfiction Novel," *The New York Times*, January 16, 1966, http://www.nytimes.com/books/97/12/28/home/capote-interview.html.

[111] Inmates Release Schedule, Kansas State Penitentiary, Lansing, KS, November 17, 1959.

[112] Jack Curtis, "I Remember Perry Smith," *Los Angeles Times*, January 28, 1968, B25.

[113] "Richard Eugene Hickock inmate case file," Parole Board Summary of Clemency Hearing, April 4, 1965, 119-24. Accessed June 8, 2013.

[114] Truman Capote. *In Cold Blood: A True Account of a Multiple Murder and Its Consequences.* (New York: Random House, 1966), 340.

[115] Tim Carpenter, "Former prison official recalls notorious case," *Lawrence-Journal World*, December 29, 2002, accessed December 3, 2014, http://www2.ljworld.com/news/2002/dec/29/former_prison_official/.

[116] Michael Bruntz, "Witness to Execution," *Lawrence-Journal World*, April 5, 2005, accessed December 8, 2012, http://www2.ljworld.com/news/2005/apr/05/witness_to_execution/.

[117] Curtis.

[118] Email interview with the author, September 23, 2018

[119] Anne Taylor Fleming, "The Descent from the Heights," *The New York Times Magazine*, July 16, 1978.

[120] Alvin A. Dewey. (1959). "Memorandum for the File: Floyd Wells Period of Employment." Garden City, KS. Kansas Bureau of Investigation.

[121] Capote was mistaken about Wells's 3-5 year sentence as quoted in his book. In an interview with Kansas reporter Ted Blankenship, Wells affirmed the longer stretch as the sentence given by the court, as also confirmed in prison reports.

[122] Bob Greer. "He Musta Done It,' Key Witness Testifies." *Garden City Telegram*, (Garden City, KS). March 24, 1960. 1.

[123] Richard E. Hickock. Unpublished letters to Mack Nations. May 24, 1961.

[124] Hickock.

[125] Hickock.

[126] Hickock.

[127] Hickock.

[128] Hickock.

[129] Don Kendall. "'Smoke Screens' Set by Hickock." *Hutchinson News* (Hutchinson, KS), March 30, 1960, 2.

[130] Kendall.

[131] Hickock.

[132] Truman Capote Papers, Manuscripts and Archives Division, The New York Public Library. Astor, Lenox, and Tilden Foundations. Box 7, Folders 1-14.

[133] Wayne Owens. (1959). Statement by William Floyd Wells. Lansing, KS. Kansas Bureau of Investigation.

[134] Ted Blankenship. "'Wells Justifies Role in Murders." *Hutchinson News* (Hutchinson, KS). April 8,

1960.

[135] Bob Greer. "'He Musta Done It,' Key Witness Testifies." *Garden City Telegram*, (Garden City, KS). March 24, 1960. 1.

[136] "Wells Denied Clemency." *Hutchinson News* (Hutchinson, KS). April 12, 1960.

[137] Sally J. Keglovits, "*In Cold Blood* Revisited: A Look Back at an American Crime." https://garymcavoy.com/in-cold-blood-revisited.

[138] Interview with the author.

[139] Rubin, Richard. *Confederacy of Silence: A True Tale of the New Old South*. (New York: Atria Books, 2002).

[140] Kevin Helliker. "Capote Classic 'In Cold Blood' Tainted by Long-Lost Files." *The Wall Street Journal*, February 8, 2013.

[141] Truman Capote, *Too Brief a Treat: The Letters of Truman Capote,* Edited by Gerald Clarke, (Knopf Doubleday Publishing Group; Vintage International, 2012), Kindle Edition, Kindle Location 6686.

[142] Ralph F. Voss. *Truman Capote and the Legacy of In Cold Blood*. (Tuscaloosa: University of Alabama Press, 2011).

[143] Alvin Dewey letter to Truman Capote, May 14, 1961. Truman Capote papers. Manuscripts and Archives Division. The New York Public Library. Astor, Lenox, and Tilden Foundations.

[144] Dale E. Saffels in letter to Col. Guy Rexroad, October 19, 1961, "Richard Eugene Hickock Inmate Case File 708," Kansas Historical Society, Kansas Memory, www.kansasmemory.org.

[145] Dale E. Saffels to Col. Guy Rexroad, October 19, 1961, "Richard Eugene Hickock Inmate Case File 708," Kansas Historical Society, Kansas Memory, www.kansasmemory.org.

[146] Gerald Clarke. *Capote: A Biography*. (New York: Simon and Schuster, 1988), 343.

[147] Colonel Guy Rexroad to Dale E. Saffels, November 1, 1961, "Richard Eugene Hickock Inmate Case File 709," Kansas Historical Society, Kansas Memory, www.kansasmemory.org.

[148] "KSIR Well-Managed, Investigation Shows." *Hutchinson News* (Hutchinson, KS). November 3, 1961, 1.

[149] Mack Nations to Warden Tracy Hand, January 13, 1962.

[150] Truman Capote. *Too Brief a Treat: The Letters of Truman Capote*. Edited by Gerald Clarke. (New York: Knopf Doubleday Publishing Group; Vintage International, 2012). Kindle Edition, locations 6482-6486.

[151] Kevin Helliker. "'*In Cold Blood*' Killer's Never-Published Memoir Raises Questions About His Motive." *The Wall Street Journal*, March 17, 2017.

[152] Richard Hickock as told to Mack Nations, "America's Worst Crime in 20 Years," *Male* magazine, December 1961, 30.

[153] Kurt Hoffman, email message to redacted recipients, October 9, 2003.

[154] Wayne Owens. (1959). Statement by William Floyd Wells. Lansing, KS. Kansas Bureau of Investigation.

[155] Wayne Owens. Off the Record Supplement to Signed Statement of William Floyd Wells. Topeka, KS. December 10, 1959.

[156] "Key Witness Recalled Here." *Garden City Telegram*. March 23, 1960.

[157] Ted Blankenship. "Wells Justifies Role in Murders." *Hutchinson News* (Hutchinson, KS), April 8, 1960.

[158] Bob Greer. "Key Witness Recalled Here." *Garden City Telegram*. March 23, 1960.

[159] Ellsworth Lapham Fersch. Thinking About Psychopaths and Psychopathy: Answers to Frequently Asked Questions with Case Examples. (Bloomington, IN: iUniverse), 2006.

[160] As noted in the *Case File* chapter, this scene is portrayed quite differently in *In Cold Blood*.

[161] Richard Eugene Hickock, Letters to Mack Nations, June 5, 1961.

[162] Duane West. "'In Cold Blood' prosecutor recalls Kansas family murders." Produced by Fernando Salazer, *The Wichita Eagle*, November 17, 2017. Video, 4:45.

http://www.kansascity.com/news/local/crime/article1852716
63.html.

[163] The knife and shotgun were recovered, of course, but those had been thoroughly cleaned of blood and fingerprints after the crimes.

[164] For a deeper dive into the Walker family murders, read J.T. Hunter's *In Colder Blood: True Story of the Walker Family Murder as depicted in Truman Capote's* In Cold Blood (RJ Parker Publishing, 2016).

[165] Emailed to the author in April 2013.

[166] David Hickock and Linda LeBert-Corbello. *In the Shadow of My Brother's Cold Blood*. iUniverse. Kindle Edition, locations 493-496.

[167] Hickock and LeBert-Corbello, location 465.

[168] Bob Greer. "'He Musta Done It,' Key Witness Testifies." *Garden City Telegram*, (Garden City, KS). March 24, 1960. 1.

[169] Richard Eugene Hickock, Letters to Mack Nations, June 5, 1961.

[170] Interview with the author, December 2018.

[171] Charles D. McAtee. *Memorandum to File: Interview with Hickock, Richard Eugene*. Lansing, KS. Kansas State Historical Society. (1964)

[172] "Inmate Files – Executed Prisoners," Kansas State Penitentiary. Operations Division – 1962-1965, Kansas Historical Society, accessed December 13, 2017, http://www.kshs.org/archives/197780.

[173] George Plimpton. "Some Thoughts on Capote." *The New York Times*, August 26, 1984, http://www.nytimes.com/1984/08/26/us/some-thoughts-on-capote.html.

[174] Alvin Dewey as told to Dolores Hope. "Brutal murders awakened sleepy southwest Kansas town." *Salina Journal* (Salina, KS). November 11, 1984, 1.

[175] Ralph F. Voss. *Truman Capote and the Legacy of In Cold Blood*. (Tuscaloosa: University of Alabama Press, 2011), 197-198.

[176] Truman Capote. *In Cold Blood: A True Account of a Multiple Murder and Its Consequences*. (New York: Random House, 1966), 87.

[177] Capote, 84.

[178] Voss, 205.

[179] Duane West. "'In Cold Blood' prosecutor recalls Kansas family murders." Produced by Fernando Salazer, *The Wichita Eagle*, November 17, 2017. Video, 1:40. http://www.kansascity.com/news/local/crime/article1852716 63.html.

[180] Matt Campbell, "As TV revisits the 'In Cold Blood' case, here's how The Star originally reported it," *The Kansas City Star*, November 17, 2017, http://www.kansascity.com/news/local/crime/article1852530 28.html.

[181] Dick Parr and Joe Wellington. "Four in Family Slain." *The Kansas City Star*. November 16, 1959, 1.

[182] Ken Curtis, telephone interview with the author, January 28, 2015.

[183] Jack Curtis, telephone interview with the author, January 29, 2015.

[184] National Affairs. "In Cold Blood." *Time*, November 30, 1959.

[185] Don Kendall. "Pastor Will Note Quieting of Rumors." *Hutchinson News* (Hutchinson, KS). January 10, 1960, 25.

[186] Houdyshell, V. (1959). Interview of Doctor Austin J. Adams. Wichita, KS. Kansas Bureau of Investigation.

[187] Truman Capote. Research Notes, undated. Truman Capote papers. Manuscripts and Archives Division. The New York Public Library. Astor, Lenox, and Tilden Foundations.

[188] Robert Barron, "Enid man recalls scene of 1959 murders," *Enid News & Eagle*, January 29, 2012, https://goo.gl/TxTFBU.

[189] Truman Capote. *In Cold Blood: A True Account of a Multiple Murder and Its Consequences*. (New York: Random House, 1966), 191.

[190] Truman Capote. Research Notes, Acknowledgments, undated. Truman Capote papers. Manuscripts and Archives Division. The New York Public Library. Astor, Lenox, and Tilden Foundations.

[191] Steve Walker, "Drawing Blood," *The Pitch*, October 4, 2001, https://www.pitch.com/arts-entertainment/movies/article/20614232/drawing-blood.

[192] Smith and Hickock filed four appeals through March 1965, three of them to the U.S. Supreme Court. All were denied.

[193] Email interview with the author, September 23, 2018

[194] A&E Television Networks, "American Justice: Murder 'In Cold Blood'," 1997.

[195] Joe Stump, "Kansas gets F grade in 2015 State Integrity Investigation," *The Center for Public Integrity*, November 9, 2015, https://www.publicintegrity.org/2015/11/09/18397/kansas-gets-f-grade-2015-state-integrity-investigation

[196] Editorial Board, "Kansas Attorney General Derek Schmidt grants a license to secrecy," *The Kansas City Star*, April 29, 2015, https://www.kansascity.com/opinion/editorials/article19900083.html, accessed May 12, 2015.

[197] Laura Bauer, Judy L. Thomas and Max Londberg, "'One of the most secretive, dark states': What is Kansas trying to hide?" *The Kansas City Star*, November 12, 2017.

[198] Derek Schmidt, News Release, "AG Schmidt asks court to stop online auction of KBI files, order files returned," Office of the Attorney General of Kansas, October 1, 2012. ** NOTE: the AG's use of the word "returned" is incorrect, since Harold Nye originated his own personal notebooks.

[199] Although since removed following the embarrassing disclosures revealed in our defense, the actual page has been preserved for historical posterity on the Internet Archive Wayback Machine, at https://web.archive.org/web/20120625094156/http://www.gcpolice.org:80/History/Clutter/Pictures_for_Clutters.htm.

[200] Larry Welch in letter to Andrew Holland, Producer, Tower Productions, December 29, 1997.

[201] K.S.A. 45-221(a)(30).

[202] Kansas assistant attorney general in letter to

Capote Productions (Manitoba) Inc., September 30, 2004.

[203] Gerald Clarke, ed. *Too Brief a Treat: The Letters of Truman Capote.* (New York: Random House, 2004).

[204] Truman Capote. *Too Brief a Treat: The Letters of Truman Capote.* Edited by Gerald Clarke. (New York: Knopf Doubleday Publishing Group; Vintage International, 2012). Kindle Edition, locations 5896-5911.

[205] Columbia Pictures Corp., Contract with Truman Capote for film rights, dated November 9, 1965.

[206] George Plimpton. *Truman Capote: In Which Various Friends, Enemies, Acquaintances, and Detractors Recall His Turbulent Career.* (New York: Nan A. Talese, Doubleday, 1997), 171.

[207] Ralph F. Voss. *Truman Capote and the Legacy of In Cold Blood.* (Tuscaloosa: University of Alabama Press, 2011), 205.

[208] Kevin Helliker. "'In Cold Blood' Killer's Never-Published Memoir Raises Questions About His Motive." *The Wall Street Journal,* March 17, 2017.

[209] Interview with Ron Nye, in conversations with his mother Joyce Nye, who related Peggy Johnson's account of the occasion.

[210] Voss., 229.

[211] *Kansas Bureau of Investigation: 1939–1989.* Topeka: Jostens, 1990, 59.

[212] *Kansas Bureau of Investigation,* 77.

[213] Mike Shields. "State's top cop has developed a long arm." *Lawrence Journal-World,* July 14, 2002 (Archive). Web.

[214] Shields.

[215] "Kansas Bureau of Investigation: 1939–1989." 83.

[216] Lee Davidson, "FBI files shed light on Ezra Taft Benson, Ike and the Birch Society," *Salt Lake Tribune,* November 16, 2010. http://archive.sltrib.com/article.php?id=50349153&itype=CMSID

[217] Associated Press, "Kill Ike's Farm Program His Aim," *Hutchinson News,* January 5, 1960, 40.

[218] George Plimpton. "The Story Behind a Nonfiction

Novel." *The New York Times*, January 16, 1966.

[219] Memorandum, "Concerning FBI Evidence Results," December 3, 1959. Harold R. Nye Personal Journals.

[220] Ashley B. Dreff PhD, Entangled: A History of American Methodism, Politics, and Sexuality (Nashville: New Room Books, 2018).

[221] Email interview with the author, February 2018.

[222] See *Sirrell v. IMS Health Care, Inc.*, 564 U.S.___, 131 S.CT. 2653, 2667 (2011).

[223] See *New York Times Co. v. United States*, 403 U.S. 713, 91 S.CT. 2140 (1971).

[224] State of Kansas v. Ronald Nye, Gary McAvoy et al (2014)

[225] Interview with the author, July 2018.

[226] State of Kansas v. Ronald Nye, Gary McAvoy et al (2014), Final Memorandum Decision and Order.

Printed in Great Britain
by Amazon

16488029R00176